New Register
of Caribbean
English Usage

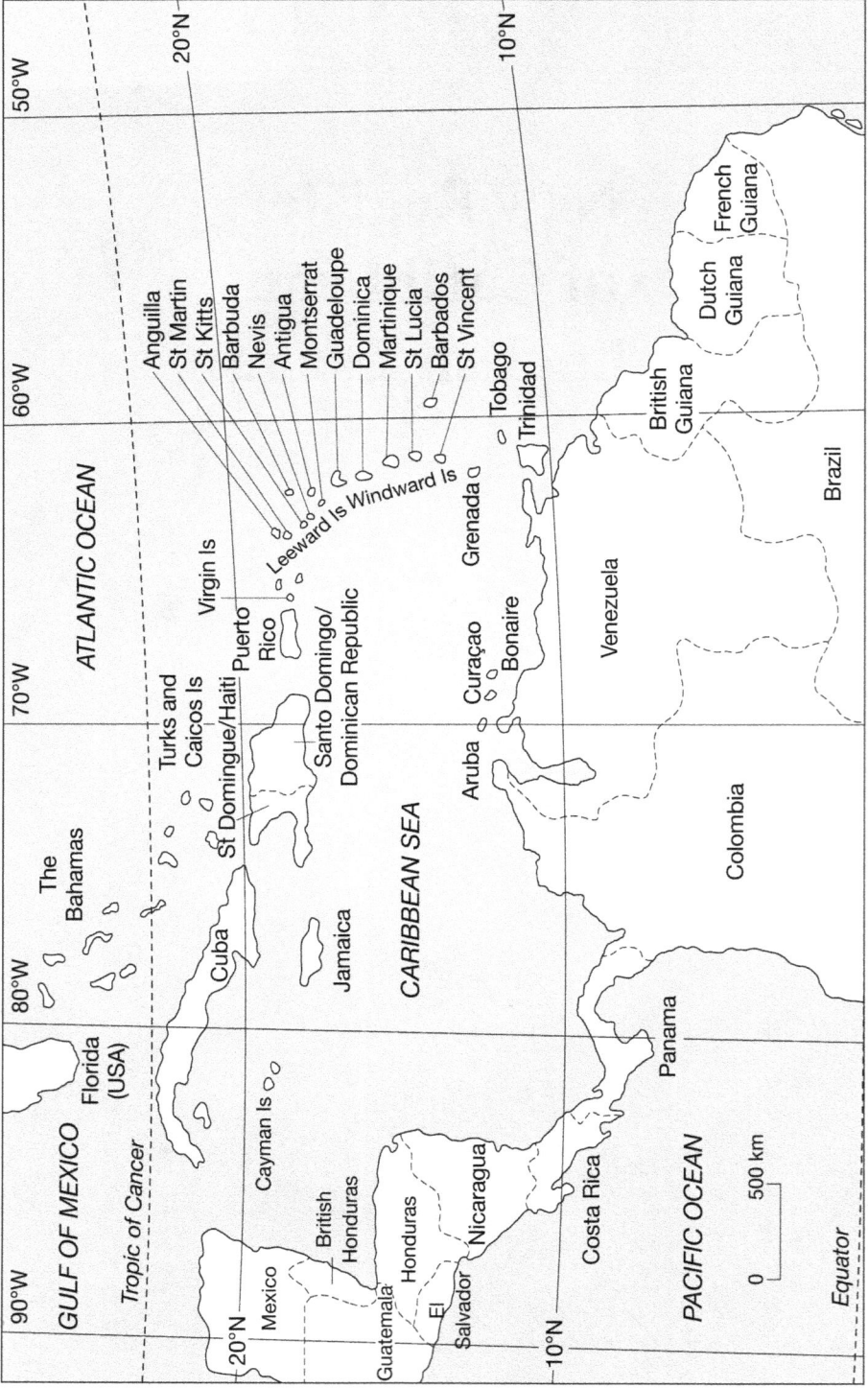

90°W 80°W 70°W 60°W 50°W

GULF OF MEXICO

Tropic of Cancer

ATLANTIC OCEAN

20°N

Florida (USA)

The Bahamas

Cuba

Cayman Is

Turks and Caicos Is

St Domingue/Haiti

Santo Domingo/ Dominican Republic

Puerto Rico

Virgin Is

Anguilla
St Martin
St Kitts
Barbuda
Nevis
Antigua
Montserrat
Guadeloupe
Dominica
Martinique
St Lucia
Barbados
St Vincent

Leeward Is

Windward Is

Grenada

Tobago

Trinidad

Jamaica

CARIBBEAN SEA

Aruba Curaçao Bonaire

British Guiana

Dutch Guiana

French Guiana

Mexico

Guatemala

British Honduras

El Salvador

Honduras

Nicaragua

Costa Rica

Panama

20°N

10°N

PACIFIC OCEAN

0   500 km

Equator

10°N

Venezuela

Colombia

Brazil

New Register of Caribbean English Usage

Edited by
Richard Allsopp

University of the West Indies Press
Jamaica • Barbados • Trinidad and Tobago
&
Centre for Caribbean Lexicography
University of the West Indies

University of the West Indies Press
7A Gibraltar Hall Road   Mona
Kingston 7   Jamaica
www.uwipress.com

CATALOGUING-IN-PUBLICATION DATA

Allsopp, Richard (Stanley Reginald Richard).
New register of Caribbean English usage / Richard Allsopp.

p. cm.
Includes bibliographical references.

ISBN: 978-976-640-228-0

1. Caribbean Area – Languages – Dictionaries. 2. English language – Caribbean Area –
Dictionaries. 3. English language – Dialects – Caribbean Area – Dictionaries. 4. Creole dialects,
English – Caribbean Area – Dictionaries. I. Title.

PE3304.D33 2010   427.972903

Map of the Caribbean on page ii courtesy of Macmillan Publishers.

Book design by Interscript.
Cover design by Robert Harris.

Printed in the United States of America.

Dedicated to Jeannette, my wife

CONTENTS

FOREWORD

This is a small work in the context of professional lexicography, but it is hoped that it will have at least two positive effects. First, it should serve to keep alive in the academic world, the claim of Caribbean lexicography to serious scholarly recognition as established by the pioneer regional work by this author, the *Dictionary of Caribbean English Usage* (Oxford University Press, 1996; reprinted by University of the West Indies Press, 2003); and that is by no means meant to discount the impact of two earlier Caribbean works, the *Dictionary of Jamaican English* (Cambridge University Press, 1967; second edition, 1980, reprinted by University of the West Indies Press, 2002) and the *Dictionary of Bahamian English* (Lexik House, 1982). Further there have been produced volume one separately of Dr Jeannette Allsopp's pioneering *Caribbean Multilingual Dictionary* (Arawak, 2003); two dictionaries of St Lucia Kwéyol, *Dictionary of St Lucian Creole* (Mondesir, Mouton de Gruyter, 1992) and *Kwéyol Dictionary* (David Frank, SIL International and Ministry of Education, St Lucia, 2001); a Dominican *Diksiyonné* (Marcel Fontaine and Peter Roberts, Folk Research Institute, 1991); most recently a *Beleez Kriol–Inglish Dikshineri* (Belize Kriol Project, 2007). Together they should be considered as making a worthy academic bibliography of Caribbean lexicon to date.

Second, it is hoped that the manageable size of the present *New Register of Caribbean English Usage* will both encourage younger Caribbean scholars in linguistics to give their professional skills to this field of work, as being not such a forbidding task, and possibly also the University of the West Indies authorities to look at continuing publications as feasible, proving to be a defining asset in the development of the Centre for Caribbean Lexicography at Cave Hill.

For all and in all, thanks be to God.

SRRA
Advent 2007

ACKNOWLEDGEMENTS

The principal, Sir Hilary Beckles, his predecessor, Sir Keith Hunte, and the University of the West Indies at Cave Hill are hereby gratefully thanked for the continued provision of an office and secretarial service for the Caribbean Lexicography Programme.

The Barbados Ministry of Culture is also duly thanked for its annual subvention from 2002 of US$15,000 for Caribbean dictionary and language study, which was shared between the anglophone and multilingual divisions of the Caribbean Lexicography Programme. It enabled the purchase of supportive and reference literature, the payment of part-time office assistants and a computer programmer, and attendance at conferences; and it facilitated the physical production of the present work.

My personal gratitude is also warmly extended to the following persons to whose interest and service the present product owes so much.

Supervisory assistant: Dr Jeannette Allsopp (Senior Research Fellow in Lexicography, University of the West Indies, Cave Hill). Dr Allsopp also reviewed the finished text.

Adviser in formatting: Ms Barbara Niles

Keyboarders: Ms Janelle Applewhaite; Mrs Patricia Duprey; Ms Sharon Estwick

Part-time assistants: Ms Janelle Applewhaite; Ms Sharie Best; Ms Lisa Prescod; Ms Karen Primus; Ms Kelli-Ann Reid

Information or guidance was requested and received from a number of persons, listed below, at various times, besides others identified at citations in the text. (The list is unfortunately not complete, but omissions are regretted and unintentional.)

BAHAMAS: Joy Delaney; Dawn Marshall

BARBADOS: Adonijah (*Nation*); Kevin Arthur; Mark Byer; Lennox Chandler; Tony Cozier; Rudolph Hinds; Richard Hoad; Dennis Kellman; Latchman Kissoon; Jeannette Layne-Clark; Dr Rosina Maitland; Professor W.K. Marshall; Debra Ramsay; June Roach; Andy Taitt; Dr Roland Toppin; The Librarian, Caribbean Development Bank; The Librarian, Nation Publishing Company

GRENADA: Myrna Taitt; Claire Clouden

GUYANA: O'Donna Allsopp; P.A.D. Allsopp; W.H.L Allsopp (Canada); Stanley Greaves; Dr Ian McDonald; Michael Ramessar (Department of Biology, University of Guyana); Dr Rupert Roopnarine; Leslie Slater (Barbados)

JAMAICA: Dr Pauline Christie; Dr Velma Pollard

NEVIS: William Glover (USA)

ST VINCENT: Marcia Hinds (Barbados); Kathleen Huggins

TRINIDAD: A.R. Lewis; Earl Lovelace; William Hutchins (USA)

UNITED KINGDOM: Tim Gosling; Professor John Wells

INTRODUCTION

THE PRESENT WORK

The title *New Register of Caribbean English Usage* (*NRCEU*) chosen for this work indicates that it is a continuation of the author's previous lexicography begun in the *Dictionary of Caribbean English Usage* (lxviii + 697 pages) which was first published by Oxford University Press in 1996. The decision to publish at this time is due in part to the lapse of time, some eleven years since the *Dictionary of Caribbean English Usage*, in part to a considered need to hand over the arduous task of continuing lexicography to a promised Centre for Caribbean Lexicography now being set up by the University of the West Indies, Cave Hill, and in part as a conclusion to some six decades of the author's work in Caribbean lexicography. Such considered conclusion was also stimulated by the recognition that competent leadership is available for the planned centre which, it is hoped, can make this publication central to its initiation.

Another opportune consideration is the fact that 2007 is a historic year in the development of Caribbean civilization, from the end of transatlantic enslavement (1807) through miscegenated plantation life to an articulated regional English with a brand of world literature in English of its own. Caribbean lexicography is therefore a chronicle and inventory of some two hundred years of linguistic development whose achievement in developing a Caribbean civilization is absolutely undeniable.

When the *Dictionary of Caribbean English Usage* was published in 1996 there had been a cut-off point in data-editing in 1992; and that means that there has been a decade and a half—some fifteen years!—of accumulated additional Caribbean lexicon. Furthermore, the immense pressure to produce the dictionary, which had been in hand since 1971, had forced the elimination, conceding 'necessary selection' as expedient, of a high number of items which it was hoped could be matter for a second edition. In the circumstances that developed, the second edition did not come about.

Accordingly, a decision has been taken to present another selection of the additional lexicon as the *New Register of Caribbean English Usage*. It comprises about seven hundred items (headwords, with new senses or usages, acronyms and so on) that have emerged from the ecological and cultural domains of the CARICOM territories, from Guyana round the archipelago to Belize. That amount, by no means immense, is offered mainly to demonstrate the fact that there is a great remainder of the inventory and chronicle of Caribbean culture and history which make us who we are that needs to be noticed. Continued Caribbean lexicography demands consideration.

A modestly funded team of online assistants researching data on the Internet Caribbean-wide is an urgent cultural obligation. But example should be more persuasive than pleading, so let a selection of items from discrete domains challenge the querulous as to whether they are not eligible candidates for listing in international lexicography (some perhaps with due status-labelling) although none can yet be found in current British or American standard desk dictionaries:

Abbreviations commonly used: ACCP, ACP countries, CBI, CDERA, CSME, ECCA, RNM, RSS, SVG

Ecology: bunchy top, cane hole, eco-lodge, fermentary, fogging machine, mealy bug, pond grass, skeet, wisdom weed

Entertainment: bashment, carnivalize, quad pans, dinki mini, pooch back, dutty wine, iwer, midi pan, rapso, rhumba-box, ringbang, socaholic

Folk inventions: backative, bariffle, blenza, broughtupsy, duck sense, invitement, livety, movementation, shit-work, shopaholic, sistren, spraddle out, squingee, stupse, teachment, tucko tucko, warrisome, wopsy

History: Arrival Day, diasporic, free coloured, kanari, Mandinky priest, orature, pataki, Pitchy Patchy

Politics: black clothes police, garrison communities, negrocrat, party paramountcy, Shiprider Agreement

Religion: revivalist, Spiritual Baptist, Nyabinghi, entrification, heartical, Zion

Social scene: Afric, Afrikan, barrel-child, biggety, dungle, earbang, eye-supper, foop, groundation, hickie, jambust, nemakharam, poor-rakey, quarrel-missy, texturized hair, weave-on

Sport: blackwash, fly-stick, sitoo, tief-out, voop

Indeed, the period of the last two decades, embracing the turn of the century, has seen an immense growth in Caribbean writing in English at all levels, from the folk variety, commonly called 'the dialect', to the formal variety of published collections of verse and poetry, short stories and novels. I have distinguished 'verse' in order to draw special attention to lyrics and comic verse of an increasingly carnivalized Caribbean with entertainment evidently dominating our culture. There has also been an increase in consciously written newspaper folk columns. Indeed newspaper sources have made up the largest part of the citations used in this *New Register of Caribbean English Usage in* which, again, written material has dominated.

INTERNATIONAL ENGLISH

The English language is a multi-national language, used, that is, by a number of Nations as their accredited mother tongue or official language. It used to be anchored in Britain, but that is no longer so: the United States, called 'America', Canada and Australia come readily to mind as territorial and population giants together with the computer, in the making of today's English; but it is a mistake to forget that every independent nation, from Britain and those largest three to each of the small island states of the Caribbean, is entitled to recognition of its own standard variety of English, technically equal in status, unrelated to political and commercial national standing or historical seniority.

The term Standard English, particularly as a spoken medium, thus becomes confusing. One only has to listen to the accredited presenters of the news and various features on the BBC and CNN, for simple but full enough example, to realize that, in the domain of spoken language, the term Standard English, as *linguistically centralized*, is unacceptable.

In the domain of writing, however, the situation is different. The sturdy, all-service Subject-Verb-Object (SVO) framework with a practical set of principles and conventions, and attractively simplified morphology that homeland English 'grammar' developed in the fourteenth to the sixteenth centuries before its gradual political spread to the Southern and Western world gave it a functional advantage in *grammatical structure* that provided an accepted core for its forthcoming international body. It is this grammatical core, with liberal regional additions of vocabulary and usage, that has become the whole intercommunicable Internationally Accepted English (IAE). It is essentially a written medium, and admits of little confusion once it is clearly understood that it is the core of many national varieties and sub-varieties. Caribbean English is one such variety. It is this term IAE, in preference to SE (Standard English), that prevails in this work. Language, however, is fundamentally talk and in human-to-human language-contact situations English resulted internationally in pidginization and creolization on a scale that no other adventuring European language was able to achieve. Signal, in the context, was Creolized English right across the West Atlantic, embracing the sprawling Caribbean archipelago.

CARIBBEAN ENGLISH USAGE

Usage, simply defined as the distinctive way in which words and phrases sourced in Internationally Accepted English with borrowings from other linguistic bodies have come to be used in Caribbean territorial varieties/sub-varieties of English, is the determining factor in identifying Caribbean English.

However, there are different levels of usage, determined by social circumstances and situations, and in this work they are recognized and identified briefly (in the context of Caribbean English being a part of the core of Internationally Accepted English), with bracketed italic abbreviations after territorial identification of headwords, as follows:

[F]	Formal: Educated usage, acceptable as IAE. (This indication may be taken for granted when no identification is given.)
[IF]	Informal: Casual usage; often called 'colloquial' in some lexicographical contexts.
[AF]	Anti-formal: Familiar usage ranging from 'friendly' through 'jocular', 'derogatory' to 'vulgar'; often called 'slang' in some lexicographical contexts.
[AF—Cr]	A dialectal 'Creole' item
[AF—Joc]	Jocular usage
[AF—Derog]	Derogatory usage
[AF—Vul]	Vulgar usage
[X]	Erroneous or disapproved: Often an error of overcorrection. Reference may be made to the introduction to this author's previous work, the *Dictionary of Caribbean English Usage*, for a full exposition of Caribbean English (p. xxxix ff).

Professor Richard Allsopp CHB, PhD, Hon DLitt
Centre for Caribbean Lexicography
University of the West Indies, Cave Hill
December 2007

EXPLANATORY NOTES

1. The structure of an **entry** is as follows (items following the Headword being optional):
Headword, [pronunciation], /pitch and stress/, *part of speech*, Territory, [*status label*]. ///
primary or // secondary **allonym** (+ territory).
Gloss 1 (Roman font) *citation(s)* (italics) *a, b, c*
Gloss 2 *citation(s)* etc.
[Etymology]
□ Notes
Phrases (numbered, with notes below as relevant)
2. An **allonym** ('other name') is the name of an *identical item* or an *equivalent term* in another territory.
Thus *apasote* (Belz), *semi-contract* (Jmca), etc. are allonyms. (N.B. Whereas allonyms are 'identical', *synonyms* are only 'similar', e.g. (IAE) 'beautiful', 'lovely', 'pretty')
2.1 A **primary (or main) allonym** (symbol ///) is the headword chosen to carry the gloss, to which other **secondary allonyms** (symbol //) are referred
Thus ... (**crop Lisbon**) is a primary allonym to which ... (*lisbon yam*), (*water yam*), ... (*white lisbon*) are referred.
3. In this work **singular 'they'** is the recognized pronominal form in place of (IAE) *he/she/ s/he, him/her*, etc. Hence **they, them, their(s) themself** replace, f. ex, *He or she knows that what belongs to him or her is his or hers. Anyone can speak for himself or herself* becomes **they know that what belongs to them is theirs. Anyone can speak for themself.**
4. An alphabetical list of bibliographic sources of citations is given at the end of the book.

FONTS

The fonts used in the *New Register of Caribbean English Usage* are as follows:

Boldface is used for all headwords in the *New Register of Caribbean English Usage*.
Boldface is also used to denote all words that are cited from other dictionaries such as the *Oxford English Dictionary*, the *Dictionary of New Zealand English*, etc. Other words referred to that occur in entries, but are not necessarily taken from a particular dictionary are also put in **boldface**.
Boldface italics are used for all headwords that occur in the *Dictionary of Caribbean English Usage*. They are also used for all secondary allonyms.
Italics are used for all citations, and for words referred to either in English or words from other languages that are used in usage notes or etymologies in entries.
SMALL CAPS are used to refer to headwords in the *New Register of Caribbean English Usage*.

PRONUNCIATION

CARIBBEAN ENGLISH

Vowels (CE)

Key word (CE)	Phonemic symbol	Phonemic spelling
beat	[i]	/ii/
bit	[ɪ]	/i/
bait	[e]	/ee/
bet	[ɛ]	/e/
but	[ʌ]	/o/
bat	[a]	/a/
bath	[aː] [aˑ]	/aa/
bite	[aɪ]	/ai/
Bob	[ɒ]	/o/
bout	[ɒʊ]	/ow/
boy	[ɒɪ]	/oi/
bo	[o]	/o/
boat	[oː] [oˑ]	/oo/
buff	[ʊ]	/u/
boot	[u]	/uu/

Note: The phonemic spelling system is adapted from that used by F.G. Cassidy. See *Jamaica Talk* (Cambridge: Cambridge University Press, 1980; repr. Kingston: University of the West Indies Press, 2006), 433.

Nasal Vowels
Nasal vowels are marked with a tilde [˜]above, thus [ũ, ĩ, ã, ɔ̃, ɒ̃, õ, ɛ̃].
The **voiceless vowel** occurring medially in *eh-heh* is represented as [h].

Consonants
The sounds [p, b, t, d, k, g; m, n; l, r; f, v; s, z, h; y, w] are rendered, generally speaking, in the same way as in Internationally Accepted English, and are represented by the same letters, whether in phonetic or phonemic spelling. Symbols are used to represent other \ sounds as follows.

Key word	Phonetic symbol	Phonemic spelling
church	[č]	/ch/
judge	[ǰ]	/j/
sing	[ŋ]	/ng/
thing	[θ]	/th/
this	[ð]	/dh/
shoe	[š]	/sh/

Jouvert [ž]   /zh/
Eh! Eh! [ʔ]   /ʔ/ (glottal stop)

Two pitch phonemes, using numbers /1 2/, and one stress phoneme, using an acute accent /1´2/ are marked in this work.

The reader is referred to the sub-section on sound, under General Characteristics (pp. lxiv ff), in the introduction to the author's previous work, the *Dictionary of Caribbean English Usage*, for a fuller exposition of the phonetic/phonemic character of Caribbean English, which also applies to the present work.

SYMBOLS

/   *In a phrase entry*, separates alternatives in sense or structure.

    along wid/with sb
    buck up to/(a)gainst sth

    In a citation, indicates the start of a new line or paragraph in the original text:

    Poor fishermen still out to sea / No agreement with T & T / De reason for all the pool sharking / It's de poor man who is netting / So a know that yuh seeing red.

///   Indicates that a primary or main allonym follows.

//   Indicates that secondary allonym follows.

/ /   Virgules enclose phonemic spelling: /raas/ /klaat/

[ ]   Light square brackets enclose pronunciation given in phonetic symbols.
    In a spelling, indicate that the sound which would be represented if the letter(s) so bracketed were 'pronounced' is absent in the speaker's articulation.
    Enclosing words at the beginning of a gloss, indicate an explanatory phrase or sentence.

[ ]   Heavy square brackets enclose etymological information.

~   Swung dash indicates that a variant pronunciation follows.

( )   *In a spelling*, indicates that the sound, the letter, the part of a word or of a phrase so bracketed is sometimes included in the pronunciation, spelling or form of the word or phrase: **(a)bout here**, **los(t)**, **rob (sb) blind**.

>   Becomes; develops into.

<   Is derived from.

☐   Indicates that a usage note follows.

GENERAL LIST OF ABBREVIATIONS
USED IN THE TEXT

AAVE	African American Vernacular Eng	fem	feminine
abbr	abbreviated/abbreviation	folk	folk etymology
Ad	advertisement	foll	following
adj	adjective	fr	from
adv	adverb	Fr	French
AF	Anti-Formal	FrCr	French Creole
AmE	American English	ft	feet
Amer	America	gen	general
aux	auxiliary	Gk	Greek
Bhoj	Bhojpuri	(H)	Headline
Br	British	Hin	Hindi
BrE	British English	Hist	historical
C	century	IAE	Internationally Accepted English
/-c-/	consonant	id	idiomatic
CarA Cr	Caribbean Creole	ideoph	ideophone
/-cc-/	consonant cluster(final, intervocalic, initial)	IF	Informal
		incl	included/ing
CE	Caribbean English	Ind	Industry
cit(s)	citation(s)	infl	influence(d)
comb	combined/combining	intr	intransitive
Cp	compare	Irel	Ireland
Cr	Creole	Joc	jocular/ly
defn	definition	Ling	Linguistic(s)
Derog	derogatory/-ily	mag	magazine
Dev	Devo	ME	Middle English
dial	dialect/-al	metaph	metaphorical/-ly
Du	Dutch	ModE	Modern English
E; Eng;	English	Ms	manuscript
EE	Earlier English (c. 1625–c. 1837 for the purpose of this work)	n	noun
		N; No	North
		naut	nautical
esp	especially	neg	negative
etym	etymology/-ical	NT	New Testament
evid	evident/-ly	obj	object/-ive
Ex(s)	example(s)	Obs	obsolete /-escent
excl	exclamatory; exclamation	orig	original/-ly
F	Formal	OT	Old Testament
f. ex	for example	pa. part	past participle

pa. t	past tense	Sg; Sing	singular
perh	perhaps	Sp	Spanish
pers info	personal info	spec	special
phr(s)	phrase(s)	sth	something
pl	plural	suff	suffix
poss	possible/-bly	Sus	Sussex
possess	possessive	tr	transitive
prec	preceding	trans	translation
prep	preposition/-al	us	usage
pres. part	present participle	usu	usual(ly)
pres. t	present tense	US	United States
prob	probably	vb	verb
pron	pronoun	vocab	vocabulary
pronunc	pronunciation	Vul	Vulgar
Prov	proverb	W Afr	West African
ref	refer; reference	wd	would
Sb; sb	somebody	wh	which
Sc	Scottish	Yks	Yorkshire
SE	Standard English		

LIST OF TERRITORIAL CODES
FOR DICTIONARY ENTRIES

Antg	Antigua	Guyn	Guyana
Austral	Australia	Jmca	Jamaica
Baha	Bahamas	Mrat	Montserrat
Bdos	Barbados	NZ	New Zealand
Belz	Belize	Panm	Panama
BrVi	British Virgin Islands	StLu	St Lucia
CarA	Caribbean Area/Region	StVn	St Vincent
Dmca	Dominica	Trin	Trinidad
ECar	Eastern Caribbean	UniK	United Kingdom
Gren	Grenada	US	United States
Grns	Grenadines		

A

A.ba.co.ni.an *adj; n* (Baha) Of or belonging to one of the islands of "The Abacos", a curved cluster of seven Family Islands of the Bahamas, the furthest north of Nassau and about 175 miles from the Florida coast; the largest of the group, Great Abaco, gives its name to the whole. *Historically different from other areas in the Bahamas, the population of the Abacos descended from Loyalists during the war of Independence from the United States. These blond-haired, blue-eyed Abaconians have given up wrecking and rum running, but still work at traditional occupations—farming, fishing and boat building.*—AdV (Mag) (2004.03.26, p.6)

ab.or.i.gi.nal (// *aborigine* n) *n; adj* (Guyn) **1.** *n* (One of) the original inhabitants or native Amerindian population of Guyana. *There can be little doubt that the time has come for Government to review and revise its policy towards the aboriginal inhabitants of the country. The existing Aboriginal Protection laws are ... only enforced spasmodically, and ... although it is a criminal offence to supply an Aboriginal with intoxicating liquor, and to harbour an Aboriginal female on one's premises without the specific permission of the Protector, it is still possible to see drunken Indians in the riparian sections of the city.*—Sport and General (vol.1, no.1, July 1939, p.32) [< ABORIGIN(E) + adj. suff -al (as *COD* 10) 'relating to'] **2.** *adj* Of, belonging or related to such person(s), or to indigenous people of non-European continents. □ Both BrE (as *COD* 10) and AmE (as *WCD* 10) current usage identify the terms **aborigine, aboriginal** as applying to the indigenous peoples of Australia. However *SOD* (4th ed., 1993) includes "Existing in a land before the arrival of (European) colonists". The *Guyn* usage would be among the earliest E usages.

ab.or.ig.in.e [aborɪʤini] *n* (Guyn) // *aboriginal* n. [< Anglicized usage of Latin *aborigine* 'from the beginning']

(a)bout here *adv phr* (Bdos, Guyn) [AF] In these parts; in/to this country. **a.** *Tom, you was in Canada good good, then for no reason at all you ups and come bout here for the staging of your book.*—AdV (1993.11.05, p.9) **b.** *Wunna so does think that cause wunna went way for two days wunna does know more than the people 'bout here!*—NaT (1996.09.06, p.22) [< IAE *about*, by popular aphesis of /a-/ + *here*, nominalized adv, 'this place, these parts'] □ Sometimes > *n phr* on its own. See BOUT HERE.

A.C.C.P (ACCP) *abbr* (CarA) Assembly of Caribbean Community Parliamentarians; a non-legislative body comprising up to four representatives drawn from government and opposition in each of 13 CARICOM member states; its main function is that of a consultative body on the process of regional integration; it was inaugurated in *Bdos* in 1996. *"The ACCP will not deliberate on matters of domestic policy, which are rightfully the province of national parliamentarians," Carrington said.*—AdV (1996.05.28, p.2)

Ac.com.pong Ma.roon(s) *n phr* (Jmca) Descendant(s) of the successfully rebellious slaves in the western parish of St Elizabeth (Jamaica), occupying terrain ceded to them by the British authorities in 1739; their leader carries the traditional title of COLONEL. See SAZJ: 1. *Colin Rowe ... was elected leader in September 1993. He is seeking a declaration that he is the legitimate head of the Accompong Maroons and he has the right to administer his powers under the Treaty.*—DaG (1996.09.25, p.A10) [*Accompong*, name of the founder of the Maroon settlement, < Acheampong, a (Ghanian) Twi personal name. For "Maroon" see *DCEU* **maroon¹** n]

AC-DC *n* (Bdos) [AF—Joc] A hetero- and homosexual male. *By de way, I notice dah auntie man, de Reveren' Jeffrey John, dat did get appint as de Bishop a' Readin' had de presence o' min to wifdraw ... But imagine how summuch ethuh Anglican priests, an' even de Archbishop o' Canterbury, like duh din see nuh partic'lar issue in de fack dat he was AC-DC.*—NaT (2003.07.09, p.9A, Lickmout' Lou) [AF—Joc metaphorical ref to an electrical accessory that can accommodate either alternating (AC) or direct (DC) current]

a.cious [ešʌs] *adj* (Guyn) [AF—Joc] **1.** [Of dress] Splendid looking. **2.** [Of food] Delicious; very tasty. **a.** *Well yo(u) really lookin(g) acious in dat wedding dress.*—(Guyn) **b.** *Dis pepperpot tas' acious, man.*—(Guyn) [By suggestive analogy. Cp 'capacious, spacious', etc. expressing intensity emotively]

ACP coun.tries [esipi-] *abbr; n phr* (CarA) Africa, Caribbean and Pacific countries; a group of 71 former British, French and other European colonies (47 African, 15 Caribbean, 9 Pacific) which became independent in the latter half of the 20C, and which have been collectively considered, by the European Economic Commission and later the European Union, for preferential economic and aid relationship. [Acronym from first letters of Africa Caribbean Pacific]

ACTI [akti] [*acronym*] (CarA) The Association of Caribbean Tertiary Institutions, an educational body representing over 40 member institutions—universities, colleges and teacher training institutions in English-speaking Caribbean countries; it was inaugurated in Kingston, 90/11/08, with the aim of coordinating and improving the quality, quantity and organization of tertiary education in the region. *Holder said the main focus of ACTI since 1992 has been the development of a regional mechanism for equivalency ... in collaboration with the CARICOM Secretariat.*—AdV (1996.11.15, p.15) [Acronym representing 'Association of Caribbean Tertiary Institutions']

act.ing white *adj phr* (Bdos) [*IF*] Pretending to be (a) white (person) *He has poisoned white people's dogs, black people's dogs, and a dog belonging to a man who is neither white nor black—a so-called acting white man.*—SuS (1993.11.20, p.11)

Ac.tor Boy *n phr* (Jmca) // **koo-koo** (Jmca) A traditional figure of the Junkanoo Festival in *Jmca*, played by a young man. Also called **Koo-Koo**. See cit. *Actor boy wore a white mask and a wig of heavy long curls. His fancy headdress, complete with jewels, feathers and glittery materials, offset with the small face mask, combined with an elaborate European-style tiered skirt with frock-coat.*—Caribbean Festival Arts (1999.10.15, p.48) [Because of his costume and comical role in the show]

a.do.do *n* (Gren) [*Obs*] See cit. *She tole me to put it in the flask in the adodo, the shed outside.*—SDP: 90

Af.ric¹ *adj* (CarA) // **Afrikan** (Bdos) **1.** Belonging to the continent of Africa (esp. sub-Saharan Africa). *Whenever I travel in Africa, I always look for some sign of an Afric god, with "thick lips and woolly hair", but so far my search has been in vain. The Afric god had straightened his hair, lightened his skin and had plastic surgery on his nose and lips, and was indistinguishable from the Grecian, Arab, and all the other gods. The major faiths in Africa—Christanity and Islam—have been imported.*—SBWW:186 [*OED* 2 **Afric** (arch) (adj), 'of or pertaining to Africa', *sb* + cits 1590–1956] □ Now *Obs* in Mod E, the term is being usefully revived, as in cit. See next. **2.** Pertaining to anybody of the African DISAPORA (see AFRIC²) regardless of inter-racial mixture, or of complexion. **a.** *The dread epic has developed and worsened in Guyana for the last half-century of this millennium which has been dominated over its latter 500 years by the gruesome reality of white enslavement of Afric peoples.*—AdV (1998.06.28, p.12) **b.** *Today, the culture practiced, and developing on St. Vincent is British based, overlaid—and infiltrated by more and more deliberate means—with a resurgence of Afric tempos, and the implantation of some others.*—HSOH:viii **c.** *Slavery had in fact instituted its own mentality. It had left a population of Afric people who wanted to dissociate themselves from Africa and others who hated themselves to the point where they went around killing people who looked like them.*—NaT (2003.05.10, p.8A)

[By analogy with such geo-cultural phenotype *adjs* as Asiatic, Hispanic, Indic, etc.] □ **1.** In ref to the diaspora **Afric** is a useful contradistinction from *African*, allowing the latter *adj* to apply restrictively to the continent of Africa. See App III. **2.** See AFRIKAN.

Af.ric² *n* (CarA) // **Afro-brother** (Trin) Any person wholly or partly of African descent who is native to a place (esp. in the Western Hemisphere) outside of sub-Saharan Africa; any member of the African DIASPORA, regardless of racial inter-mixture. **a.** *Pele, Colin Powell and Derek Walcott are three distinguished Africs of modern times.*—Bdos (Ms) **b.** *It all started over 200 years ago when a group of black captives revolted against the might of France and defeated the mighty forces of Napoleon. The fact is that that victory should have been the beginning of a glorious liberation for Africs everywhere.*—NaT (2001.01.04) [By functional adj > n extension of **Afric¹**. See also note to sense 2 there]

Af.ric hair.style *n phr* (CarA) Any of the varieties of hairstyle and design such as *Afro, corn-row, Nubian knots, twiggies*, etc. which can be created only by exploiting the natural spring or coil in an AFRIC person's hair; they are especially used by black women. [See *Afric¹* adj]

Af.ric.an¹ *adj* (Gren) [Religion] Associated with aboriginal, continental African spirtualism. *Another evening a fellow came with a hand-bag. He greeted me, he told me he is from an African church, does African work, and he heard of me, he was very glad to greet me, and he came to spend the night with me.*—SDP:97 [Understood as originating in Africa as motherland] □ Restrictive usage, relating to the early Spiritual Baptist belief system.

Af.ric.an² *n* (Jmca) [*AF/IF*] Of African blood by descent. *She and Mama were of mixed blood—Indian and white. Dem never even waan me seh me have African in me.* [They never even warned me that I have African [blood] in me]—SSLG:144 [A semantic extension of the IAE *African n* 'a native of Africa' to refer to the 'basic racial quality of such a person']

Af.ric.an feast *n phr* (Gren) [*Obs*] [Religion] A communal, ceremonial feast for thanksgiving with accompanying prayers to an aboriginal African deity; it involves the sacrificial killing and eating of fowls or a lamb, and is accompanied by night-long drumming and religious singing and dancing. *The first time I wanted to beat drum, I went for a permit in the police station at Point Fortin, and the sergeant asked me what it is I am carrying on, if it is Shango feast or African feast. I told him what I know of is African feast, and I related to him how it happened that I should give that feast.*—SDP:98 □ Cp **break a table** (Jmca)

Af.ric.an.i.ty *n* (CarA) One's being of African descent as a significant aspect of one's personality; the particular quality of being of African descent; belonging to African heritage and culture as a significant feature of identity of a person or thing. **a.** *[Eric Roach's] Africanity [which] he can claim with the same fervour [as] Claude McKay and Aimé Césaire, was only a part, though a fundamental part, of his Caribbean nature and identity.*—RTFR (Intro p.14, K. Ramchand) **b.** *One of our learned clergymen quite recently was heard expressing his views on the Africanity, or lack thereof, of black Barbadians ... People like Mr. W—— D—— can no longer confuse the youth, as African-Barbadians are becoming more aware of who they are.*—NaT (2002.07.25, p.10) [< African '(being) of Africa' + suff -ity denoting 'quality or condition', as in 'humanity', 'vanity', etc.] □ Used as distinct from AFRICANNESS, as an elevated derivative connoting significance, as in 'humanity', 'quality', 'purity' etc. The term is said to have originated in the USA.

Af.ric.an.ness *n* (CarA) **1.** The state or condition of being African, in relation to race, origin or appearance. **a.** *Some West Indians, especially those of light complexion are not too keen to be associated with Africanness, while East Indians boast of their Indianness and Chinese and whites certainly know who they are.*— (Guyn, Ms) **b.** *Shades of red he chooses, and the suggestion of squares and masks in the design mark Africanness in his Art.*—(Bdos, Ms) **2.** One's recognition of being genetically of continental African descent; the state and condition of having aboriginal African roots. **a.** *Africanness identifies Black people's place in human civilization. It is out of Africanness that comes Black people's innovative use of percussive instruments—a multiplicity of types of drum and ultimately the steelband. Jazz, break-dancing, rap are products of Africanness.*—(Bdos, Ms) **b.** *This makes him an important node for those of us who subjugate our Africanness to our Americanness. As I have often said, I feel a much stronger, more immediate, sense of connection to America (north and south) than I do to Africa.*—AdV (2000.04.16, p.9) [< African '(being) of Africa' + suff -ness 'state or condition' as in bitterness, happiness, etc.] □ The IAE suffix -ness, has a neutral connotation. However, a parallel term, AFRICANITY, said to have originated in the USA, has been in use in *Bdos*, relating to cultural identity, perhaps deriving a more elevated connotation from 'dignity', 'humanity', etc.

Af.ri.cen.tric *adj* (Bdos) Variant of AFROCENTRIC. *In contrast, in Barbados, the plantation-dominated landscape turned inward, the earth recoiling internally into numerous caves—periodic refuge for rebel Africans like Bussa who challenged the seemingly all-powerful white plantocracy, but [having] no basis for the kind of sustained Africentric cultural development that took place in the Free Villages built by former slaves in the hills of Jamaica after 1838. No mountain retreat, of course, meant no drums ... No drums meant an absence, too, of homegrown Africentric religion—Kumina, Pocomania, and Rastafari in the Jamaican context.*—NaT (2006.11.27, p.8) [Perh influenced by AFRIC]

Af.rik.an *adj, n* (Bdos) /// AFRIC (*CarA*) [Of persons] Of African descent, anywhere in the global African DIASPORA. See cit. *Hello, Afrikan! Global Afrikan*

Congress is born! ... The Global Afrikan Congress was born yesterday in Barbados, the closing day of the African and African Descendants World Conference Against Racism. The name of the new baby came after several hours of labour, and much controversy sparked by a decision to exclude non-Africans from the five days of deliberations at the Sherbourne Conference Centre ... Delegates agreed on the title Global Afrikan Congress after examining eight other suggestions ... One delegate explained that the "K" in the name of the new body followed the Pan-African spelling, and its membership would comprise Africans and African descendants, with one representative from each African region and two each from Europe, North America, Latin America, Caribbean, Oceania and a youth representative.—NaT (2002.10.07, p.48) [See cit for rationale for spelling. However '-k-' coincides with German and So Afr *Afrika, Afrikaner, Afrikaans*] □ **1.** This term was developed by consensus at an international conference in Bdos in Oct 2002. See cit. **2.** Cp AFRIC *n, adj* wh covers the same field of meaning.

Af.ro-Amer.i.ca *n* (CarA, UniK) The AFRIC population, society and culture of the USA; Black America. *Their nearest counterpart would be the Negro hipster or ghetto hustler in Afro-America.* Ken Pryce, "West Indians in Bristol" 'The black Experience in Britain',—ISER, UWI, Trin. [A back-formation from the adj *Afro-American*, 'black' (person)] □ A convenient compound perh considered more acceptable than 'Black America'. Cp f. ex '*Euro-America*' as referring to the white American population and society.

Af.ro-bro.ther *n* (Trin) /// AFRIC² (CarA) Any person of African descent, esp a male; any native of (esp sub-Saharan) Africa. *On a much more positive note, I wish to call upon all Indo-Trinidadians to join with their Afro-brothers and sisters and celebrate Emancipation Day.*—ExP (1997.08.01, p.9) [< *Afro-*, as a universal combining form, 'identified or identifying with Africa' + IAE *brother*, as a generic term for fellowship] □ May apply to the whole CarA, and intended to include **Afro-sister(s)**, but not currently regarded as ideally inclusive. See DCEU *Afro-Caribbean*, but cp AFRIC¹.

Af.ro.cen.tric *adj* (CarA) Partial to, embracing or reflecting the cultures and life-ways of (esp sub-Saharan) Africa; empathetic with (esp Black) Africa, its peoples and diaspora. *A brief observation of the styles worn by women locally would show that there is a tendency towards the Afrocentric look associated with braided hair.*—AdV (1999.09.12, p.32) [< *Afro-*, combining form 'relative to Africa' +—*centric*, combining form 'having as its specified centre'] □ OED 2 (1991) does not list **Afrocentric**, but OED Additions vol.3 (1997) relates it to 'African or Afro-American culture' + cits from 1967. The word may, however, have been in earlier use in CarA contexts by regional social scientists.

Af.ro fade *n phr* (Bdos) A man's AFRO hair-style lightened in thickness behind the head. *The guys haven't been left out. Adrian Patterson, a barber,* *reckons the favourite style among his clients was the Afro fade ... that's when they want the Afro look but don't want too much hair in the back. So you fade it out.*—NaT (1996.05.10, p.24)

Afro.gen.e.sis *n* [*Linguistics; Creolistics*] (CarA) The theory that all West Atlantic Creoles (anglophone, francophone, hispanophone and Dutch) have notable similarities of conceptual framework, idiomatic, syntactic and some phonetic and lexical structures that are historically derived from common substratum influences in the Niger-Congo family of West and Central African languages. [< *Afro* (comb. form = 'African' + *genesis* (Gk = origin) Cp (Ling) 'Monogenesis', 'Polygenesis'] □ The term was first identified by Dr Richard Allsopp in 1976.

Agro.tour.ism *n* (Bdos) The use of regional agricultural products and foods as a means to attract tourists. *Therefore, Harvey explained that in an attempt to ensure sustainable development of the sector, the Agro-Tourism Linkages Centre has been working on projects involving the development of farm sites for recreational, scientific and agro-heritage tours as well as the development of the herbals sector. ... We continue to undervalue our agriculture, our heritage and our foods.*—AdV (2004.03.26, p.5) [< *Agro* (comb. form = 'relating to Agriculture' + *tourism* (as an industry]

ahigh *adv* (Bdos) On high; in high places. *Only a few calypsos have been released so far, but some people from ahigh are going all out to ensure that certain people are not attacked in song.*—SuS (1997.06.21, p.11) [*OED* a-high (*Obs*) *adv* 1. On high, aloft' (+ Note: The full form *on high* is now alone used; + cits to 1696] □ The survival of this EE form notably in the cit 'people from ahigh' in *Bdos,* is not characteristic of general CE usage.

aji; (agi) *n* (Guyn) Monosodium glutamate, a salt much used as a seasoning in cooking Chinese food. *Look for instance roti and curry cook with agi and then the meat pressure in the pressure-pot on gas stove. Curry roti different. No agi in that, is masala.*—StN (1994.03.23, p.8) [Abbr of *ajimoto* < *ajima moto,* perh Chinese name of the substance]

all *adv* **1.** As emphasizer (CarA) [*AF/IF*] Even. **a.** *I was at the hospital and Ralston used to come visit me often. The nurses used to call me Miss Ralston. All when it wasn't visiting time him bore and come in.*—SSLG:122 **b.** *Mama say she used to work hard inna Westmoreland, weh she come from. She tek all axe and fall tree when she young.*—SSLG:159 **2.** In completive function As fully as; in as complete a way as. *It was about the things that she met me with in Trinidad. She wanted to rule them all she like. I had furnitures, I had garden, and I had money that I had worked and save.*—SDP:63 **3.** As intensifier As often as; as frequently as. *Sometimes he come all three times a day. [Even] when it wasn't visiting time him bore and come in.*—SSLG:122 **4.** *Phrases* **4.1 all about** *adv phr* (CarA) [*IF*] Everywhere. *I had been all about looking for you.* —(Pers

info, 1997.11.28 T. Gossling) **4.2 all (like) how** *adv phr* (ECar, Jmca) [*AF*] (If you look at) the way how; considering. **a.** *All how we play carnival today, is only brass bands leading the way. Hardly do we hear the melody of a lovely steelband symphony.*—LuK2 (91/07, p.29) **b.** *Christmas parties are nice though, and all like how I not so hot in the cooking department, it's a welcome opportunity to eat well for a month.*—ObS (1996.12.22, p.5) □ An additional usage to *DCEU all³* adv Phr 5.2 *all how.* 'In all ways', etc. **4.3 all (like) now; all now (so)** *adv phr* (Bdos, StVn) [*AF/IF*] At this time; at time of speaking/writing. **a.** *If we no longer have to stick to the accepted facts, there is no reason for us to even wait for history to happen—we can write the history of the future all like now.*—NaT (1990.03.06, p.9) **b.** *If the Prime Minister takes an early retirement he can enjoy himself with his family, engage in any particular hobby and write his memoirs and be spared all the constant confusion and criticism. Were I faced with those alternatives, all like now me and my dogs would be brekin' coming down Two Mile Hill.*—NaT (1991.08.16, p.9A) **c.** *They say the witness who nearly mek him gey hang, confess after, that she lied on him! Is ah pity Big Comb was not ah Lawyer, he would ah get he lickle five years an' dey out all now so.*—SeA (1996.12.31, p.9) **4.4 and all the like** *pron phr* (ECar) [*AF/IF*] And so on. *Sometimes the overseer would tell me, "Go and cut a bunch of bluggo; go and pick breadfruit", they would give me a coconut and all the like.*—SDP:57

all-Ca.rib.be.an *adj* (CarA) Belonging or pertaining to the Caribbean region, taken as a whole. *If we accept the validity of the concept, of all-American, why should we find it difficult to accept the reasonableness of action and strategies designed to establish and maintain the concept of all-Caribbean or all-Barbadian?*—SuS (1985.06.30, p.4) [As *OED* **All** E, in combinations, 1, 'the whole (body) of', as in 'all-night', All-Saints', etc.]

all-weath.er road *n phr* (Guyn) An inter-regional road with a hard surface, and wide enough to take heavy-gauge traffic in all types of weather, hence the name. *For the 17,000 inhabitants of the Rupununi, their dreams for an all-weather road link with their city Georgetown have vanished. With the coming of the long rainy season all vehicular traffic using this road will be cut off on the Mabura finished leg of the road.*—StN (1993.04.28, p.9)

all-white *adj phr* (Bdos) Exclusively for white people. *And he recalls a situation back in the '70s at the "all white" Savannah Club (located at the Garrison across from the cannons).*—SuS (2000.05.13, p.7) [Cp *OED* 2 **All** E. III and IV, special combinations as in *all-electric* 'using only electricity'] □ This shift of combinative use of 'all + adj' from the sense of 'wholly, completely' as in *all-embracing, all-wool,* etc. to 'exclusively' as in 'all-French' (finals in Tennis)' 'all-time' (record)' etc. and here *all-white,* is a development in Modern English not noticed in *OED* 1, E I, II. The added record in *OED* 2 **All** E III, IV suggests that this function of *all-* is rare.

al.men.dra *n* (Belz) The WEST INDIAN ALMOND tree and fruit. *Terminalia catappa (Combretaceae). Almendra not so plentiful this season.*—(Belz, Cayo District) [Spanish name, by influence of Guatemala] □ More common in general *Belz* folk-speech is **ha.manz.** (See *DCEU* **almond.**)

a. long wid/with (sb) *prep phr* (Jmca) [*AF*] In sexual partnership with (sb). *After ah had me second child for Foreman, ah found out he was still along wid di same Sonia.*—SSLG:150 [Cp. (*DSUE 8*) **along with** (coll. weakening of) with: late 19–20C + ex: 'Her engagement to her understanding with—whatever ... she had along with the young Henry Lee fellow—had hardened her']

Amer.i.can ap.ple *n phr* (Jmca) /// ENGLISH APPLE (ECar) *A walk to South Parade to buy American apples and grapes and the tough and sweet ropes of white candy bump ended the day in Kingston.*—DaG (1996.03, p.9A) [From the source of importation to *Jmca*, the US. See (*DECU*) **apple**]

amwé *excl; n* (Gren) [*Fr Cr*] A cry for help. *That woman take so much licks she had to bawl for amwé.*—(Gren) [Fr Cr < (Fr) *à moi!* "Help!"]

anar *n* (Trin) [*Indic*] Pomegranate; *Punia granatum (Punicaceae). The fruit rind of the anar is parched and ground for diarrhoea.*—GMPP:8 [Hindi, Urdu word] □ Restricted usage.

An.gel Ga.bri.el ri.ots *n phr* (Guyn) [Hist] See cit. *The most significant and disastrous of the riots was sparked off and instigated in February 1856 by James Sayers Orr known as the 'Angel Gabriel'—hence the 'Angel Gabriel Riots'. The riots broke in Georgetown and spread to the East Coast, Demerara and to the Essequibo. Portuguese shops and houses were sacked ... Khalill Mohammed investigating these riots pointed out in his thesis: 'The Negroes destroyed Portuguese property and not their persons' which supported his claim that these riots were seen by the Creoles as a means of lessening the economic clout of their rivals.*—MSHPG:13

ans.wer *vb tr Phrase* **answer a call of nature** *vb phr* (Guyn) // **take in short** (Guyn) (A euphemism for) to have to go and urinate or ease your bowels. *He quietly got up and went out and I thought he had gone to answer a call of nature but he never came back to the meeting.*—(Guyn)

An.ti.gua black pine.ap.ple *n phr* (Antg) A heavyish, ovoid variety of pineapple with a dark green rind (hence called 'black'); it is native to Antigua; and features in the national coat-of-arms.

An.ti.gua Car.ni.val *n phr* (Antg) See cit. *The last week of July and the first Monday and Tuesday in August are set aside for one of the Caribbean's great summer festivals—Antigua's Carnival.*—Cab (Summer 1994, p.18) □ A time officially chosen in Antigua to coincide with the historic festive significance of August 1 (Emancipation Day). See CARNIVAL.

any *pron Phrases* **1. any and any** *adj phr* (Jmca) [*AF*] Second-rate. *Standards were very high, you couldn't carry any and any dibby-dibby or fenky-fenky foods to market.*—RLTJWS:70 [A reduplication expanded for emphasis. Cp similar IAE phr 'each and every'] **2. any and any (old) how** *adv phr* (Jmca) [*AF*] Carelessly; without consideration. *Ole Nat did come in like a slave to them; anything they said he had to jump. They felt they could treat him any and any how.*—RLTJWS:6 **3. any at all** *intensifier adv phr* (Belz, Jmca) [*AF*] Why the hell did he want to tell him about his plans, did he want to involve him in this thing any at all?*—MHJT:157 *Is what kind of water pipe this any at all, Mr. Engineer? How come it is so rotten, eh? And only buy a couple years back!*—YFOC:14 □ A strongly emotive tag phrase. **4. any which part** *adv phr* (Jmca) [*AF*] Wherever. *Me notice how white man, dress up inna him three piece suit will walk out of him office wid a brown paper bag a lunch, and siddung a dutty an eat. Any which part him mind tell him, him siddung.*—Outlook (J. Keane-Dawes, 1995.06.11, p.14) [< *any* + Cr *which part* 'where', of likely Afr source. See *DCEU* **which**²; also *DJE* **which-part**]

ap.an jaat.ism *n phr* (Guyn, Trin) The practice of choosing or supporting persons of your own race, esp. for office in politics or in public administration; it is particularly associated with East Indians. (See etym, also *DCEU*, **Apan Jhaat.**) *If Western democracy means electoral arithmetic, and apan jaatism means racial arithmetic, then the common sense thing for any East Indian politician in Guyana (and soon Trinidad) to do is shout for democracy. And the Western World and the West Indies would applaud all the way.*—AdV (1998.06.28, p.12) [Bhoj. *Apan jaat* 'your kind' + IAE suff *-ism*, as *COD* 10 'ism' 2 'denoting a basis for prejudice or discrimination, e.g. racism']

a.pa.so.te [apasote] *n* (Belz) /// WORMWOOD (Jmca) /// WORM OIL PLANT (Belz) An upright bush growing to about 2 ft, with slender stems, small narrow leaves and seeds bunched along separate shoots; the crushed leaves yield a strong oily scent, and an infusion is used by some as a vermifuge for children; *Chenopodium ambrosioides (Chenopodiaeceae) A popular plant used for seasoning by many Belizeans is the apasote, the leaves of which contain chenopodium oil, an effective cure for roundworms and hookworms.*—(Belz, Ms) [Sp, from Aztec *epazotl, epatl* + *zotl,* 'little fox + dirt', a prob ref to the smell when crushed for use. See *SGDA* 1:614] □ Spanish name used in Belz from Lat. Amer. infl. It is better known in CarA as **semi-contract, semen-contra** etc. (See *DCEU.*)

Ap.pren.tice.ship *n* (CarA) [Hist] A state of extended conditional enslavement on CarA plantations after the act of Emancipation (1834), legislated by the British Parliament. See cits. **a.** *The British Law provided for a period of compulsory 'apprenticeship' to follow slavery and precede complete emancipation. This required the ex-slave to remain at his job under his old master for a period of years. The chief distinction from slavery was that he now received wages. In Jamaica apprenticeship was abolished abruptly in 1838 and nowhere did it work* *very well. The new freedmen considered it a trick to avoid the freedom they had been promised ...*—M. Ayearst: The British West Indies (London, Allen & Unwin, 1960; p.24) **b.** *Under the terms of the Emancipation the children of slaves born after the Act was passed and all slave children under the age of six were freed; but children older than six and their elders had to serve a four year apprenticeship before being freed.*—SSHL:24 **c.** *It appears evident that the negros in this Colony [Antigua] have gained nothing by the exchange of Slavery for Apprenticeship ... (The special Magistrate) has power to punish an Apprentice on the complaint of any person whatever.*—SHWI (App xxi) [By transfer of the normal 19C English system of 'apprenticeship' (or preparation) of minors in the legal and moral introduction to a craft or trade] □ Often capitalized in Hist writings.

arc eyes *n phr* (Bdos) See cit. *And for all who don't know, you get arc eyes when you gaze too long at that bright whitish blue light you see when those fellows are welding.*—AdV (1998.10.23, p.10)

Ar.ri.val Day *n phr* (Guyn) The 5th day of May, celebrated annually as a public holiday to commemorate the arrival in *Guyn* of the various races of people as immigrant plantation labourers. The choice of dates relates historically to the arrival of the first ship of East Indian immigrants in *Guyn* in 1838. *Arrival Day should be a time for unity knowing that collectively all our peoples have contributed to the gains and freedoms achieved in trying to fashion a truly free and democratic society. So stated President Bharrat Jagdeo in his Arrival Day message yesterday.*—StN (2006.05.05, p.15) □ See **Indian Arrival Day** (Trin)

au.vent [ovǎ] *n* (Dmca) // **windward side** (Dmca) [IF] The east or windward, Atlantic coast of the island. *You could see she come from auvent.*—(Dmca) [FrCr < From au vent 'windward'] □ Considered to indicate 'far away' country, the capital Roseau being leeward on the Caribbean coast.

B

back to *prep phr* (Jmca) [*AF—Cr*] [Of time] continuing up to; through to; from that time to. *She was a higgler. She always deh pon di road from Tuesday night back to Saturday. When she gone a market me and me grandfadda gone a bush.*—SSLG: 98 □ This is prob unique *Jmca* Cr usage, with 'forward-looking' sense. In IAE *back to* is always backward-looking, whether in ref to position or time.

back.a.tive *n* (Jmca) [*IF*] Reliable support; influential backing. **a.** *She start call down all who live inna di yard fi backative.*—SSLG:184 (cited PRJW:233) **b.** *Most of what Garvey preached was a true thing, a good thing, only he never got the backativ.*—RLTJWS:52 [Perh a nominalized blend of IAE *back-up* + *relative, supportive*] □ Established after becoming a folk vogue word in the 1980s.

bag.gy *n* (Jmca) [*AF—Joc*] Female underpants or panties. *A was runnin(g) an(d) stoppin(g) to haul up me baggy.*—(Jmca) [Familiar blend of *bag* + (pant)*y*]

bail.iff *vb tr* (Jmca) [*AF*] To levy, as a bailiff, on the furniture and household items of sb (who is usu in default of payment of rent). *Di people dem next door say, "Yvonne dem bailiff yuh. Bailiff come and tek out stove, machine and dressing table fi di rent. Ah was shock."*—SSLG:151 [By typical Cr functional n > vb shift of IAE *bailiff* 'a sherrif's officer authorized to levy on a person's household items']

bam.sie/bam.sy *n* (Trin) [*AF—Joc*] // **boongy** (Baha) // **botsie** (Bdos) The buttocks. *She hair long to she bamsie.*—(Cso line, 1970s) [Hypocoristic variant of *bam-bam* 'the bottom', [*child-talk*] esp of children and women] □ By infl of Trin Cso by 'Sparrow', originally adapted fr child talk. ***Phrase* roll yo(ur) bamsy** *vb phr* (ECar) [*AF—Joc*] [Dancing, esp of a woman] To vigorously wiggle your backside; make your buttocks move in a rolling motion. *Buh wait / We culture does include dem tings / Like roll yuh bamsy, wuk-up / And behave rude?*—MMSC:30

Bap.tist *n; adj* (Bdos, Jmca, Trin) [*IF*] **1.** [IF] (An informal reference to SPIRITUAL BAPTIST) *Both the Spiritual Baptists and Shango are syncretic in that they borrow from other religions. A major difference in Shango and Baptist belief systems is that Baptist rituals are directed toward their version of the Holy Trinity, while Shango rituals are directed toward African or African-derived gods. Spiritual Baptists are (ostensibly?) Christians and, in the words of one informant,* "don't worship the mothers". *This is not to say that Baptists do not believe in the existence of African gods. In sixteen years I never met a Spiritual Baptist who did not believe in the power of Shango deities. Baptists do not feel that African gods should be venerated.*—KACR 1:109 [See SPIRITUAL BAPTIST] **2.** (Jmca) A member of or relating to an early (18C) black post-Emancipation Christian religious movement similar to the SPIRITUAL BAPTISTS of the *ECar. The Baptists were the first to advocate minimum wage legislation and to call for the establishment of a university as early as the first half of the 19th Century? The Baptists were also the first to establish free villages in Jamaica. They solicited money from England to buy land for the settlement of land-hungry ex-slaves.*—JJRW:6 □ The *Jmca* use of the name (sense 2) prob predates the *ECar*.

Bar.ba.di.an ba.o.bab [be·obab] *n phr* (Bdos) See cits. *Adansonia digitata (Bombacaceae)* [pers info, Prof S. Carrington] **a.** *According to Rashford these [Barbadian Boabab] trees have been known by locals as "flower tamarind" trees. The baobab tree has been also known as the "bottle tree", "Judas bag", "monkey tree" and, along with the silk cotton tree, was believed in folklore to harbour spirits. Rashford said that Reverend Griffith Hughes, in the Natural History of Barbados, 1750, identified the baobab as the "Corn-Tree" and noted that the tree at Warrens was brought to Barbados from Guinea in 1738.*—AdV (1995.07.18, p.9) **b.** *The two best known Barbadian baobabs are located in Queen's Park and on the Warrens Estate. Others are located in the flower forest.*—AdV (1995.07.18, p.9)

Bar.ba.dos(ed) *vb* (Bdos) [Hist] [Of British whites] (To be) deported from Britain to Barbados, originally as penal punishment. See cit. *During the initial stage of sugar production, when the white servants found themselves toiling in the same field as gangs with black slaves, they became wild and unruly in the extreme. Some of the English and Irish youths shipped over in the 1640s and 1650s had been kidnapped. To be "barbadosed" in the seventeenth century meant the same as to be "shanghaied" in the twentieth. It would be hard to say whether the London thieves and whores rounded up for transportation to "the Barbados Islands" or the Scottish and Irish soldiers captured in Cromwell's campaigns and sent over as military prisoners were any less hostile and rebellious than the Negroes dragged in chains from Africa. Irish Catholics constituted the largest block of servants on the island, and they were cordially loathed by their English masters.*—DSAS:69 [By

functional n > vb shift of 'Barbados' as destination] □
A unique IAE occurrence of verbalizing a country's
name. Cp *COD* 10 *shanghai* 1, though this has a shifted and later (19C) sense. 19C British penal deportations to Australia and New Zealand did not generate
parallel lexical usage.

bare joke *n phr* (Bdos) [*AF—Joc*] Something absurd.
*The resident raised her voice angrily: "I went for a job
and I couldn't give the Orleans as my address. And if you
ask a taxi driver to bring you here it is a bare joke. He
ain't coming!"*—SuS (1991.08.18, p.1B) [< *bare* (Bdos,
IF) 'pure, absolute' + *joke* (Bdos IF) 'an absurdity')]

ba.rif.fle *n* (Bdos) [*AF*] A bundle; a lot. **a.** *An' de
newspapers gine still be featurin' a bariffle o' Press re-
leases day after day.*—AdV (1992.12.27, p.8) **b.** *Mean-
while, de lis' o' candidates from de diff'rent parties
got-in a bariffle o' onknown quantities..some names
yuh never hear 'bout yet.*—AdV (1994.07.08, p.9) [<
IAE *barrelful* by reduction of intervocalic /-cc-/, -'lf']

bar.rel-child *n* (Jmca) [*IF*] A young child, usu not yet
a teenager; left behind in Jamaica in the care of a relative or close friend, while the mother goes to find
work in North America, sending back remittances
and food and clothing in a barrel-sized container of
compressed cardboard; hence the nickname. *I was
the traditional barrel-child, as my mother had to leave
my siblings and me behind and go up to New York to
work in order to support us.*—(Jmca)

bash.ment *n* (ECar; Jmca) [*AF*] An enjoyable party
with plenty of food and music; [by extension] any
entertainment or enjoyable sensual experience esp in
young people's social life. (See cits for variety of extended senses.) **a.** *"It's all about 'bashment'. It's the
latest slang which has taken a firm place in the language of young adults in the Corporate Area. The
party is 'bashment', and the sex is also more 'bashment' ... the slang is used in local terms to mean big
'excitement' or simply 'big things a gwaan'. Some feel
that the slang originated from bus conductors in the
Corporate area, who will say "bashment!" as a com-
mand to their driver to "drive now!" Young people
picked it up readily from there. People use it for different reasons—if they are going on a move, work or
party. Most dancehall disc jockeys say 'run the bashment (rhythm)' and they use it to promote dances, and
parties." Eighteen-year old Simone of Rollington Town,
[said] the first time she used the word bashment was
after sex, when her boyfriend asked her "how was I?"
Her reply? "That was a good bashment."*—ObS (Teen
Age, 1996.12.29, p.3) **b.** *Family, friends and a massive
crowd of fans rubbed shoulders on the grounds of the
Versailles Hotel in Clarendon last week Friday night as
they turned out to celebrate Freddy McGregor's Earth-
day in bashment style.*—Xnews (1997.07.2–8, p.16) **c.**
*"Bashment rides" with loud, vulgar, and violent music
need to be stamped out ... "When I was going to school
it was the secondary schools that were into the bashment music. Now from the time they are seven or eight
years old they stand up on the road and [wait] until

vans with the loudest, rudest music come out."*—NaT
(2004.05.27, p.3) [Perh orig a characteristic CE com-
pounding of [*Rastaf*] *bashi* 'a calabash (of food)' +
CE intensifier *suff* -MENT. PDT:54 comments: *bashi*,
'diminutive form of affection for the calabash ...
[which] can be seen at all "irations" as large mixing
or serving bowls ... [and] small eating dishes'] □ The
term has shifted in sense from its *Jmca* source and
gained wide (*CarA*) acceptance through the entertainment culture and teenage *AF* usage, associating it
emotively with pleasure.

bat.ty boy *n phr* (Trin) [*AF—Vul*] A homosexual
male. [< *batty* 'buttocks' (see *DCEU*) + **'boy'**]

bawl *vb tr* (CarA) [*AF*] *Phrase* **bawl eye water** *vb phr*
(Jmca) [*AF*] To cry long tears. *Caribbean Literary Festival organiser, Colin Channer and Kwame Dawes,
"bawled living eye-water" before a large audience at
Treasure Beach, St. Elizabeth, recently. The tears were
tears of joy and the audience empathised; at least one
member cried, too.*—DaG (2001.06.16, p.B9) [< *bawl*
'weep', by exaggerated reduction in sense (see *DCEU*
bawl 1.) + *eye-water* 'tears' (CarA, see *DCEU*)] □ A *Joc*
transfer of the characteristic CE idiom *cry long tears.*

be *vb* (Gren) [*Obs Cr*] (Monoform link vb, pres. or
pa.t) *I had to go back and beg them to teach me. I weren't
successful in doing anything, I just be lazy.* (= was
lazy).—SDP:100 [Prob a survival of Irish Engl: Cp
MCUD **be** vb '1. The present tense with be ... is used to
express a habitual or normal state of affairs', ex. "It
doesn't always be a problem"—See *DCEU* **be¹** 1, 2, but
the pa.t. usage is not attested as here] □ **1.** Normally in
CarA Cr or *IF* CE, the vb 'to be' is omitted in such
expressions. The usage here to signal "a state of affairs" is prob *Obs* in ECar though it is still found in
Baha (see *DBE* **be¹**) □ **2.** Prob a grammatical feature
of general early *CarA Cr*, though currently rare in
ECar. Note, however, its occurrence in *Baha*. See
DBE **be** 1, **be** 2. □ **3.** Not normal in writing. The cit is
from a biographical transcript.

bear.ing-wheel skate *n phr* (Jmca) A scooter made
from scrap lumber and wheel bearings.—DPJP:5
[< wheel-bearing skate]

beat *vb tr* *Phrases* **1. beat drum** *vb phr* [*IF*] (Gren) To
beat a ceremonial drum with one particular rhythm,
related to the rituals of an aboriginal African religion.
*Oshun ordered me to keep a thanksgiving in April and
a drum-beating. I kept that thanksgiving and I beat
drum for one day.*—SDP:104 **2. beat up** *vb intr phr*
(Gren) [Religion] To beat your own body with flailing arms and/or roll on the ground with feet also
flailing, in the experience of spirit possession. *A girl
came and did not want to dance, she did not want any
Powers to manifest her, and when Oshun came ... I saw
she fall, and she start to roll and beat up and beat up. I
did not worry with her. I leave her there till Oshun
gone.*—SDP:86 [< IAE *beat* + phrasal frequentative
up] □ The *intr* use of this phrase is not unusual in Cr
usage. Cp *DCEU* **wuk-up**.

beg yo(u) *vb phr* (Jmca) [*AF*] Please. '*Beg yuh come out a me yard!' And dem lef.*—SSLG:162 [< *Courtesy phr A beg yo(u)* 'I beg you', with aphetic loss of '*A*'] □ Courtesy subjuncts (see *Q & CGEL* 8.90) like IAE. 'Please ...', kindly ...' etc., function to persuade. **Beg yo(u)**, however, is unusual in being always initial in its sentence.

bel.la *n* (Jmca) A large round-bottomed cooking pot. *... and another bella would be used to cook the hard food; yam, banana, breadfruit, co-co, dasheen, badoo, corn, pumpkin and the big 'cartwheel' dumplings.*—RLTJWS:48 [Prob an abbr of *belapat* 'a huge cooking pot', as *DJE*, < *bela* 'a greedy person' + *pat* 'pot']

bel.ly *Phrase*—**dash (a)way belly** *vb phr* (Jmca) [*AF—Vul*] To have an abortion.—DPJP:8 [IAE, *dash away* [AF] 'to throw away' with Cr. aphesis of /a-/, + *DCEU* **belly 2.** 'a pregnancy'; and cp such *DCEU* id phrs as 3.7 '*belly is a burying-ground'*]

be.ne [bɛnɛ] *n* (Gren, Tbgo, Trin) A sticky sweet made from sesame; see *DCEU* **benne**. *And she told me "Get milk, don't forget pumkin; and bene, I must have bene, sugar-cake, coconut".*—SDP:85 [< Mandingo *bene* 'sesame'] □ This rare spelling more closely reflects the Afr. origin.

big.get.y *adj* (Baha) [*AF—Joc*] Self-confident; assertive; pushy. *Coming to work late and telling a short-staffed supervisor that you didn't come in to stay is "biggety".*—GMMTB:20 [< IF IAE *big* 'self-important' + *suff* -y; 'having the quality of'. Cp 'bossy', 'showy'; also cp *DCEU* **biggitive**] □ Cp **biggitive** (Guyn) wh rather connotes 'pretentiousness'.

big-up¹ /1´2/ *adj* (Baha, Bdos) [*AF—Joc*] **1.** [Of a person] Highly placed; important. *The handsome fellow who is known to frequent certain big-up circles, talks and deals with certain big-up women, told one of his big-up male homosexual friends that life is not so easy for him these days.*—SaS (1994.04.09, p.11) **2.** [By extension, of an event] Very significant. *E suppose to be gine to Germany 'cordin' to de newspapers, to sign some big-up loan agreement wid de European Investment Bank concernin' de construction o' de Souf Coas' Sewerage Projeck.*—AdV (1993.03.26, p.9, Lickmout' Lou) [< *big* + intensifier *up*. See *DCEU* **big-up¹**] **3.** (Baha) Pregnant. *So if you hear that a friend is "big up", start knitting gift bootees.*—GMMTB:21 [< *big* 'grown in size' + intensifier suff *up* as in 'high up'] □ The *Bdos* usage is often hyphenated, the *Baha* usage usu not.

big-up² *n* (Bdos) [*AF—Joc*] An important, socially significant person. **a.** *We even heard that one big-up is planning to hold a Press conference to protest the results.*—SaS (1993.07.10, p.11) **b.** *Now that he is being asked to identify all his sexual partners, in recent years, he is running down a who's who of big-ups both male and female.*—SaS (1994.04.09, p.11) [By functional adj > n shift of BIG UP¹. See *DCEU* **big-up²**]

big-up³, big up *vb (phr)* (Bdos, Jmca) [*AF/IF*] **1.** To make important; to treat as worthy. **a.** *It's nice how they*

big-up the teachers on Teachers' Day.—(Jmca). **b.** *Countries today need positive influences, not sellers of songs "bigging-up" drugs, sex and murder.*—AdV (2002.06.23, Jmca letter-writer). **c.** *To our own golden boys Barry Forde and Obadele Thompson, let me say, well done, you have made Barbados proud, the two o' wunna really big we up to the whole world.*—SaS (2004.09.04, p.11) [By functional adj > vb shift of **big-up¹**. Also cp *EDD big* vb 1 'To make big; to magnify'. + cit from sWor '*E's a good un to big 'esself*'] **2.** [By extension] To puff up (yourself). *The situation is made worse by the high promotion of festive activities and the never-ending advocation for youths to just have a good time. This is helping create some of the hopelessness among them and signalling that the only thing for them to do now is to party and big-up themselves.*—NaT (1996.06.24, p.9A) [By extension of sense, and functional shift of **big-up** adj & n 'important (person)'. Adv extension **up** functions as intensifier, as often in *CarA* Cr]

big-up⁴ *adv* (Bdos) [*AF—Joc*] With a show of personal confidence; boastfully. *I wonder how Major feel, neh, after 'e did talk so big-up 'bout how he wife, Norma, did decide dem should stay at No: 10!*—AdV (1997.05.03, p.12, Lickmout' Lou) [By functional adj > adv shift of BIG UP¹]

bigup⁵ *greeting* (Jmca) [*AF*] Hello! (With respect, see cit) *Bigup is used mainly by young people, and in the most formal of circumstances. At a wedding in an up-scale neighborhood, and high-status guests, the young man toasting the groom, began with the greeting "Big-op to all a unu, so that I won't leave out anybody".*—K. Shields-Brodber (MS, 2004/8)

bin.gi [bɪŋgi] *n* (Jmca) A familiar *Rastaf* term for a festive NYABINGHI gathering that may last some days. *During the 1974 celebration of the Ethiopian Christmas ... Dreadlocks from all over Jamaica met in the far reaches of the Bull Head Mountains in Clarendon for a Bingi. [They] swarmed the grounds ... puffing the holy herb ... . [There were] four sets of drums, lead singers, priests, dancers.*—MSMCDB:242 [Abbr of NYABINGHI]

bird-speed *n, adv* (Bdos) With the speed of a bird. *When dem lights change to red fuh drivers gine 'cross de road to go up by CBC, it does be two an' t'ree cars sometimes dat fly t'rough bird-speed, mekkin' de drivers dat got de green light wait or risk meetin' duh Maker!*—AdV (1995.04.08, p.12, Lickmout' Lou) [Cp IAE *post haste* with (the) haste of (the) post]

bird-watch.ing / 1´22 / *n* (Trin) [*AF—Joc*] [Usu of a group of idle young men] Looking sensually (and whistling) at passing young women. *He was among the boys on the block bird-watching, not expecting his own girl friend would pass.*—(Trin, 1995) [Metaph. transfer of the IAE term in reference to an adult hobby, + *CarA* Cr usage of *bird* 'an attractive girl' as *DCEU* **bird 2** [*AF*]]

bitch lamp /1´2/ *n phr* (Jmca) [*IF*] A small oil lamp made out of tin. *The young man acted bravado before* *he got up and stumbled round to the back in the dark till smaddy called him and offered him a bitch lamp.*—RLTJWS:1 [Perh shared with AmE slang. Cp *RHDAS* I p.170 *bitch n.6* West 'a makeshift lamp made from hardened grease' + cits 1904–1936] □ Compare *DCEU* **slut lamp**.

black clothes (police) *n phr* (Guyn) A special male police strike force, developed in the late 1990s, identified by their black wear, hence the name. **a.** *They were told by an officer that the police were doing their duties, and that she would have to return later. "At around 6:30 [am] the black clothes police came and ransacked the house and removed the colour television. They took photographs and left." Shivgobin said.*—StN (2001.08.15, p.3) **b.** *I have in my possession a list in excess of 135 people killed by the Black Clothes. I only offer a partial list of citizens shot to death and otherwise unlawfully killed by "black clothes" and some other rogue elements in the Police Force 1993–2002.*—SuS (2002.09, p.10A) □ The term is popular and journalistic, not official.

black fly *n phr* (ECar) See CITRUS BLACK FLY

black.wash[1] *n; adj* (CarA, UniK) [AF/IF—Joc] [Cricket] **1.** The winning of an entire series of matches by a West Indies cricket team (whose players are mostly AFRIC, i.e. 'black' and hence the name) playing against England or another white team. *"As they progressed to what several placards in the West Indian section of the ground proclaimed as their 'blackwash', the West Indies again showed their spirit in overcoming adversity".*—(T. Cozier, in W. Indies Annual, 1985) [By *Joc* analogy < WHITEWASH. See also cit.] □ Cp WHITEWASH; BROWNWASH; WASH **2.** [By extension and *Joc* inversion] The loss of an entire series of matches by a West Indies side (i.e. of black players) to an opposing side of white or Indic players. See BLACKWASH[2]. *All sports are promoted by great players, without whom a day at the beach would be a better alternative. You may recall that Ali Bacher, the South African cricket chief, insisted that Lara and Carl Hooper be part of the West Indies touring party on that devastating "Blackwash" series in 1998.*—NaT (2000.08.17, p.4B)

black.wash[2] *vb tr* (CarA) [AF/IF—Joc] [Cricket] **1.** [Of the West Indies Team] To beat an opposing national (English, Australian or Indic) side in the entire series of matches of a tour. *We long for the glory days of the 1970s when the Windies, under Captain Clive Lloyd, our cricket Lord, blackwashed the world twice in World Cup matches in 1975 and 1979.*—Bdos (Call-in radio, June 2004) [By functional n > vb shift of BLACKWASH[1]] **2.** [By extension and *Joc* inversion] [Of an Indic team] To beat a West Indies team in the entire series of matches of a tour. (See note.) *Pakistan became the first team in 69 years to blackwash the West Indies yesterday, winning the third and final cricket Test by 10 wickets with more than a day to spare.*—NaT (1997.12.10, p.33A) [A shift in usage due to the inapplicability of WHITEWASH to an Indic team] □ This use

duplicates WHITEWASH, the term originally used in this context. There is evidently a popular confusion in the use of these terms. See BROWNWASH.

blen.za; blen.zers [blɛnzʌ / blɛnzər(z)] *n (pl) / collective* (Bdos) // **blindza; dunny; dunsa; dunsie; dunza** (Jmca) [*Rastaf*] Money. **a.** *He would brek all the world records and start getting contracts from big-shot names he never ever hear 'bout, and he corning blenza.*—SuS (2000.05.20, p.11) **b.** *I want a villa in de souf o' France an' a roun'-de-worl' trip 'pon de QE2—so ef yuh come into any blenzers, yuh know wuh to do!*—NaT (1991.05.03, p.9) [The variant is a spelling pronunc of (*Jmca Rastaf*) BLINDZA (see), prob developed from Bdos folk pronunc ɪ > ɛ shift (as in + "if" > /ef/) + characteristic CarA loss of syllable final [-d] + Bdos syllable final [-r] as in 'water']

blind *adj* **Phrase** **rob (sb) blind** *vb phr* (CarA) [AF] To cheat or steal from (sb) without scruple. *Winkie never stopped lamenting how Sommerville did hoodwink and rob him blind.*—RLTJWS:169 [By shift of AF usage as an adverbial intensifier, as in IAE *'blind drunk'*]

blin(d)za [blaɪnzʌ ~ blɪnza] *n* (Bdos) /// **blenza** (Bdos) [*Rastaf*] **a.** *"Blinza" (money) is another agent of "low lively" and has no place in their society. Nevertheless, since their philosophy dictates that they must not steal, beg nor rob nor be parasites, this is one part of Babylon that they cannot shake off. So they plant food and produce art, some of which they sell to get enough "blinza" to buy those necessities which do not grow out of the eart.*—NaT (1977.02.13, p.14) **b.** *I would like to get a copy of 'calling rastafari' everytime it comes out and just write and tell us how much it cost and how to send the "blinza".*—(Letter to editor, April 1979; cited in PDT:49) [... the Jamaican process where, so far, "blind" has been used to replace word sounds involving "seeing" (e.g. /siigaret > /blainjaret/p.6). "Blinza" indicates here that Rasta perceives money as a negative thing.—PDT:49, 50] □ See BLENZA (BLENZERS) for development commoner in Bdos.

block *vb intr* (Bdos) [AF] To create a rough, noisy, brawling scene; to row and (perhaps) fight. *The businessman who got hooked on a St. Lucian female dancer has moved out from his house. Some people who are accustomed to seeing him at the night club, said that since the Lucian turned his head, he has even travelled to her homeland. They say the last time she was in Barbados his wife went to the night club and 'blocked'.*—SaS (1999.05.22, p.11, Pudding & Souse) [Perh notionally 'to block, i.e. put a stop to everything' by your rage. Cp *DSUE* 2 p.1010 BrE *do one's block* 'to become angry' ca 1918. Also *RHDAS* I p.189 AmE *put the blocks to* 2 'to victimize, treat maliciously, do for']

blouse an(d) skirt! *excl* (Jmca) [AF] (An exclamation of surprise or amazement.—DPJP:7) [A euphemism for an oath]

boas.y [bwosi] *adj* (Jmca) [AF] Pleased with yourself. *Mr. Jones was a very boasy man. You could see it in the* *way he dressed.*—(Jmca) [< IAE *boas(t)* + (familarity suff) *-ie, -y,* as in *snowy*]

boo¹ *n* (Bdos) [*AF*] **1.** Small droppings or specks of dirt left by houseflies, or small bits of dung of a lizard or bird; hence **bird-boo, fly-boo, lizard-boo.** *He flicked some lizard-boo off the patio table and wiped the surface.*—(Bdos) [Perh ultimately from a Br dial source. Cp (*DARE*) Amer dial Eng. **boo** n1. Also **boo boo** '(Dried) mucus in the nose' 1892 KS 1901 NY. Also (*DNE* 2) Newfoundland Eng **boo** n **3.** 'Nasal mucus'] **2.** [By extension] Rubbish; nonsense; junk *I mus' remember nex' time I write to tell yuh 'bout de tas'eless pap CBC servin'-up to viewers 'pon Channel 8 dese days. Bare boo, girl! Unadulterated, undiluted boo!*—NaT (1998.02.04,—p.9A, Lickmout' Lou)

boo² *vb intr* (Bdos) [*AF—Joc*] [Of a housefly, small bird, or house lizard, or bird.] To defecate or leave bits of dung (on sth). *If you park yo(ur) car under these trees, pigeons sure to boo (u)pon it.* —(Bdos) [By functional n > vb shift of **boo¹**]

boon(g).gy [buŋgi] *n* (Baha) // **bamsie** (Trin) // **botsie** (Bdos) [*AF*] **1.** [Child talk] The buttocks. *Move yo(ur) boonggy from there (= Move your backside from there).*—(Baha) [Cp (*RHDAS*) Amer Eng [*Vul*] **bung** n. 1 'The anus' + cit 1788 from Grose *Vulgar Tongue*; also **bunghole** n. 1.a 'the anus' + cit 1611 from Cotgrave. Thus the word, prob pronunced [buŋ] can have entered *Baha* colonial Eng early, through dial Br Eng, and undergone similar child-talk familiarization to BAMSIE, BOTSIE. □ Often occurs in casual adult speech. Other spellings occur (see *DCEU* **boungie**) but '-oo-' seems to occur oftener. **2.** [By extension] [Vul] [Used as a swear-word] Arse! *Yo(ur) boonggy!*—(Baha) *Phrase* **peas and rice boonggy** (Baha) [*AF—Vul*] Large buttocks (esp. of a woman). (See cit.) *In the Bahamas the 'boongy' is truly 'maximus', credited to the overindulgence in the national dish peas and rice—thus the term 'peas and rice boongy' for the more generously endowed.*—GMMTB:22

boss *adj* (ECar) [*AF—Joc*] The best, most exciting of his/its kind. **a.** *Trinidad is where you'll find boss calypsonians like Mighty Sparrow and Kitchener.*—(Bdos) **b.** *An(d) de drug kings driving boss cars yo(u) know, Mercedes-Benz and t(h)ing.*—GMMTB:22 [By functional n > adj shift of AF **boss**, as in *DCEU*]

bot.sie *n* (Bdos) /// BOONGGY (Baha)

bounce *vb tr Phrase* **bounce your foot** *vb phr* (Gren) [*AF*] /// STUMP YOUR TOE (ECar) See *DCEU* ... *and if it is not for the Conductor you could be easily damaged, for you bounce your foot on something.*—SDP:98

bout here *n phr* (Bdos) [*AF*] This place/area/country. *But that is what I like 'bout 'bout here, when we put you in to run the country that is all we want, so so long as you running the country good and ain't involve in no kinda corruption, we don't look into your personal*

business.—AdV (2006.08.18, p.12) [By functional adv phr > n phr shift. See *(a)bout here*]

bow-man [bɒumʌn] *n* (Guyn) See cit. *The 'tacouba' is one of the prime terrors of river boat-men in the interior and is one of the main reasons for the "bow-man"—the one who stands at the bow with an enormous paddle to look out for danger and signal to the 'captain', while trying to pull the boat's bow away from the obstacle with the huge paddle.*—Ms (M. McWatt, 2003.12.02) [< *bow* + *man*, 'man at the bow' analogy of IAE *boatman, oarsman, helmsman* etc.]

box out *vb phr* (Baha) [*IF*] To do a quick ironing of clothes without being thorough. *Le(t) me box out dese clothes before I lie down.*—(Baha)

bra.cers [bre·sərz] /1´2/ *n pl* (Bdos, Guyn) Braces; a man's over-the-shoulders suspenders for his trousers. **a.** *She had bought him a presentation box of a fine new pair of bracers for Xmas.*—(Guyn) **b.** *... an' I notice 'e did wearin' bracers (or suspenders as duh's call dem now), ...*—AdV (1993.11.05, p.9, Lickmout' Lou) [An *Obs* E name for 'braces'. See *OED* **bracer** 1 'also a pair of braces' (*Obs*) + cit (1799) 'a bracer or sling for keeping up breeches'. The term evid survived longer in AmE: See *WCD*:10¹ brace, braces 4 c. pl 'Suspenders'] □ **'Bracers'**, the name still used by men of the older generation, is still understood in stores, though 'suspenders', perh influenced by AmE, is commoner.

braid.ed hair; braids *n (phr)* (CarA) Hair styled in **corn-rows** (see *DCEU*) or one of its many varied presentations. *Braids are a popular option for many black women, conscious of the plaited styles of their grandmothers before the intrusion of chemical processing. A brief observation of the styles worn by women locally would show that there is a tendency towards the Afrocentric look associated with braided hair.*—AdV (1999.09.12, p.32) □ Different from IAE *braid* 'a length of hair made up of interlaced strands' (see *COD* 10, sense 2). The *CarA* item, properly **corn-row**, is a thin, tight plaiting of short hairs in a row. The Br and N. Amer word is perh considered elevated usage by *CarA* journalists.

bram! *excl* (CarA) [*AF*] Look out!; suddenly; Lo and behold! **a.** *At 12.00 on the dot, it was show time. Bram! Stage lights up. Bram! Music starts. Bram! Dancing girl appears.*—AdV (1992.10.09, p.9 Eric Lewis) **b.** *Her machine she says would work good, good all through the year but as soon as Xmas comes around and she is trying to meet deadlines, bram! everything done. It doesn't want to spool, the needle breaks, it drops stitches and some days it just doesn't start.*—AdV (1994.12.23, p.13A) [By shift from function as ideoph, indicating an unexpected happening]

bra.sion [brešʌn] *n* (Bdos) [*Rastaf*] A visit, a move, or an action with some personal motive. *I just hey pon a brasion, so I say I gine mek a turn and gi' ya a hail.*—NaT (1998.03.05, p.7) [< *vibration*, with loss of initial syllable by aphaeresis] □ **Vibration** is a positive term in Rastaf talk indicating 'a good feeling'.

break *vb tr* (Jmca) *[IF]* To break into. *Three shops broken.*—DaG (H) [Journalistic omission of phrasal prep. Cp current IAE *'arrive, depart'*, etc.' < 'arrive at, depart from' etc.]

bright *adj* (Baha) /// ***clear-skinned*** (ECar) See *DCEU* *[IF] Don't bring no black woman round me. I like bright women.*—(Baha)

bring *vb tr* (Gren) *[AF—Cr]* To carry; take *Ogun came with a long paper, he told me, "Bring that letter to this man, and he going to sell you seven acres of land".*—SDP:102 [Possibly a combination of Irish Eng and perh infl of extended sense of Fr *porter* 'to bear, carry, take' via Gren Fr Creole. See note at *DCEU* **bring** 3. (ECar)]

brin.gle *adj* (Jmca) *[AF]* Angry. *Mrs Brown got bringle when she discovered that they had broken her window again.*—(Jmca) [Prob < *OED* **brindle** 'to be irritated' by /d > g/ velarization, with characteristic loss of IAE pa. part /-d / in CarA Cr]

brok-down¹ [brʌk-dʌŋ] *adj* (Baha) *[AF]* // **brok up** (ECar) Looking sickly; showing loss of colour and flesh in face and body. *Boy since she gone to drugs, she looking brok-down eh?*—(Baha) [< IAE *broken down* 'collapsed, distressed' (with ref to person's appearance)] □ **brok** (*bruk, bruck*) 'break, broke, broken' is one of a small group of monoform CarA Cr base vbs taken from IAE pa.t. forms. Cp *los(t), lef(t)*.

brok-down² [brʌk-dʌŋ] *n* (Baha) *[AF]* A brawl; a big fight *De two o(f) dem had one hell of a brok-down over de woman.* —(Baha) [By functional vb > n shift < IAE (*relations*) 'broken down']

brok-up [brʌk-ʌp] *adj* (ECar) *[AF]* /// BROK-DOWN¹ **a.** *The marriage didn('t) agree wid her. The husband treat her real bad an(d) she lookin(g) real brok-up.*—(Bdos) **b.** *The weeding of the yard was too much for me. A feel real brok-up.* —(Guyn) [< IAE *broken up*, with informal exaggeration] □ Sometimes also *[IF]* **'broken up'**.

bro.ther.man *n* (CarA) *[Rastaf]* (Your) fellow man/woman. *Would you let the system/Make you kill your brotherman/No Dread No.*—Bob Marley (Reggae lyric "Coming in from the Cold":1980) [Compound *brother* + *man*, with extended sense = 'humankind']

brought.upcy; brought.upsy *n* (CarA) // ***manners*** (CarA) Good manners (esp. in young poor people); training in how to behave respectfully on social occasions. **a.** *Poor but decent, that was our watchword. We had to wear patchy clothes, that is true. But we had culture, we had brought-upsy. Not like these prodigals that walking 'bout now.*—NaT (1990.05.04, p.9) **b.** *No manners people have no "broughtupcy", or are of questionable upbringing.*—GMMTB:24 [< (Well) brought

up + *suff* -cy (< decency) or -sy (< courtesy), whence variant spellings]

brown.wash *n* (CarA) [Cricket] The winning by one side of the entire series of matches by a touring team of Indic (Indian, Pakistani, Bangladeshi) cricketers. *And two of the worst series in Lara's 48-Test career were in the 2–3 loss to Mark Taylor's Australians and the recent 0–3 Whitewash/Blackwash/Brownwash at the hands of Wasim Akram's men.*—NaT (1997.12.17, p.14B) [By *Joc* analogy < WHITEWASH, BLACKWASH, Indic players being considered brown of skin] □ By analogy, BROWNWASH, vb tr, may be assumed. Cp BLACKWASH².

buck *Phrase* **buck your foot/toe** *vb phr* (Baha, Jmca) /// ***stump your toe*** (ECar)

buck up to/(a)gainst sth *vb phr* (Baha) To bounce against sth through carelessness. *He start to back-back de car and buck up (a)gainst de fence an(d) damage it.*—(Baha) [Perh an extension of 'bucking' of a horse, in wh act it rears, moving back somewhat, with its forelegs up]

bunch.y top *n phr* (Bdos) A disease affecting papaya/pawpaw trees, causing mottled, greasy-looking spots to develop on the leaves and stems, and shortening of the topmost internodes, so giving the appearance of bunching (hence the name); the leaves rot and the fruit usu ripen prematurely with poor food value; it is believed to be caused by a bacterium transmitted by the LEAFHOPPER bug (*Empoasca spp*). *Poor pawpaw tree / falls victim to nature's disease. / Death visits in a show of / beauteous triumph, / insidious disarming, / green leaves turn gold, / now brown then fall, / fruit rot and die. / Bunchy top ... brought by leafhopper.*—MMSC:16

burn *vb tr* *Phrase* **burn somebody's cakes** *id phr* (Bdos) *[AF—Joc]* To expose sb's secret behaviour. *He was one of those used to go to that house on Friday nights till a neighbour burned his cakes and his wife found out.*—(Bdos, 1963) [Prob misled ref to the well-known Br historical tale of King Alfred's identity being revealed when he let a peasant's cakes burn. The story appears in one of the series of "The Royal Readers", popular in school use in the *CarA* in the early 20C]

bu.tu (bhut.to) [butu] *n* (Jmca) *[AF—Derog]* A person of low social status. **a.** *Mind you, plenty bhutto go see Pavarotti and nuff topanaris visit Rae Town.*—DaG (2001.08.16) **b.** *A butu in a Benz is still a butu.*—R. Nettleford. [By functional shift of *DJE* **butu** vb 'to stoop down', prob from (W Afr) Akan, Ewe]

by.catch *n* (CarA) (Properly **fish by-catch** *n phr*) Unwanted marine catch taken in a trawler's net. See cit. *"The use of the term 'bycatch' originated in British Guiana in 1950 when I was first shown the large discards of catfishes (which were called 'skinfish'), caught incidentally by local fishermen in their nets and abandoned as* *unmarketable ... When a trawling survey, conducted off Guyana in 1957, found large resources of penaeid prawns, the situation became much worse. Soon, over 200 US, Japanese, and Guyana-based trawlers started jettisoning their bycatch. However, the FAO declined to help ... It was only when I resigned from FAO, and started the IDRC fisheries program in 1972, that there was hesitant approval to undertake a bycatch utilization project in Guyana (Allsopp 1982). My new word—'bycatch'—was first questioned, but eventually accepted as replacement for 'trash fish'. It also beat cute ('bye-catch') and boring ('non-target species') as alternatives ...*

The word bycatch was then adopted by European environmentalists, by the Inter-American Development Bank, UNEP, and finally by FAO, which made the reduction of bycatch a good thing under their Code of Conduct for Responsible Fisheries. In fact, they have just published the second edition of a 'Guide to Bycatch Reduction in Tropical Shrimp-Trawl Fisheries' (Eayrs 2007)."—Sea Around Us Newsletter (no.44, Dec. 2007, pp.1, 2) [By analogy with IAE *by-product* 'incidental or secondary product'(of fishing), or by blend with *'fish-catch'*] □ The originator of the term, W.H.L. Allsopp, was fisheries officer in (Br) Guyn, 1950 ff.

C

ca.mal.ly/ca.mol.ly bump *n phr* (Baha) A swelling on the head caused by a blow.—GMMTB:27 *Look de big camally bump I get from de piece o(f) wood hit me on my forehead.*—(Baha) [Perh related to (*EDD*) Br dial Eng **commony**, sb. (Nhb etc.; Amer) 'A boy's common (coloured) marble']

cane hole *n phr* (Bdos) [Hist] (In former times.) A cone-shaped hole, about 1 ft in diameter at the top, and about 1 ft deep, made by hand in the ground, sometimes rimmed by sweet-potato leaves to form a "vase", to receive a planted cane-cutting; cane holes were set out in rows by labourers. (See cits.) **a.** *"I drive mule and cow carts and dig cane holes at eight cents a hundred right there," said the sprightly 91-year-old former labourer at Hopefield and Spencer's Plantations as he pointed to a spot mere feet away from his home.*—SaS (1996.12.28, p.20) **b.** *Certainly from the 1950s, such restoration work was undertaken and it was a continuous struggle especially when cultivation of sugar cane shifted from cane holes to tractor delineated cane rows.*—NaT (1998.03.09, p.6A)

can.teen *n* (Bdos) A removable roadside stall at which fruit, food-snacks, and any small ready-to-hand domestic items are on sale. See cit. *I have located a canteen to rent. One of your very kind readers has given me one but I still am in great need. First, for a location. So I am begging your caring readers if they have a space on a construction site, factory yard and so on, to please help me. It's a 12ft by 6ft canteen with plumbing and electrical installations.*—NaT (2005.06.14, p.21) [By extension and modification of IAE sense of a 'convenience' restaurant, esp in a school]

ca.pa.dul.la *n* (Guyn) See KAPADULA.

CAREC *Acronym* (CarA) **C**aribbean **E**pidemiology **C**entre; it provides laboratory reference and epidemiology services to 21 member countries, including all CARICOM states, Bermuda and the Netherland Antilles; it was instituted in 1975, with headquarters in Port of Spain, Trinidad. *CAREC has an experimental mosquito colony.* —Bdos (Ms)

car.ni.val.i.za.tion; (-isa-) *n* (Bdos) **1.** The wilful creation of an atmosphere characteristic of a (Trinidad) carnival in any ordinary cultural event, whether indoor or outdoor; the habit of promoting the celebration of any organized cultural event with (usu open-air) loud popular music, inciting uninhibited displays of dancing and exhibitionist conduct. **2.** [By extension] The frequency of, or popular preference for such shows in a community or country. *Mr. Arthur did not need to spell out the problems that plague and worry the nation today—crime and lawlessness without appropriate punishment, cultural penetration of the worst kind, rap songs that degrade women, crass ill manners everywhere, total permissiveness at all levels in pursuit of what I have labelled in the past "belly and bumper culture" or the Carnivalisation of Barbados.* —NaT (2000.03.13, p.8, H. Fraser) [< *Carnival* 'the annual pre-lenten bacchanalian festival of Trinidad' + suff -*ization*, 'making sth become such'. Cp f. ex '*Americanization*']

car.ni.val.ize; (-ise) *n* (Bdos) **1.** To create an atmosphere typical of a (Trinidad) carnival in a cultural event. [Prob a back-formation from **carnivalization**. < (Trinidad) *carnival* + suff -*ize* 'make or become such or like'] □ The vb and n-forming suffixes -*ize, -ization* have become prevalent in post-independence (1960s) CE with strong connotations associated with IAE *nationalization*. Cp *DCEU* **Bahamianize/-ization, Barbadianize/ization**, etc. **2.** [By extension] To encourage the habit of (often open-air) exhibitionist, physical displays of personal conduct in a community or country. *For years we in Barbados were known as the square West Indians—straight-laced, moralistic, bookish and boring, even stingy. A massive media campaign to Carnivalise us has had phenomenal success. The gratuitous indulgence of our newpapers, fighting for sales, in lewdness for the sake of lewdness—without redeeming features, lack of conscience in the name of profit, has taken its toll.*—NaT (2000.03.13, p.8)

ca.roach.es *n pl* (Jmca) [AF—Joc] A number of small items of little or no real value; personal knick-knacks. *"Lady, if Me was fe tek time wid every smaddy ..." / "I know mi love, but see wid me nuh, do!" all the while lumbering her caraoches, piece by piece, into the bus.*—LSDSY:9 [< Amer Sp as (*SDGA*) *corotos* 'scraps', etc. See *DJE* **carochies** + cits 1877–1956] □ **1.** Conjectural spelling prob infl by IAE 'roach'. **2.** Compare **georgie-bundle** (Bdos) (*DCEU*)

carry town *vb phr* (Bdos) [AF] To take (a load) from the country to market in town. *I used to carry town the produce from the plantation. I used to carry town syrup, mek two trips, sometimes three trips. Yes, in the early days,"* he recalled.—AdV (1998.05.03, p.16) □ For omission of prep *to* cp the phrase *went school*. [AF] (Bdos)

cat(s') moth.er *n phr* (BrVi) [*AF—Joc*] Sb who is smug, who thinks much of themself. *She always dress up. Me 'n know who she lookin(g) out for. She de cat mother.*—(Tortola) [Cp IAE [*IF*] *the cat's whiskers* 'an excellent person or thing']

cat pas.sion *n phr* (Bdos) [*AF*] [Often of a woman] A very bad temper; violent behaviour. *She go wid she cat passion fightin(g) up an(d) bitin(g) anodder woman, an(d) dey call de police to come an(d) hol(d) she.*—(Bdos) [A ref esp. to the biting and clawing of cats fighting]

catch *vb Phrases* **1. catch a cow.boy** *vb phr* (Baha) [*AF—Joc*] To make a quick towel-wash of your face and body parts. *I had got up late and just had to catch a cowboy, grab some breakfast and get out of the house.*—(Baha) [Perh < a truncated phr *cowboy wash* 'a hurried informal wash'. Cp (*RHDAS*) Amer. E slang *cowboy*, adj 'rash; reckless'—used prenominally] **2. catch(ing) your posterior** *n phr* (Bdos, Trin) [*AF—Joc*] To have/having a very hard time of it; to suffer great privation. *In Trinidad and elsewhere, when things are bad, people talk about catching their posteriors although the word used is different and considered vulgar. In polite company they speak of catching among other things, their "tail", "nennen" or "royal".*—AdV (2004/5) [A *Joc* euphemism for CATCH YOUR ARSE (See *DCEU* **catch** Phr 8.6 for many // //)]

cat.gut *n Phrase* **turn catgut** *vb phr* (Baha) // **skin the cat** (Baha) // **skin cuffins** (Bdos) To somersault. *He was so happy when (h)e hear de result dat (h)e turn catgut through de corner. [= in the street]*—(Baha) □ The // // given refer esp to somersaults while swimming.

cat-piss-an(d) pep.per *n* (Bdos, Guyn) [*AF—Vul*] A noisy, unrestrained, brawling row. *Ef Lickmout' Lou did buy a $10 ticket fuh a show, an' when she get to de place she fin' a mob-o-ton o' people payin' at de door and she couldn' get in wid she ticket, dog-bite-dem! It would be cat-piss-an'-pepper bout dey, hear wuh I tell you?*—NaT (1978.01.20, p.5) [An imaginary mixture of domestic unpleasantness of the worst kind. Perh also notionally related to CAT PASSION]

CBI *abbr* The **C**aribbean **B**asin **I**nitiative (CBI) remains a vital element in the United States' economic relations with its neighbours in Central America and the Caribbean. The CBI, launched in 1983 through the Caribbean Basin Economic Recovery Act (CBERA), currently provides 24 beneficiary countries [all CARICOM plus 10 Latin American] with duty-free access to the US market for most goods. (Its expiry date is September 2008.) *Under the Caribbean Basin Initiative, the [Angostura] company will enjoy duty-free entry status into the United States, supplying them with fuel ethanol up to seven per cent of their requirements.*—TrG (2005.09.13, p.6)

CDERA [sɪdera] *Acronym* (CarA) The **C**aribbean **D**isaster **E**mergency **R**esponse **A**gency is a regional inter-governmental agency established in September 1991 by an Agreement of Heads of Government of CARICOM to be responsible for any disastrous event affecting any participating state, once requested. The participating states are sub-regionally grouped into operational units as follows: Antigua responsible for: Anguilla, British Virgin Islands, Montserrat, St Kitts. Barbados responsible for: Dominica, St Lucia, St Vincent. Jamaica responsible for: Bahamas, Belize, Turks & Caicos. Trinidad & Tobago responsible for: Grenada, Guyana. *Co-ordinator Jeremy Collymore said one of CDERA's focuses this year was examining how to provide more tangible support for media coverage. He added CDERA was investing in technology to allow it to operate independently of services in regional territories.*—NaT (2005.06.03)

chat *vb intr; n* (Jmca) [*IF*] Say; tell; talk idly or unwisely. **a.** *"Perhaps the most serious offence within Bongo law is the chatting of Kumina secrets .... Chatting is one of the more important taboos enshrined in the law."*—PRJW (cit dd 1984) **b.** *Super Sass warns all youth that when they face the judge it is either they get away or go to prison. Courthouse is not a place where you 'siddung an reason, [like] the dj chats.'*—Xnews (1996.07.13, p.30) [Prob a vb tr extension of IAE *chat* vb intr, 'to talk idly'. Cp Perh also *EDD chat* sb2 'chatter, gossip' + functional n > vb shift]

cheap(er) *adj* (Baha) [*AF*] (It is/would be) better to. **a.** *"Cheaper you go to work dan stay home."*—GMMTB:29 **b.** *"Cheap as well you go to work, dan stay home."*—GMMTB:29 [Prob by shift of sense 'cheaper' > 'preferable']

cheese on/an(d) bread! *excl* (Bdos) [*AF*] /// *jeezan peace! Cheese on bread! You en see dat you nearly hit the car next to you?*—(Bdos)

chi.chi [ši-ši] *adj, n* (Jmca) See cit. *I know that the word 'chichi' (pronunced sheshe) can be used to denote overrefinement, pretentiousness or an excessive emphasis on fashion or elegance, or to describe something that is arty.*—DaG (Mag) (2002.04.09, C. Millsy) [Prob by reduplication of BrE loan from Fr *chic*, 'elegant, 'stylish' pronounced [šik]] □ **1.** The spelling **chi-chi** as one word, for this pronunc (like 'sheshe') is a useful way of distinguishing the different origin of this word fr **chi-chi**[1, 2] (which is like 'chee-chee') □ Also not to be confused with SHE-SHE.

chi-chi[1] [či-či] *n* (Jmca) [*IF*] **1.** A termite that eats out the inner substance of woodwork; it excretes a fine light-brown dust by which it is detected; *Cryptotermes brevis (Isoptera). The wall only looked good but it was full of chi-chi.*—(Jmca) [Perh from a W Afr source. See *DJE*, and CHI-CHI[2]] □ **1.** A hyphenated or two-word spelling may usefully distinguish this form, like 'chee-chee', fr **chichi**. See preceding. **2.** The dust so produced, also called **chi-chi dust.** □ **2. Chi-chi bird** and **chi-chi bus** (see following), fr imitative sounds, are unrelated to CHI-CHI[1, 2] but perh so spelled by convenience.

chi-chi[2] [či-či] *adj; n* (Jmca) [*AF—Derog*] **1.** *adj.* Contemptible; of a low sort. *What kind of chi-chi* *mentality is that?*—DaG (Mag) (2002.04.09) [Prob by association with dirt, dust, excrement, homosexuality being held in great contempt in *Jmca*] **2.** *n* **chi-chi man** (Jmca) [By extension] A homosexual man. **a.** *Me (h)ave me own queen. Me no (h)ave chat wid chi-chi dem. ('I have my own woman. I don't talk familiarly with homosexuals.')*—(Jmca) **b.** *How yo(u) a flex like a chi-chi so?*—DaG (Mag) (2002.04.09)

chi-chi³ [či-či] *vb intr* (Jmca) [*AF—Derog*] [Of a man] To have sex with another man. **a.** *A chi-chi dem man de a-go chi-chi (= It's sex those men are going to have with each other).*—DaG (Mag) (2002.04.09) **b.** *Mi no chi-chi with man (= I don't have sex with another man).*—DaG (Mag) (2002.04.09) [By functional n > vb shift of CHI-CHI²]

chi-chi bird [či-či bʌrd] *n phr* (Jmca) Any chirping, 'cheeping' or singing bird. *Chi-chi bud-o! Some o'dem a halla, some a bawl.*—Jmca folksong. [Imitative from 'cheep cheep cheep'] □—See note 2 at CHI-CHI¹.

chi-chi bus [či-či bʌs] *n phr* (Jmca) [*AF—Joc*] A large white omnibus, imported from the USA and so called from the hissing sound of its airbrakes (i.e. like a chi-chi bird) [See note 2 at CHI-CHI¹]

chi-chi man [či-či ma.n] *n phr* (Jmca) /// CHI-CHI² [*AF—Derog*] **a.** *During the JLP campaign for the N.E. St. Ann Election, the JLP campaigned using the 'Chi Chi Man' song to fan homophobic fears.*—DaG (Mag) (2002.04.09) **b.** *It's amazing the kind of garbage that is being played on our radio station today. Every next line has something derogatory and violent in nature whether it concerns women or the "chi-chi men".*—DaG (Mag) (2001.06.10, p.E11) [Perh a combination of CHI-CHI¹, by shift of the sense 'corrupt, rotten, unwanted' (there being a very strong resentment of homosexuality in *Jmca*) + an overlapping of the originally separate form *chichi* (pronunc 'sheshe') with a suggestion of effeminacy.

chi-chi.ness [čičines] *n* (Jmca) [*IF*] Male homosexuality. *Some people have even coined the word 'chi-chiness' ... which means the state of being a chi-chi.*—DaG (Mag) (2002.4.09) [CHI-CHI²,³ + IAE suff -ness as in COD]

chick.en-in-the bag *n* (Baha) Fried chicken served with fried potato chips as fast food (usu in a brown paper bag).

chi.na-bump(s) *n; vb tr* (Jmca) **1.** *n* The small clumps into which a black woman's hair is rolled as a temporary way of keeping it before it can be finally styled. See (*DCEU*) **cork-screw**. *Then I put on my white socks and my best pair of shoes. And I tied my 'china-bumped' hair in a new scarf—the china bumps, which a friend had done last evening, had held up well through my night of restless sleep; I had tied my head in a thick cloth.*—JT-GDD:49 [Prob a literate overcorrection of the folkform *'chinee-bump'* (see *DCEU*), 'china-/chinee-' prob serving as a diminutive folk prefix: Cp (*DJE*) **Chiney apple/-banana/-guava/-yam** for small varieties of

those fruit in *Jmca*; + [*Joc*] 'bump'] **2.** *vb tr* To so style (a black woman's) hair. See cit above.

chi.nee [čaɪnɪ] (CarA) *n; adj* [*AF—Derog*] Chinese. *Phrase* **not/never in a Chinee world** *id phr* (Bdos, Guyn) [*AF—Joc*] Impossible; wholly unacceptable. *I wun be happy wid dat 'cause de impression it gi' to de public is dat de sentence impose by a judge shun get tek serious an' dat cyahn be right—not in a Chinee worl'.*—AdV (1992.01.31, p.9) [From the popular notion that Chinese language and culture are beyond comprehension. The phr originates in *Guyn*. Chinese immigrants came to Br. Guiana as indentured labourers in the mid 19C]

cit.rus black fly *n phr* (ECar) A shiny black, mothlike insect with a waxy body about 1 mm long; it lives in groups on the underside of leaves of citrus and coffee plants, seriously damaging the yield (whence the name); *Aleurocanthus woglumi* (Aley rodidae). *A current dry spell being experienced in Dominca is helping the spread of the citrus black fly now affecting the country's citrus industry, an agricultural offical has said.*—NaT (1998.03.18, p.16A)

clear-skin(ned) *adj* (ECar) [*IF*] // **bright** (Baha) Of light complexion; having the complexion of a quadroon. *He was tall and clear-skin and the girls used to rush he.*—(Gren)

clide [klaid] *vb* (Jmca) [*IF*] To cloy. *She needed water to drink so that the parched corn wouldn't clide her.*—RLTJWS:131 [Perh a corruption, from IAE pa. t. form 'cloyed'] □ For the occurrence of IAE past tense form of vb as a base form of Cr vb cp **brok, lef(t), marrid**.

cock tax *n phr* (Bdos) [*AF—Vul*] A man's monthly financial support, as legally determined by the law courts, for a child he has fathered by an unmarried mother. *An w(h)en yo(u) go for yo(ur) money at de court, yo(u) can('t) get it becau(se) de dam man ain('t) pay de cock tax.*—(Bdos) [*Vul* ref to a (punitive) tax on the man's 'cock' or penis, as bearing responsibility for the child]

co.co pa(n).yol *n phr* (Trin) [*AF—Derog*] A northern Trinidad peasant of Hispanic descent. See *DCEU* **cocoa-panyol**. *Moreover, this composer was, for a particular period, a respectable interpreter and singer at May Cross or Cross Wakes, a cultural expression introduced by the coco panyol to the island.*—SuG (1994.11.27, p.19) [< *Coco(a-plantation)* + (Sp) *(es)pagnol, Spanish* (linked to) 'Venezuelan immigrants'. "They arrived as political refugees, as peasant farmers called 'peons', as wage earners or even as owners of cocoa estates ... . Their experience in cultivating cocoa in particular was the basic reason why they got the name coco-panyol"] □ The spelling variants and the regular absence of pluralization (see cit) reflect the Derog status of this Creole term.

col.lec.tion box *n phr* (Baha) [*AF—Vul/Joc*] The vagina of a mature woman. *Always appears in the phrase "your* ma collection box". If you use this most fearful of insults hurled, be prepared to run for your life.—GMMTB:32 [A Vul ref to a woman's use of her vagina as a means of making money. Cp *DCEU* **hairy bank** (Guyn)]

colonel [kʌrnɛl] *n* (Jmca) [Restricted usage] The elected leader of all four Maroon comuunitites: Scots Halls, Mooretown, Charles Town and the ACCOMPONG MAROONS. (Jamaica)

col.our pre.ju.dice *n phr* (CarA) **1.** A social preference for persons, esp those of African descent whether pure or mixed with other races, who are of lighter shades of skin; a despising of persons of darker skin in the same range of shades. *In addition to and perhaps more psychologically destructive than white/black racism, what we have in the Caribbean is a rooted and pervasive legacy inherited from slavery, of colour prejudice. Light-skinned people, no better endowed with talents or intelligence than anybody else, are visible choices for jobs, for respect, for marriage ... in every field of human activity.*—(Bdos, Ms) [< IAE *colour* (of skin) + *prejudice* 'irrational opinion of or preference for'.] □ Cp COLOURISM **2.** [By extension] The selection or exclusion of persons on such a basis; discrimination on grounds of skin colour.

col.our.ism *n* (CarA) **1.** Recognition of persons, esp those of African descent whether pure or mixed with other races, according to shades of skin colour. *There is colourism all over the world with human beings. The colour disease is systematic, widespread, pervasive and needs to be extradited by an action plan and strategy, which I assume was what that Conference was all about. I'm an educator on colourism.*—NaT (2002.10.13, p.10A) [< *colour* (of skin) + suff as *COD* 10 *-ism* **2.** 'a basis of prejudice or discrimination', as in *racism*] □ See COLOUR PREJUDICE. **2.** [By extension] Discrimination based on preference for persons of lighter colour in the range of shades of skin; COLOUR PREJUDICE. *'The issue is "colourism", not racism. I came to Barbados for the Conference because in New York where I am from, I've been working against colourism. We call it that because there is only one race',* said the founder of the Institute for Interracial Harmony.—NaT (2002.10.13, p.10A)

com.bo.lo /2´21/ *adj* (Jmca) [AF/IF] A crony; a pal. *From what I can recall, he always used to dress up most agreeable to go to meetings clear over yonder with his Garveyite combolos.*—RLTJWS:51 [Prob of Afr orig. See full note in *DJE* and note also as likely intermediary, Cuban Sp *cumbila* 'comrade, friend']

come *vb intr* **Phrases 1. come forward** *vb phr* (Bdos) [*Rastaf*] To advance (spirtually). *All the time I came forward to Rastafari I had to run to the caves to heed the call.*—SuS (Mag) (2001.07.22, p.8) [**Forward** is a term with a particularly positive connotation in *Rastaf* talk] **2. come in like** *vb phr* (Jmca) [IF/AF] To seem as if; to be like/as if. **a.** *... it come in like they had offended one of our closest friends.*—RLTJWS:146 **b.** *Picnic day was something special; it would come in like sports day combined wid harvest festival. All kinds*

of merry-making would go on.—RLTJWS:18 [Cp *DJE*—**come²** dial 'To become, come to be']

con.fud.dle up *adj phr* (Baha) [AF—Joc] Confused. *When your brain seems to be overheating and you can't think straight enough to remember your own name, you are doubtless "all confuddle up".*—GMMTB:26 [Blend of IAE *confuse* + *EDD* (deal) *fuddle* 3 vb 'to drink heavily; to get drunk ... Hence (1) *fuddled* ppl, adj, 'confused, stupified with drink' + cits from many counties. (4) vb to confuse, stupefy with drink] □ Cp *DCEU*—**cuffuffle** (Bdos, Guyn)

cool *vb tr* **Phrase cool your liver** *vb phr* (Bdos) [AF—Joc] To drink (liquor). *Then, later at [Christmas Eve] night, the drum and kettle men would come around asking for something to cool their liver.*—AdV (1998.12.20)

cop.pet *n* (Baha) A stand of trees and bushes, or a piece of land.—GMMTB:33 *After he worked all them years, you mean he never even own a coppet?*—(Baha) [Perh an unrecorded diminutive of (*EDD*) **cop** sb' 7. (Obs) 'Any enclosure that has a ditch 'copped' or cast up around it'—(Chs). Cp also *OED* 2 *coppice* sb 1.a. 'A small wood or thicket consisting of underwood and small trees' + cits 1538–1867]

corn.beef and bis.cuits pol.i.tics *n phr* (Bdos) [AF—Joc] The practice of seeking to capture the votes of persons who are needy by offering them gifts of corned beef, biscuits and rum during political campaigning; also sometimes called **rum and corn-beef politics**. *There's no doubt that the days of corned beef and biscuit politics are over. Barbados has ushered in a new political era where pizza, snack boxes, rum, brandy and stouts are the orders of the day. This was amply represented by the fare available when the Bees swarmed to Deacon's Primary on Monday night to endorse their main man Mark as the candidate for St. Michael North West. There was so much food and drink around that it easily could have been mistaken for a moonlight picnic.*—SaS (1996.11.02, p.11) □ **1. Corned beef** ... (cit) is a journalistic refinement of the regular basic phr. **2.** Also called **rum and roti politics** (Trin). See *DCEU*.

cor.ner *n* (Baha) [IF] Street. *I live through McPherson, that's the corner I live through.*—(Baha) □ The regular phrs are *Through which corner?* 'On which street', *Through that corner* 'On that street', etc. However, "it also has the Standard English meaning of an angle of a building or the meeting of two streets". — GMMTB:33

cor.por.a.tion *n* (Baha) //**manager belly** (Guyn) [AF—Joc] A paunch; a man's big belly. [Prob by association with the corpulence of executive men of big business corporations, popularly called the 'Bay Street Boys' in Nassau, *Baha*]

coul woche [kul-woš] *n phr* (Dmca) [AF] A blow with a stone; a pelting (with a stone). *Dat dam véwa still troublin(g) de young girls. (H)e deserve a good* *coul-woche. (= That damned old wretch (is) still mo-lesting the young girls. He deserves a good stoning).*—(Dmca) [By folk etym < Fr Cr *koul-woche* < Fr *coup de roche* 'blow with a stone'] □ One of the many Fr Cr loans in *Dmca* folk speech. Sometimes written 'cool wash', by anglicization.

cow.boy *n* See CATCH, *Phr.*1

crab.bie *n* (Baha) [*AF—Vul*] The vulva and pubic area of a young girl. [A prob ref to the crab-like smell of the unwashed condition. Cp *DCEU* **bacalao** (Trin). See also SALT-FISH (ECar)]

crash pro.gramme *n phr* (Jmca) A scheme devised by the Jamaican government during the 1970s where-by numbers of unemployed persons were given jobs to clean up the sides of roads, etc. *But the work what a gwaan now is more like crash programme work that can put some money inna wi pocket.*—(Jmca) [From *crash-* as a combining form with sense 'emergency' as in to 'crash-land'. + IAE *programme*] □ The term has come to be used for jobs for which payment is given for little work.

crop Lis.bon *n phr* (Bdos) // *Lisbon yam* (ECar), // *water yam* (Belz, Guyn, Jmca, StVn), // *white Lisbon* (Bdos), // *white yam* (Dmca) A large branched yam with white flesh of floury texture, widely cultivated for its food value; *Dioscorea alata (Dioscoreaceae). The yam most severely affected by the anthracnose is the crop Lisbon or 'White Lisbon' (as it is more familarly known to Barbadians).*—AdV (1992.10.25, p.34) ['*Crop*', from its being the preferred variety for cultivation '*Lisbon*' (yam), name of a popular large variety]

cross wake *n phr* (Trin) // *May Cross* A night-long cel-ebration, with Hispanic music, singing and dances dedicated to a religious thanksgiving or a petition for some special purpose; the holy Cross, decorated and adorned with fruit and flowers is its centre piece, hence the name. *The event ends with the throwing of a bouquet of flowers which is to be caught by one of the participants from the crowd in attendance, whose commitment it will be to hold the next year's Cross Wake.*—SuG (1994.11.27, p.19) □ It was introduced by immigrants from Venezu-ela where it is celebrated in the month of May, hence also sometimes called *May Cross*.

CSME *abbr n* (CarA) **C**ARICOM **S**ingle **M**arket and **E**conomy: A single economic system embracing all CARICOM states, initially agreed on in 1989, inaugu-rated 30th January 2007 and meant to allow free move-ment of persons, goods, services and capital, a right to establish business, and a common external policy within a harmonized legal framework, throughout the member states. **a.** *He said he expected that in 2004 at least three states—Barbados, Jamaica and Trinidad & Tobago—would be in complete "CSME readiness", while all the other member states should be in such a position in 2005.*—SuS (2003.02.16, p.1) **b.** *As we initiate a CSME any agreement signed by a single country in the region will have implications for others in the CSME.*—ExP (Mag) (2002.01.06, p.9)

cud.joe [kʌjʌ] *vb intr* (Jmca) [*AF—Cr*] To be tight-lipped; not to say what you know. *"Is a secret plant, we nuh know whe it come from, an what is in it so, but it powerful bad and man know de use of it ... (but) me a fe cudjo. De Maypole is a secret dance."*—cit dd 1984 by PRJW:240 [Prob by functional n > vb shift of *kojo* (loosely spelled 'Cudjo(e)' name of a Jmca maroon whose successful resistance in the 18C to enslave-ment is legendary in *Jmca* history] □ Being tight-lipped, for reasons of security, was a crucial element in the organizing of slave resistance.

cun.ke.rer [kuŋkʌrʌ] *n* (Guyn) [*AF—Joc*] A blunder-ing, ill-trained technician. *Don't take it to that cunkerer in Leopold St., he messed up the wiring of my radio.*—(Guyn, 1939) [From "cunk" imitative of metallic sound of a clumsily handled tool] □ Perh obsolescent.

cuss.ment *n* (Guyn) [*AF—Joc*] A loud, abusive quar-rel, with an exchange of curse-words; a "cussing out" between two or more persons. *A tell yo(u), when de cussment start in dat yard, yo(u) have to shut yo(u) windows so the children won('t) hear.*—(Guyn.) [< CE *cuss* (see *DCEU*) + CE intensifier suff -MENT]

cut *vb tr* (Gren) To suppress, undo; to remove the ef-fects of (some supernaturally imposed evil). *Ogun is St. Michael, that is a powerful saint, because he would cut anything.*—SDP:101 □ This usage of **cut** occurs commonly in contexts of supernatural beliefs and practices. See *DCEU* **maldjo**[1] Phrase 3.1 *cut maldjo* etc. **Phrases cut and drop; cut and load** *vb phr* (Guyn) See cit. *But the most significant strike was that at En-more in 1948. Cane cutters objected to the introduction of a system whereby the cane cutters had to cut the canes and take them to the punts themselves ("cut and load" system) whereas previously the cutters would cut and leave the canes, and others would collect the canes and load unto punts ("cut and drop" system).*—GCROG:21

cut arse / -tail *n / n phr* (ECar) See CUT HIP.

cut-down *adj, n* (Bdos) /// DONE-GROW (Baha)

cut-hip *n* (Baha) // *cut arse / -tail* (ECar) [*IF*] A thrash-ing; a sound beating. *[Mother to son] If yo(u) don('t) behave I will let yo(ur) pa give yo(u) a good cut-hip when (h)e come home.*—(Baha) [< *cut* 'to cause the flesh to cut from the lash of a whip' + *hip* (Baha) [*IF*] 'the but-tocks'] □ **cut** 'to lash (sb's skin) very severely' came into milder metaph use in CE than the actuality of cutting the skin of a slave with a cat-o-nine tails as illustrated in the following account: *When we arrived, [the women] had been up about three minutes, and the brutal driver was flogging them with the cat with as much severity as he had previously flogged the men; he cut them wherever he listed, and as often as he pleased ... A black girl, appar-ently about eighteen, ... was moaning piteously. Her moans were answered by the cut of the whip... I observed the driver cut her across the naked ankles, leaving the mark of his cat visible ...*—SHWI:6, 8

D

dash *vb Phrase* **1. dash (a)way belly** *vb phr* (Jmca) [*AF—Vul*] To have an abortion. [< *dash* (see next) + *belly* 'a pregnancy' (Jmca)] —**2. dash (away) sb** *vb phr* (Jmca) [*AF—Joc*] To fail to visit or look up somebody. *Yuh dash mi way.*—DPJP:8 [= throw out (sth). DJE notes. "In common use in Jmca where *throw, fling* would be preferred elsewhere. Also const *away, out* etc."] □ Usu with inanimate obj. This construction + animate obj. is particularly emphatic.

day *n* (StLu) A weekend festive event organized by a rural community and usu beginning Friday evening, sometimes continuing into a holiday Monday; it features the sale of a wide variety of local foods and drink at roadside booths and tents, to the accompaniment of loud DJ music. *Don't miss Cul-de-sac day 2002, November 29–December 1.*—((StLu), Poster pinned to utility post, 2002) [Perh extension of the notion of observance of a religious Saint's Day, some of which are marked by local festivities] □ In the cit, Cul-de-sac is a place-name, identifying a village festivity. *Phrase* **day be.fo(r)e** *adv phr* (Bdos) [*AF*] The day before yesterday; two days ago (at time of speaking/writing). *Well, an investigation still gine on, but day-befo' two young police officers get charge in connection wid de incident.*—AdV (1997.02.01, p.12, Lickmout' Lou) [A truncated adv. phr] □ Abbr. phrs are common in Bdos talk. Cp **August Bank, Christmas Bank** (holidays) etc.

dead-yard *n* (Jmca) // *dead yard* (Guyn) The yard in wh an open-air wake and related pre and post-burial rites for a deceased person are held, with singing and ritual dancing. *Momma loved 'dead-yards'—a home where somebody had died and wasn't yet buried (The term, 'dead-yard', had its origin in the fact that before the early seventies, poor rural folk kept their dead at home on large blocks of ice). What drew momma to dead-yards was the nightly singing of hymns and the gossip groups. She had a lovely tenor voice that was perfect for dead-yard singing.*—JTGDD:10 [< (DCEU) CE *dead* 'a corpse' + *yard* 'the open space around a dwelling, used for general gatherings']

dead-an(d) wake [ded-an-wek] /1'12/ *adj* (Jmca) [*AF*] [Usu of a sickly child] Looking or becoming physically stronger. *One time when me was still 'lickle bit' a woman named Hannah Mitchell saw me coming from Redpan with a two-and-sixpence pudding pan ful o' water pon me head and she bawled out, 'Look Dead and Wake!*—RLTJWS:4 [< (was) dead and (is now) awake]

deal.er *n* (Gren) A person believed to be capable of supernatural feats through witchcraft. See cit. *Dealers is something different to loupgarou. Dealers will form themselves into many things—all sorts of animals,—and they get money ... They have certain prayers so that they can stand up outside and the door will open and they will enter, and you cannot stop it.*—SDP:91 [< *deal* (as in 'dealing with the devil, or the spirit world'.) + IAE *agential suff* -er 'one who—']

dear mer.chant /1'22/ *n phr* (Guyn) [*AF—Joc*] One who charges what is considered a high price for their service, produce or item for sale. *I pass and see some nice dresses hang up there, but I di(d)n('t) stop 'cause I know what a dear merchant she is.*—(Guyn) [< *dear* 'costly' + *merchant* (in particularized sense) 'a retail trader'] □ In similar *Joc* use re a propensity, cp. *IF* IAE *speed merchant*.

dee.jay; dee.jay artiste; DJ *n; n phr; abbr* (CarA) [*IF*]// *radio DJ* (Jmca) A singer of popular lyrics, particularly as developed out of the DANCEHALL culture of *Jmca*; a successful composer of such lyrics for whom personal CDs are "cut". See cits. **a.** *The overflowing stadium crowd was eager for a promised clash between the island's two top deejay artistes, Ninjaman (Desmond Ballantyne) and Shabba Ranks (Rexton Thomas). The deejays are no favourites of Wailer. "What they are bringing to the music can't work", the entertainer told the Caribbean News Agency. Reggae has more class. These deejays don't sing in keys. They don't know chords and changes.*—AdV (1991.01.19, p.2B) **b.** *But one of the things that irritates me about the station is the fact that announcers rarely identify the singers and DJs whose work is aired. So when I hear clever word-play I'm never sure who the artiste is. Sometimes the DJ rather cleverly identifies him/herself; or I'm lucky enough to catch the voice.*—ObS (1996.10.11, p.7, Woman Tongue) **c.** *Fans hunger for Jamaica's DJs for whom sell-out concerts beckon as soon as they cut a single.*—Cab (97/3–2, p.12) [By extension, with semantic shift, from the popular abbr DJ (pronounced deejay), for (COD 10) **disc jockey**, as a surrogate performer. This identifies the actual performer of the recorded music in a distinctive and more nationalistic way] See DEEJAY MUSIC □ This usage increasingly doubles with the original and still current sense of DJ, the earlier common abbr for 'disc jockey' (see COD 10, DJ¹)

dee.jay mu.sic *n* (CarA) Any music for dancing in the CarA played by disc jockeys and seen as western in character, but not specifically Caribbean. See cit. *He is critical of deejay music. "We have to be careful about what is stored in our archives as our cultural legacy", he said. "If you leave things without substance, they will rot. Deejay music has little substance. It cannot be the most prominent aspect of the music."*—AdV (1991.01.19, p.2B) [< pronunc of DJ (= disc jockey(s)) + (recorded) music broadcast by them]

dem-so *pron, 3rd pers. pl.* (Bdos) [*AF—Cr*] People like them; people of that sort or class. *Politicians awright; dem could get, / Good Bajan brown sugar to use; / Dem-so got contacks ... / Um is me an' you dat cyahn choose.*—AdV (1993.05.28, J. Layne-Clark) [See *DCEU so²* sense 1, + etym note]

de.port.ee *n* 1. (CarA) A person forcibly returned to the country of their birth by the law authorities of the country to which they had emigrated (esp. N. Amer.), as a penalty for having been convicted of a criminal offence. *The Administration and law enforcement authorities often argue that deportees have contributed to the surge in violent crime. Although statistics have shown that there continues to be a consistent influx of deportees from North America to Guyana over the last seven years, there have been no matching statistics to indicate their involvement in crime.*—Gyr vol.12, no.135, 2004/3, p.24 [< IAE *deport* 'expel' + suff *-ee sb*, object of the verb.] □ The term (sense 1) has gained wide currency in the *CarA* from the 1990s, with the high number of deportations by the US Immigration authorities to the *CarA*. **2.** (Jmca) // **recon** (Bdos) // **roll-on-roll-off** (Trin) A used car bought from Japan for sale in *Jmca* or *Trin*. *This latest iteration of the Swift is set to make waves as a deportee. First of all, let's make no bones about it; The Indian engineers who designed this car must have been BMW Mini owners.*—DaG (2006.11.12) [Perh by *Joc* transfer of sense 1, the used car being seen as sth unwanted and disposed of by the country of origin]

der.ricks *n pl* **Phrase** **in derricks** *prep phr, functioning as adj phr.* (Trin) // **in ducks guts** (Bdos) In serious domestic trouble and having grave hardship. *Mamitz saw to it when she moved that you would miss none of her [sexual] charms, but for the last nine weeks she had been 'in derricks' ... The tram conductor who used to keep her ... had accused her of infidelity and beaten her ...*—OBCSS:36 (CLR James) [Perh related to (*EDD*) Br dial Eng **derricks** *sb pl* (Dev) 'A name for a species of dwarfish fairies' + cit: "The wood ... is haunted by the derricks or dwarfs, evil beings who seem of darker nature than the 'pixies'"—1887] □ Cp *DCEU duck¹* (*Phr*)

di.as.po.ra *n* (CarA) **1.** (A collective reference to) the descendants of sub-Saharan African peoples living anywhere in the Western Hemisphere. **a.** *There exists a certain indifference/lack of understanding by Africans in the Diaspora as to the reality of conditions within the continent, expecially as regards the reality of Afro-Arab as they 'play-out' in the borderlands from Mauritania, through Sahel, through to the Sudan.*—Ms letter

(2002.11.25) **b.** *Speaking to the* DAILY NATION, *the author said the monthly Light in The Diaspora, which had its debut last month, was created to shed light on the issues affecting Africans in the diaspora, particularly Barbadians.*—NaT (2002.12.04, p.7A) [Orig. in use in the Gk version of the Bible, Deut 28:25 = 'dispersion' (of the Jews among the Gentiles as punishment), and thereafter in the OT and NT = 'scattering' (of Jews, also of Christians). See *OED* + cits 1876–1889, for entry of the Gk word into Eng. However the term re-emerged in the late 20C used by historians in specific ref to the forced dispersion of enslaved Africans in the Western Hemisphere] **2.** [By extension in recent times] Masses of persons of any race, culture or nation who have migrated fr their orig homeland (usu in the CarA) to better developed countries (usu in the Northern Hemisphere). **a.** *... [W]e have reached out to the people and they have come forward to meet us in large numbers and with unreluctant voices; but, more important, with hearts open to West Indian unity. And we have looked beyond the region to the diaspora. We have talked with West Indians from all the same sectors in Britain and with the community at large in London and Birmingham.*—S. Ramphal, To Be a Canoe (1991:6) **b.** *Sue-A-Quan's "Cane Reapers" tells the story of the early Chinese "diaspora" settled in Br Guiana, and the descendant diaspora established in Canada in the latter half of the century.*—Review Ms (May, 1999)

di.as.por.ic *adj* (CarA) Of or relating to the DIASPORA or global spread of sub-Saharan African peoples and their descendants, particularly the spread of such peoples in the Caribbean and continental North and South America. *I have chosen and very seriously offer the term 'Afric' as one that, in my considered view, recommends itself to embrace all diasporic peoples who are ethnic descendants of the peoples of Africa who are native to the continents and islands of the West Atlantic (or emigrants therefrom to Europe).*—BACP: Intro, p. xiv [< diaspora, 'scattering', originally ref. to the dispersion of the Jews out of Palestine, + *adj suff* '-ic', as in Britannic, Islamic, etc.] □ '*diasporal*', '*diasporan*', '*diasporical*' also occur in some writings with the same reference.

dib.by-dib.by¹ *adj* (Jmca) [*AF*] **1.** (Jmca) Second-rate; of low quality. *Standards were very high, you couldn't carry any and any dibby-dibby or fenky-fenky foods to market.*—RLTJWS:70 **2.** (Bdos) [Of a young woman's dress] Intended to attract the male, but in poor taste; indecorous (esp in ref to a very short skirt.) *A young schoolgirl shocked shoppers in a supermarket last Saturday night when she walked in wearing a dibby-dibby skirt, barefooted and a towel wrapped around her upper body.*—NaT (1997.09.20, p.11) [Perh from a folk-pronunc of **divi-divi**, popular name of a wild looking wind-swept tree often found in rough terrain, with shift of sense to 'appearance of things and persons']

dib.by-dib.by² *n* (Bdos) [*AF*] (Bdos) A young woman whose style or arrangement of dress is in poor taste. *But wait—you vyin' wid de lil' dibby-dibbies* *now, wearing' dem blon'-streaks an' t'ing in yuh hair?*—AdV (1996.11.10, p.8, J. Layne-Clark) [By functional adj > n shift of DIBBY-DIBBY.¹, 2]

die back *n* (CarA) // **wither tip** (CarA) A disease affecting citrus trees causing the gradual death of branches, shoots or roots, starting at the tips and drying progressively backwards, hence the name; it is thought to be caused by a fungus, *Phytophthora spp,* or insects. *Wither tip' or 'Die back' was first noticed in Jamaica in the early 1900's. It partially destroyed the Dominica citrus industry in the 1930s. It is a fungus that attacks most citrus as well as other members of the Rutacea.*—Pers info, M. Phillip, Ministry of Agriculture (Bdos) □ Also known as **wither tip** because of withering of the tips of a branch as the first signal of the disease.

dig *vb* To mind, care. (See note at *phr.*) *Phrase* **ain't diggin(g) not(hi)n(g)** *neg vb phr* (Bdos) [AF] Not letting anything bother you; not minding or being bothered by sth. *[Your minibus driver] would even kyar de parcel home fuh yuh / and wudun dig nutten.*—MMM:21 [By folk diffusion, with shift in usage, fr AAVE *don('t) dig not(h)in(g)* 'not understand anything', 'not to care about anything', hence 'not mind', as in cit]

Din.ki; din.ki mi.ni; din.ki min.ny; ding.ki mi.ni [dɪŋki-mɪni] *n (phr)* (Jmca) 1. A folk-dance of the ring-game type, characterized by hip and foot movements, and accompanied by folk instruments; it was traditional after funerals as part of the **nine-night** (see *DCEU*) celebration for the repose of the dead person; esp. preserved in the parish of St Mary, but now 'popular among school children'. **a.** *Dinki Mini is unique to the parish of St. Mary where the musical accompaniment includes an instrument called 'Benta', and is the only one of its kind.*—DPJP:9 **b.** *Daddy, on the other hand, who wasn't much of a singer, was casual about this popular rural entertainment of singing, feasting and the famous 'Dinki-Mini' folk dance.*—JT-GDD:10 [Perh < (*CBCD*) Congo *ndingi* 'a dirge or funeral chant' + mini (prob a verbal particle)] □ See *DJE* for fuller descriptive cits. **2.** [By extension] Songs and singing associated with or copied from the event.

do *vb (semi-tr) Phrase* **Wha(t) do yo(u)?** *id phr* (Guyn, Jmca) [AF—Cr] What is wrong with you?; What is happening to you? *But wha(t) do dem at all? Dey ain('t) know is Christmas an(d) people want de(ir) money?*—Guyn) □ This semi-trans use of '*do*' in 'absolute' function sets it apart from *OED* **do** (slang) 'To beat up, defeat' or *do down* 'bring to grief'. Its sense relates to (*Guyn*) *do for do* 'tit for tat' and may be W Afr in origin.

does.n't *monoform neg aux* (ECar) [X] Don't. **a.** *They told me it was a woman came in the station and made the report, but I doesn't know her.*—SDP:99 **b.** *They doesn't talk to each other.*—(Guyn) [An overcorrection recurring in the mesolectal stage of post-creole development, prob infl by wide occurrence of *does* as

a habitual aspect marker in *ECar* Creoles. See *DCEU* **does**]

dog¹ *n Phrases* **1. do the dog** *id phr* (Bdos) [AF—(*Vul*)] // **pooch back** (Bdos) **1.** [*Vul*] [Of a couple dancing] To have the male partner making pelvic thrusts behind the female while she bends forward with her buttocks against him (in the manner of dogs copulating, hence the phrase). *How much more shocking is young people's dancing going to get? Can they not enjoy a dub fete without doing the dog? Does the young woman not feel shame?*—NaT (1998.05.05, p.9) **2. dog bite dem!** *vb phr (functioning as oath)* (Bdos) [AF—Joc] Let hell break loose!; Hell would break loose! *Ef Lickmout' Lou did buy a $10 ticket fuh a show, an' when she get to de place she fin' a mob-o-ton o' people paying' at de door and she couldn' get in wid she ticket, dog-bite-dem! It would be cat-piss-an'-pepper bout dey, hear wuh I tell you?*—NaT (1978.01.20, p.5) [< [May the] dog bite them!] □**1.** The keeping of ferocious dogs for security purposes in walled yards was once a common *CarA* practice esp. in *Bdos* and *Jmca*, in post emancipation times. **2.** The phr, with pitch pattern / 2 '22 /, became an oath in Bdos. **3.** [By extension, esp. of partying] To enjoy yourself greatly; to party with some abandon. *Man that was a great party. Nice girls, first class DJ, I really did the dog.*—(Bdos) **4.** [By extension] To display attractive talent esp involving the body. *Boy he played like Pele, A tell yo! Scored three-goals—he really did the dog.*—(Bdos) **5.** [By extension] To act in an irritating, aggressive or quarrelsome manner. *Ah tell you, when she was in the doctor's office, she did the dog.*—(Bdos)

dog back *vb phr* (Guyn, Trin) // **beg back** (See DCEU **beg** *Phr*) [AF—Joc] To say sorry and try to recover the lost favour of a lover. *Irene gathered that Nicholas had come 'dawgin' back to Mamitz the night before, and [she] was drivin' him dog and lance, but Celestine beg for him and Mamitz let him come in.*—OBCSS:48 [By functional n > vb shift, ref. to a dog coming back 'home' with its tail between its legs].

dog dump.ling *n phr* (Bdos) The soft, potato-sized, yellowish fruit of a small tree that grows wild. (See cit.) It is used as a folk-medicine and is known by several names in the CarA. See (*DCEU*) **jumbie-soursop** for // // // *I like the names "Dog Dumpling" and "Monkey Dumpling" for the introduced, naturalised small tree* **Morinda Citrifolia,** *which I know as "Wild Pine" or "Forbidden Fruit".*—AdV (Mag) (1994.02.27, p.11) [< *dog,* a *Joc* prefix for sth contemptible (the flesh of the fruit has an unpleasant smell) + *dumpling,* from its shape] □ Its medicinal value has been turned to account by some herbalists in a product called '**Noni**' which has given another name to this fruit.

dog.gie *n* (Baha) [AF—Joc] [Children's talk] The penis. [Perh from Amer E. slang. Cp (*RHDAS*) *dog n* 1 a 'penis' + cits 1600–1989]

dog.hunt.er, dog-hunt.er *n* (Bdos) A whip made of plaited strips of leather; it was commonly used on mules in the plantation era in *Bdos. Miranda screamed when the next blow landed. The instrument of pain was a doghunter—a short whip, about two feet long, which sprouted three thin tails of plaited leather.*—NSWOM:70 [Perh a *Joc* metaphor < Early Eng slang *dog* 'penis' (See *RHDAS dog* n. 1) + **hunter**. (See *DCEU*.)]

dol.ly-ba.by *n* (Jmca) [*IF*] A doll. *I never expected to just skip through life only making dolly-baby clothes.*—RLTJWS:174 [< child talk "*dolly*" 'doll' + *baby*, by *CarA* redundant compounding]

Don; don *n* (Jmca) [*AF*] See cits. **a.** *The Don is a community leader with doubtful reputation. He represents a kind of alternative authority, is usually well off (is sometimes a drug dealer or other character considered shady by constituted authority) and has his own system of justice which sometimes requires him to "execute" offenders. The police consider him a menace and a threat. Politicians sometimes court the Dons and depend on them to ensure them access to the communities whose support they desire.*—Jmca (Ms, 2002.10.17) **b.** *The Jamaican garrisons have long been identified by several local scholars as tight political fiefdoms of miniwarlords or dons. For example their community 'justice system' prescribes death for rape, and bodies-in-barrel executions.*—DaG (2002.10.19, Ed.) [Perh a survival of an old BrE slang term, as *DSUE don*. 'A swell; an adept, a pretentious person' (19C). But the later infl of Amer slang fr Italian immigrants, as *WCD* 10 2 don. **4.** 'A powerful Mafia leader', is more likely] □ Capitalized in sociological literature.

Don Gor.gon; (Dan Gor.gon) *n phr* (Bdos, Jmca) [*AF*] See prec. + cits. **a.** *A Don Gorgon is recognized as a don or big shot.*—DPJP:15 **b.** *Barbados' biggest teachers' union has condemned the "dan gorgon" lifestyles of many young males as a threat to this country's stability ... Unlike most others in the community, the "dan gorgons" who stand aimlessly on street corners have no appreciation for morality.*—AdV (1992.12.07, p.1) [*Don* + *Gorgon*, compounded for intensity, *Gorgon* connoting 'dread ruthlessness'. See PDT:43] □ The form *Dan Gorgon* is a *Bdos* variant pronunc of *Jmca* speech.

done-grow /1´2/ *adj; n* (Baha) // *cut-down (Bdos)* // *small-one (Jmca)* **1.** *adj* [Of a person] Of noticeably short stature. **2.** *n* Such a person. *She kinda tall, and he is a done-grow, so the two o(f) dem look a sight dancin(g).*—(Baha) [< [*AF—Cr*] pa. part *done* 'finished, ended' + *grow(ing)*]

don.key-hair *n* (Bdos) [*AF—Joc*] Any artificial hair used in braiding, plaiting or making additions in a black woman's hair styling. *Ness, you should see some o' dem—de boys in big, obzocky pants dat droppin' halfway down de behines an' de girls in short, tight uniform-skirts, earrings, lipstick, rouge an' paint—an' mo donkey-hair 'pon duh head dan a jackass got in 'e tail!*—NaT (1999.09.23, p.9A, Lickmout' Lou) [Fr *Joc* comparison with the dry loose long hair of a donkey's tail]

don('t)-care.fy [donkerfɑi] *adj* (Baha) /// *don't carish (ECar)*, [*AF—Joc*] *The liquor like it makin(g) him real don('t)-care-fy; he don('t) care how (h)e look (u) pon de street.*—(Baha) [< *DCEU don't-care*² 1 adj (CarA) 'indifferent' etc. + IAE *suff* -(i)fy, reduction of -*ified* 'made, caused (to be), as in 'magnify'. Cp *DCEU Englishfy*]

don't carish *adj phr* (ECar) [*AF—IF*] // *don('t)-carefy (Baha)* // *pa mélé (StLu)* Irresponsible; indifferent to criticism or appeals. See *DCEU*.

down-fall *n* (Bdos) A bird-trap made as box-shaped, with a slatted frame of light wood, or a light cardboard box, either one being raised a few inches at one end on a small stick to which a string is attached. Bird seed or grains are put underneath to attract a bird, and the string is pulled to bring down the trap when a bird is underneath. *As boys we used a down-fall or fly-stick to catch birds.*—(Bdos) [From the trap's falling down on the bird]

dread.er *adj (comparative)* (CarA) [*Rastaf*] More frightening; more terrible *Dread ... Dreader than dread I say / Dread ... Dread in every way / Dread ... Dreader that an uzi in the night / Dread ... Dreader than a drive by killing / Dread ... Lord it is so chilling /*—Cso, David Rudder [< Rastaf *dread* + IAE comparative *suff* -*er*]

duck's guts *n phr* **Phrase** **in duck's guts** *prep phr functioning as adj phr* (Bdos) [*AF—Joc*] —// IN DERRICKS (Trin) □ Cp *duck*¹ in *DCEU*.

duck sense *n phr* (Guyn) [*AF—Joc*] Natural or god-given wisdom (as being better than common sense). *Yo(u) mus(t) (h)ave real duck sense to get on in dis life.*—(Guyn) [A ref to the fact that ducks seem to know how to move safely with their young through the muddy water of the drainage trenches and canals of coastal Guyana without being caught by snakes or alligators that can be lurking unseen just below the surface] **2.** *Phrases* **2.1 don(t) make duck sense (in water)** *id phr* (Guyn) To seem to be an unwise decision in clearly doubtful circumstances. *I ain'(t) goin(g) married a man dat got to stay livin(g) in (h)e mother house. Da don't mek duck sense in water.*—(Guyn) **2.2 have duck sense** *vb phr* (Guyn) To be naturally sensible. **2.3 make duck sense** *vb phr* (Guyn) To seem to be surely the right thing to do.

duh [dʌ] *existential adv* (Bdos) [*AF—Cr*] There. *One a we people at de top a de wite people big expensive church! Duh in nuh higher officer.*—MMSC:30 ... . (= *There ain't no higher office*) [This monoform folk pronunc of 'they, their' in subj position is, in this and like contexts, transferred to the function of IAE initial existential '*There*']

dun.gle *n* (Jmca) A slum of Kingston, so called because it was built on the city dump. **a.** *As for the fellow, she never caught sight of his house in town, only some old boarding house him put her up in clear inna* *dungle.*—RLTJWS:62 **b.** *Plenty bone a dungle a come from good man table.*—Jmca (Prov. ACJPS no.909). (= *Many a bone in the dung-heap was once on a rich man's table*) [Pronunc of *dunghill,* popular name of the slum < *dung* 'raw sewage' + *hill,* and perh reinforced by IAE 'jungle']

dun.ny; dun.sie; dun.za *n* (Jmca) /// BLENZA (Bdos) [*Rastaf*] **a.** *You 'av di dunny? Di big man say ah two thou.*—DaG (2001.04.23) **b.** *'I a look a money, Buzza; / come fahwood wid some dunny/ di breddah seh him bruk/ him seh him naw wok.*—JMRF:4 [An invented Rastaf word (see PDT:38). Perh by association with IAE vb *dun* (sb for money) + reinforcement of rhyming slang < 'money']

dun.sie *n* (Jmca) /// BLENZA (Bdos)

dunza (Jmca) /// BLENZA (Bdos) See cit. *Dunza in Jamaica Rasta Talk falls within [Pollard's] list of innovations generated within the milieu of Rasta. In Barbados it is an adopted Jamaican word submitted to the process of replacing the existing initial sound with a negative sound. So "dun" [represents] "blind", [in blindza"].*—PDT:49 [< *done,* connoting negativity, ruin (see *DCEU done*[1] vb, esp Phrs.), or 'too soon finished' (PDT:48), + *za,* evid a disapproval suffix, as in // **blindza.** The form **dunny** is derived 'rhyming slang' for 'money']

dut.ty wine *n phr;* **dut.ty wi.ning** *vb phr; n phr* (Jmca); (Bdos) An exhibitionist dance done by an individual, usu a young woman. See cits. **a.** *"The dutty wine dance is a head rotation dance and you have to use your head and neck to do it. But, you have to move your neck both ways. I am seeing too many girls here only moving their heads in one direction. That is even more dangerous. If you keep on spinning you head in one way it might be easier to crack your neck," she cautioned.*— NaT (2006.11.10, pp 12, 13) **b.** *However, Falanta said she was happy the girls dutty wining in Barbados were not as 'risky' as dancers in Jamaica who hang from the ceilings. Falanta does not try this. «I din't do it because it is a risk,» she said.*—NaT (2006.11.10, pp 12, 13) ['*dutty*' < (dial pronunc of '*dirty*' [*AF*] 'vulgar' + *wine* (CarA, Cr) 'dance by gyrating the hips and buttocks suggestively']

E

each.way; each.wey *adv* (Bdos) Whichever way you turn. *Dese is difficult economic times eachwey; unemployment rife, an' hardship all about.*— NaT (1992.02.07, p.9, Lickmout' Lou) [Prob a shift in use fr betting in horseracing, wh *COD* spells '**eachway**']

ear.bang¹ *n* (Bdos) [*IF*] A blow on the ear with a flat object (such as a book), delivered as a punishment or torture. *B—— said that he told the officers he did not know anything about the woman's death, and W—— who was there with S—— R—— and other officers, started beating him by giving him two earbangs and asked him if he intended to talk.*—AdV (1990.05.05, p.5) [< IAE *ear* + [*IF*] *bang* 'hit, clout' on the word-formation pattern of *body-blow*, 'blow to the body' etc.]

ear.bang² *vb tr* (Bdos) [*IF*] To hit sb on the ear(s) with a flat object, as a punishment or torture. *C—— said instead of letting him go, Constable F—— took him to a room and earbanged him with two big books until his ears bled.*—NaT (1994.10.07, p.4) [By functional n > vb shift of EARBANG¹ + reinforcement by IAE word-formation types such as *gate-crash, gift-wrap* etc.]

ears *Phrases* **1. ears ringing** *id phr* (CarA) Having a ringing sensation in the ears; (experiencing tinnitus) *When yo(ur) ears ringin(g) somebody talkin(g) yo(ur) name.*—Trin. **2. in somebody's ears** *adv phr* (CarA) [Of noise] Loudly and continually; with the effect of a disturbing nuisance. **a.** *The Catholic minister said that I am beating drum in his ears and he cannot rest at night, so they came to stop me.*—SDP:120 **b.** *During the August holidays the children next door play and shout whole day in your ears, so we are glad when school starts again.*—(Guyn)

East-ind.ian.ise/.ize *vb* (Guyn, Trin) To employ a majority or very significant number of East Indian (as opposed to AFRIC) persons in an institution, as a matter of administrative policy. *The East Indian population is in the majority in Guyana and Trinidad and Tobago ... Having acquired a measure of control of the agricultural and private sectors, the leadership of the political directorate of the East Indian population now sees the East-indianising of the civil service, government agencies and the small artisan class, now dominated by Africans, to be essential goals in the government programme for equal opportunity. Africans are therefore being displaced and discarded from their positions in these areas of employment.*—Internet Article (K. Nantambu) (2001.10.09) [< *East Indian*, 'Indic' + IAE vb forming suff *-ize/-ise* 'make, become, cause to resemble' (as in **Americanize** (*COD* 10)]

eas.y-so *adv* (Bdos) [*AF*] **1.** As easily as ever. *It look like the bassa-bassa between BATMAN and the NCF get resolved easy-so. I does got to wonder ef dese annual confrontations en part o' de Crop Over showcase.*—AdV (1993.06.25, p.9) *adv tag* **2.** Quite unexpectedly. *Dem people out in Southern California los' duh houses an' all duh possessions in dem turrble fires. Looka how duh fancy houses wid swimmin' -pool and t'ing gone up in smoke easy so.*—NaT (2003.10.29, p.9A) [< *easy* (adj in adv function) + (*DCEU*) *so¹* 'without warning'] **3.** As if normal; hardly causing public attention. *Dem Haitian police an' soldiers does beat-up de poor civilians over dey. Looka how one man dead from a blow, easy so!*—AdV (1994.09.23, p.9)

eat *vb tr* [*Notional*] To acquire the quality or nature of the thing eaten. □ Cp *eat* vb (CarA) [*AF—Joc*] To acquire a propensity or type of conduct from imaginary consumption of something having that quality. Cp *eat parrot*, 'be talkative', etc. See *DCEU*. *Phrases* **eat razor blades; eat wasp** *vb phrs* (Baha, Bdos) // **eat was(p)** *(Baha)* [*AF—Joc*] To be sharp-tongued; to use rough language readily (esp. in quarrelling). **a.** *You should hear the fluent cuss-words of these lil children nowadays—like dey eat razor blades.*—(Bdos) **b.** *Her mouth so sharp today, she mussee eat was'.*—GMMTB 1995:44

eat.er.y *n* (CarA) A good restaurant. **a.** *Kamau was a generous partner. He always paid for dinner when the couple went out and he often took her to some of the island's fancier eateries. Each time raised Miranda's suspicions about how Kamau made his money.*—NSWOM:59 **b.** *Alternatively, head for Vegas (Antigua not Nevada) but 20 yards from Carnival City. It's a village of bars, eateries and a reggae dance hall. You can eat good food there and find new friends.*—Cab (Summer 1994, p.18) [< *eat* + suff *-ery*, as *COD* 10, sense 1 'denoting a class or kind'] □ The word, once *IF*, indicating a place of lower commercial status, prob by association with 'grocery', 'bakery', has been elevated in status, as in cit **a.** (Cp earlier entry in *DCEU*.)

ECCA *abbr/ used as n* (ECar) [Obs] **E**astern **C**aribbean **C**urrency **A**uthority (ECCA) was established in March 1965 following the withdrawal of British Guiana and Trinidad & Tobago to establish their respective central banks. Unlike its predecessor, the ECCA was under no obligation to provide 100 per cent sterling backing for the currency which it issued. Under the 1965 ECCA Agreement the foreign exchange cover [of] the EC dollar was set at 70 per cent, but this requirement was reduced to 60 percent 10 years later. Grenada, not an original ECCA signatory, joined the Authority in 1968.

E.C.C.B.; ECCB *abbr/ used as n* (ECar) *E*astern *Ca*ribbean *C*entral *B*ank; an international Central Bank established 1st October 1983 for the maintenance of a sound banking system within seven Eastern Caribbean states: Antigua & Barbuda, Dominica, Grenada, Monsterrat, St Kitts & Nevis, St Lucia, St Vincent & the Grenadines; it issues its own common currency for those states. See also EC DOLLAR. *The ECCB came into being on October 1, as successor to the Eastern Caribbean Currency Authority, following the enactment of enabling legislation by the respective governments ... The ECCB's overall objective is the promotion of monetary stability and the building of a financial structure conducive to balanced growth and development throughout the region. At the time of writing, the ECCB is one of only four multi-state central banks in the world.*—CDB (Bdos) (Ms) 2004.09.08

EC dol.lar [isi-dɒlar] *n phr* (CarA) *E*astern *C*aribbean dollar, the unit of currency of the Eastern Caribbean Central Bank, issued as of 1984 in Country coded notes of $5, $10, $20 and $100, and a general $1.00 coin. See ECCB. *In 1976 an amendment to the ECCA Agreement was passed which shifted the link of the EC dollar from sterling to the US dollar.*—Caribbean Development Bank document, 200pp.

e.co -ac.ti.vi.ties *n pl* (CarA) Recreational pursuits involving or related to the enjoyment and preservation of a country's natural environment, culture and history. See cit. *[These] include semi submarine, botanical gardens at both Garden of the Groves and Hydroflora Gardens, cruises, deep-sea fishing, scuba diving and snorkeling, Dolphin Experience, golfing, tours, horseback riding and Nature Centre as well as the Lucayan National Park. There are many eco-activities offered on Grand Bahamas which can enlighten nature lovers to Grand Bahamas' eco-structure.*—AdV (Mag) (2004.01.04, p.23) [< *eco-*, combining form shortened fr 'ecological', + IAE *'activities'*] □ Although *eco-* is noticed by *OED* 2 as a combining form pre 1950, its special importance to scenery (e.g. re TOURISM) (see *DCEU*) and environmental issues in regard to history, culture and sustainable development in the *CarA*, has produced many hyphenated compounds such as this that have a specific focus in the *CarA* regional vocabulary.

e.co-farm.ing *n* (CarA) The industrial cultivation of land and animals in harmony with the natural environment. *As it happens, he is known islandwide not only for his acumen in wild plants ... but also for his participation in eco-farming and sustainable agriculture.*—SuS (Mag) (2001.07.22) [< *eco*, 'ecology/ical', a combining form < meaning 'related to the environment', usu with a positive connotation, + IAE *farming*]

e.co-lodge *n* (Trin) A small, secure, sturdy, well-furnished dwelling placed at a site chosen for its isolation in natural surroundings, well away from the bustle of urban life. *At the fishing village of Blanchisseuse there are a handful of eco-lodges to stay at, and the coast road peters out—it's a long hike from here to the village of Matelot, where the road resumes, but great for anyone who enjoys nature and seclusion.*—Cab (Mar/Apr, 1997, p.33) [< *eco-*(a combining form. See preceding) + *lodge* as in BrE, 'a small separate dwelling with a specific function'; as **porter's 1.**, **hunting 1.**, etc.]

e.co -struc.ture *n* (CarA) The entire make-up of a country's natural environment. *There are many eco-activities offered on Grand Bahamas which can enlighten nature lovers to Grand Bahamas' eco-structure.*— AdV (Mag) (2004.04.01, p.28) □ See also *ECO-ACTIVITIES*.

e.co.tour.ism *n* (CarA) The organisation of a country's Tourist Industry so as to conserve and market its natural environment, culture and history. See cit. *This loss of appeal is also evident from the rising search among travellers for more pristine natural, cultural and educational vacations. This nature-based or so-called "ecotourism" focusses on small-scale authentic natural and cultural experiences. It involves a variety of forms like visiting rainforests, bird and wildlife watching, participating in archaeological digs, witnessing village ceremonials, trekking, rafting and other types of adventure tourism.*—CaW (1995.12.01, p.39) [< combining form eco- (see *ECO-ACTIVITIES*) + *tourism* 'tourist industry'] □ Usu written as one word, in contrast with other generally hyphenated forms with *eco-* as pref.

Eh bien [ɛbiɛ̃] *excl* (StLu) [*AF/IF—Joc*] Can you imagine?; How curious!; Well Well!. *These days the game of Cowboys and Crooks being played in Her Majesty's Prisons is getting really confused. It is difficult to tell who are the Cowboys and who are the Crooks. The Warders are themselves confused as to whether they are Cow-Boys or Crooks. One Cow-Boy Warder riding shotgun, shot straight at a Crook then he lost his head because he couldn't decide whether he was Cow-Boy or Crook. Eh Bien ...*—CrU (Queek Quack, 1992.08.22, p.7) [Fr loan "Well, well!"] □ A conversational intimacy tag borrowed from Fr Cr, ending a remark in English, about an odd or amusing matter. It shares this "terminal space" with other Fr Cr alternatives such as *Bon djé*! 'Good God!'

else.where *n* (Bdos) Other places. *Elsewhere in Bruce Vale is tranquil. From their verandahs, some residents relish the cool breeze flowing over the East Coast.*—AdV (1996.06.13, p.17) [By nominalization of adv *elsewhere* 'in another place'. Cp similar and commoner nominalizations of IAE advs *here, there*. (See *DCEU*.)] □ A collective sg form with an understood pl function.. However IAE wd require the sequence 'elsewhere ... it is'.

El.eu.the.ra pine.ap.ple *n phr* (Baha) A very sweet variety of pineapple grown on the Bahamian island of

Eleuthera. See cit. *The pearl of Bahamian fruit is the Eleuthera pineapple, star of the annual Pineapple Festival, and rightly so. It is reported that the Eleuthera Pineapple is what got the Hawaiian pineapple industry kick started. It is smaller in shape than the Hawaiian fruit, but remarkably sweeter. If in doubt, check your fingers glued together after two or three slices.*—AdV (1998.07.26, p, 2)

Em.er.ald Isle (CarA) Montserrat. See cit. *Montserrat is known as "the Emerald Isle" from the lush greenness of the three dominant mountain ranges across the island.*—CaW (11/92, p.38)

end *n Phrase* **at ends (with sb)** *prep phr* (StVn) [X] At odds with (sb); quarrelling (with sb). *Arrindell said that she did not know her son to have been at ends with anyone. She further added that no one seems to know what could have provoked her son's murderer(s) to commit the crime since everyone in his community spoke well of him.*—ViN (2003.08.15, p.40) [By folk etym < (unfamiliar) IAE phr *at odds with*, prob reinforced by the idea of 'relations being at an end']

en.gage *vb tr Phrase* **engage meat** *vb phr* (Bdos) To reserve a particular part of the carcase of an animal that is to be slaughtered (usu in the owner's yard) and sold to neighbours whose patronage has been solicited, or 'engaged'. *I am just a simple country girl. The slaughtering I know about is the backyard kind in the days when we would "engage" meat, the proceeds of which helped send many of us to school.*—NaT (2000.03.10, p.8) □ The term "engage" applied principally to the buyer, but also, by extension (as evid in cit) to the 'solicitor'.

Eng.lish ap.ple *n phr* (ECar) // ***American apple*** (Jmca) The imported European apple; *Pyrus malus (Rosaceae)* of the red or yellowish-green variety (i.e. as different from a number of *CarA* fruits of different species and family though called APPLES).

Eng.lish.er *n* (UniK) [*IF—Joc*] An Englishman / -woman. *No doubt an ordinary ball thrown with ease would have him out in two-twos, but as I was saying, it look as if the unusual play of the boys have the Englishers in a quandary. Them Englishers never see a stroke like that in their lives ... All heads turn up to the sky watching the ball going.*—Cab (Autumn 1994:56) (Samuel Selvon) [< *English* + *Joc* IAE use of suff *-er*, by analogy with such forms as 'Londoner', city-dweller etc.] □ A word commonly used in humorous contexts by the Trin writer Samuel Selvon (as in cit).

Eng.lish Pier.rot [ɪŋglɪš piɛro] *n phr* (Trin) [Carnival] A masquerader (commoner in the early decades of the Trin Carnival celebrations) of the ***Pierrot Grenade*** type) whose performance was in English, in contrast to Fr Creole, the language used by ***Pierrot Grenade***. (See *DCEU*) See cit. *The English Pierrot recited stilted epics about great kings and battles and portions of English history, and was known to recite orations from Shakespeare: Julius Caesar, Marc Antony,*

Brutus, Othello, and excerpts from English and Classical literature.—SCL Paper, Al Creighton, (1984.05.25, p.8)

enough *adj Phrase* **enough to make a man walk and talk to himself** *id phr* (Jmca) [*IF*] Sufficiently disturbing to the mind. *It would be fascinating to find out whether what is the case in both the United States and South Africa is also true in, say Brazil ... But even the evidence that is available is enough, as they say in Jamaica, to make a man walk and talk to himself.*—SuS (1995.10.08, p.6A) □ Talking about your troubles to yourself aloud in public is a common feature of *CarA* folk life. It has been called by some sociolinguists 'cathartic auto-communion'.

en(t) *neg imperative* (Trin) **1.** Don't **2.** Variant of 'ain't' *And we were not permitted to walk on the lawns. But we pass that stage! This land is we own, and independent, yes. Ent let nobody tell me what an' what to do or ent do! If I want to carve my initials, who is you to try an' stop me?*—Trn (no.12, p.27) [*ain't*, shifted fr *'don't'*, pre-verbal aux function as in 'I ain't know', to function in imperative role] *Phrases* **1. en(t) have no time with that** *id phr* (CarA) [*AF*] See **time** *Phr.* **2. en(t) payin(g) taxes fo(r) yo(ur) mout(h)** *neg id phr* (Bdos) [*AF—Joc*] Not to be afraid to speak out; not putting a bridle on your tongue. [*Joc* ref to incurring taxes by excessive display on one's life-style]

en.tre.me.ti.a. *adj* (Trin) [*AF*] Meddlesome, pushy and interfering. *"Ah doh like she; she too entremetia for me."*—Rhona Baptiste (Trin) Calendar: 1992 [< pa.t. of Sp *vb entremeter: entremetia* 'he/she was interfering' + dial functional *vb* > *adj* shift > 'interfering, meddlesome']

en.tri.fi.ca.tion *n* (Guyn) [Religion] The entry of the (Holy) Spirit into the human body in the earth-related communion with God; spirit possession. *The various rhythms played by the drums are called 'hands'. The basic trio of drums consists of the mother drum, the jar drum and the cutter ... Any one of the hands can produce entrification, which is the term we use for spirit possession.*—Ema (2002–2003, vol.1, no.10, p.54) [< *entry* + IAE suff *-fication*, forming nouns of action] □ An emotive word-forming extension of 'entry'.

e.re.ba [ɛreba] (Belz) Cassava bread. *You know, we are abandoning Garifuna. Now, at a time when the price of ereba is up and the demand for it is high, that's when ereba bakers are vanishing. We've turned away from ... food that gave sturdiness and health to the the Garifuna man.*—CCD:5 [The Garifuna (= Island Carib) name]

Er.rol Bar.row *n phr* (Bdos) [*IF*] The $50 bill, Bdos currency, which carries the commemorative image of Errol Barrow, the prime minister who brought independence to Barbados in 1966. *"I can't stand this dropping of ten cents here and five cents there. And 25 cents here and there" he said. Complaining that there was too much noise being made by coins when* the plate was being passed, he urged his congregation to remember the church with Errol Barrows and Grantley Adams.—SaS (1996.02.03, p.11)

Er.rol Bar.row Day n phr (Bdos) 21st January, an annual holiday in Bdos, honouring the memory of Prime Minister Errol Walton Barrow (1920–1987) who brought about the independence of Barbados in 1966.

ess conj (Bdos, Guyn) [AF—Cr] [Obs] If. **a.** Befoh de yare is oba(h) uh gwine to Trinidad ... Um cahn be like Bahbados, fuh dis is uh ole hole. Uh wun stan hay nuh longah ess the streets was pave with gole.—Lizzie and Joe (1903) Rep.AdV (Mag) (1996.08.04, p.10) **b.** Ess yo(u) only say a word o(f) answer-back, dey was ready to sen(d) yo(u) home.—(Guyn) [Perh of dial Irish E infl. < pronunc of Eng, as (Erse pronunc. of 'asse, esh 'ash' Cp MCUD), thence shifting via contextual function to "if", as CarA Cr **as** /aaz /; f. ex cit b, wd be 'as (soon) as you only say a word ...'] □ This Obs form, still heard in Guyn basilectal Cr in the 1930s–1950s, is prob out of pres use in Bdos. Note that the Bdos [Joc] cit is fr 1903.

e.thuh [εδʌ] adj (Bdos) [AF/IF] Other. Ef dem was to tek a survey, dem would fin' out jes' how few people interested in dem debates as substitutes fuh ethuh programmin'.—AdV (1995.05.12, p.12, Lickmout' Lou) □ A common pronunc in current Bdos E, even among educated persons.

Et(tu) [εtu] n (Jmca) See cit. An African retention kept alive by a small group of people found in the parish of Hanover who claimed 'Yoruba' (Nigerian) ancestry. The 'Ettu' play is usually performed on the occasions of weddings, feasts, 'nine night' and 'forty night'. 'Shawling', a feature of the dance, is a ritual of appreciation for the dancer's skill and movements, and forms an integral part of each performance. The Queen throws a scarf around the neck of the dancer, who is then ceremoniously 'dipped back' from the waist for strength, then the shawler raises the dancer's arm in salutation and congratulation.—JCMAT:4 [Perh < Yoruba **e.tu**, wh has several meanings in that language incl 'a type of cloth'. The ritual "shawling" referred to in the cit may bear some relationship to this. However see also DJE wh suggests a Twi origin.]

Eu.ro-Bar.ba.di.an adj; n (Bdos) A white Barbadian person who is of European descent. My own family background includes a brother and a sister who married Europeans and I respect the contribution of those Euro-Barbadians like Sir Graham Briggs, who may have championed the cause of Afro-Barbadians.—AdV (1994.10.24, p.9) [< Euro- a combining form, current fr c.1981, signifying 'of or belonging to Europe; European' + Barbadian' of or belonging to Barbados'] □ Prob by analogy with and infl by **Afro-Barbadian**, in the same cit.

ever [εva] adj (Bdos) [AF—Cr] Every. **a.** Dey had dat long-draw out ting call de Budget pon TV, wid evvah-one gettin' up saying de same ting over an' over again.—

SaS Unicey (1991.12.21, p.9) **b.** Wha' after all, I used to be in there ever single Saturday morning and I knew actually all the old faces.—SaS (2003.09.28, p.11) [By apocopic avoidance of terminal—/ -cc // vri /]

ever since adv phr **Phrase** ever-long-time-sence adv phr (Bdos) For a long time now. But I realise ever-long-time-sence wha dis "Christun life" mean, soul—de practice o' hypocrisy. Some of de mos' prominent ones dat does be bawlin'-out de hymns when de Sunduh come does do wuh duh like an tell you de Lord will onderstan'.—NaT (1998.03.18, p.9A, Lickmout' Lou) [A blend of ever since (with an open vowel) + '(a) long time (ago)'] □ Cp also variant **every long time since**.

ex.tem.po n (Trin) Individual instrumental or vocal improvization in a musical performance. In the two major musical forms in the English-speaking Caribbean calypso and reggae, the ability to create on the spur of the moment, to improvise, is equally important, whether it be called "extempo" or "chanting".—Cab (Spring 1993, p.39) [IF shortening of IAE extemporize / -ization]

ex.tend.ed fa.mi.ly n phr (CarA) A society of blood relatives recognized within itself, and considered emotionally significant, with inter-personal entitlements. See cit. As Elder has pointed out appropriately, the term "family" in its meaning as extended family (in St. Lucian Kwéyòl "fanmi"), also relates to the group comprising ancestors and living descendants. Since all Djiné regard themselves as "children" of the deities— mainly Shango and Ogun—the ancestor cult as a whole rests upon a "family" comprising both the living and the dead "Africans" (Afwitjen in S. Lucian Kwéyòl). "Families remain bound to ancestral land not merely for economic considerations but from sentiments far more profound and powerful.—Caq (vol.39, nos. 3, 4. 1993/12, p.85) □ This basically anthropological African concept survives diluted in current Afric CarA sociological contexts.

eye n **Phrase** with the tail of your eye adv phr (Belz) Out of the corner of your eye. With the tail of his eye he watched how his neighbour, a beatific smile on his face, sipped contentedly from the glass with the coffee aroma.—YPF:41

eye game n phr (Trin) [AF—Joc] [Of young men] Looking sensuously at young women passing by on the street. □ Also called **bird-watching** [AF—Joc]

eye-ser.vant n (CarA) A person who only works, or works diligently, when being observed by a senior employer. We don't want eye-servants in this kin(d) o(f) work. Nobody ain('t) got no time to check dat de job gettin(g) done.—(Baha) □ This term is not listed in COD 9, 10, as current, but is noted in OED 2 with cits 1552–1832.

eye sup.per n phr **Phrase** take eye-sup.per id phr (Belz) [AF—Joc] To look longingly at what is unobtainable. □ Cp similar notion in IAE idiom "to feast your eyes on".

F

face *n Phrase* **(your) face set up like rain** *id phr* (Bdos; Guyn) (Having) a look of fretfulness, of vexation. *My God, the heat? Hot? Well, I thought Bimshire was hot. I used to walk 'bout here and complain; miserable and with my face set up like rain, with vexatiousness.*—CPH:186

fadge *vb intr* (Bdos) *Phrase* **fadge for yourself** *refl vb phr* (Bdos) To manage, fend (for yourself). **a.** *His wife was in hospital so he had to fadge for himself.*—(Bdos) **b.** *The service staff were on strike so everybody was fadging for themselves for two days.*—(Bdos) [*OED* **fadge** *vb* (*Obs*, senses 1–5) 5. '(Of persons) To make things fit; hence to get on, succeed'. + cits 1611–1789]

fall *vb tr* (Jmca) [*AF—Cr*] To fell, cut down (a tree). *Mama say she used to work hard inna Westmoreland, weh she from. She tek all axe and fall tree when she young.*—SSLG:159 [< IAE as *OED* 2 **fall** vb IX trans senses 51.c. 'To cut down (trees)' dial, US, Austral & NZ + cits 1891 Austral & NZ 'the trees require to be fallen; 1941, The bush was then 'felled' or 'falled'] □ The *Jmca* cit (1986) combines with those fr Austral & NZ as prob evidence of colonial Engl retentions.

fast.en[1] *vb tr Phrase* **fasten a name on sb** *vb phr* (Jmca) [*IF—Joc*] To taunt (sb who puts on airs) with a nickname. *He used to say: "Unno no call me no Count Tepple". May be that was a name his breddas fastened on him since he was so stand-offish and loved keeping his own company.*—RLTJWS:11

fave [fe.v] *adj* (Trin) [*AF*] Favourite. *Since the onset of the Alternative Thursday night music session in June at Flags Sports Bar, the trendy hangout spot for sports fanatics, many fans wanting to get a taste of their fave local music groups have flocked to Flags to satisfy their appetite for a bit of the two.*—Newsday (1997.08.25, p.47) □ Truncated form of 'favourite'.

fee-fee *n* (Jmca) A child's noise-making toy made of a rolled paper tube which extends to full length when blown, making the sound indicated by the name. *[W]hile some were beating a drum or blowing a fee-fee ...*—RLTJWS:20 [Imitative] □ Also called a **blow-out**.

feel *vb intr* (ECar) To suffer the consequences of disobedience. *Tornado? Wunna mekking sport, wunna hard ears, so wunna now have to feel. Repent.*—AdV (1992.05.15, p.9) [Reduction of phr 'feel pain'] □ *Hard-ears yo(u) won('t) hear; own-way yo(u) mus(t) feel* is a well-known ECar parental admonition.

fer.ment.ar.y *n* (Trin) **1.** A large wooden bin in which cocoa beans, fresh from the pods, are put to 'sweat' or 'ferment', loosening the thin white skin covering the actual bean, under the heat of a gable roof of galvanized iron. **2.** [By extension] The place where the process of fermentation of cocoa beans collected in wooden bins takes place, followed by the placing of the sweated beans in huge trays to be exposed to sunlight for a week and tramped on by naked feet to help clean the beans of their dry skin before they are bagged for sale. *I know when the cocoa is to pick, and when it is to prune, and how long it must remain in the fermentary, and how long to dry in the sun.*—LTS:11 [< IAE *ferment* + *-ary* 'connected with' place of (as in granary, sanctuary, etc.]

fine-leaf thyme /1´21/ *n phr* (Guyn) **1.** A woody herb about 2 ft tall, with small serrate leaves wh have a mint-like smell, and are used as seasoning; it is "closer to a marjoram than to a thymus" (C. Springer, pers info, 2002); *Lippia Spp.* □ Both varieties named for their small leaves, by contrast with THICK-LEAF THYME. **2.** A slender aromatic, branching shrub, often over 6 ft tall; it is hairy and bears little white flowers; an infusion of the leaves is used by some to control vomiting; *Lippia micromera (Verbenaceae).* Also known as **Spanish Thyme** (GMPCG:168)

fing.er waves *n phr* (ECar) A black woman's hairstyle in wh the hair is fixed in low moist-looking waves, about the thickness of a finger apart (hence the name) and following the shape of the head. □ The vb form *fingerwave* also occurs in talk.

fire *n Phrase* **put the fire under sb's tail** *id phr* (ECar) [*IF*] To use means to frighten or force sb to get a move on; to make sb begin some necessary action. *The boy won('t) study up in England until the father had to go up there and put the fire under his tail and threaten him.*—(Guyn) [Perh a ref to the practice (f. ex in Guyn) of driving monkeys away fr farm land by firing the bush in which they hide]

fire.side *n* (Guyn, Jmca, Trin) [*IF*] [In rural areas] A cooking place; (Guyn, Trin) a hearth made of clay or mud mixed with cow-dung. **a.** *You could hear her chopping wood to make her fireside. The old woman had to do this because she hadn't a kerosene oil stove.*—Jmca (Ms.) **b.** *Christiana was at the fireside looking at the bake roasting in the pot, with her back turned to the door.*—LTS:97 [By shift of sense fr 'place around the fire' to 'fire-place']

fish by.catch *n phr* (CarA) See BYCATCH.

fit *vb* (Jmca) To suit (a situation); to be right for (sth). *Phrase* **it don(t) fit yo(u)** *id phr* (Jmca) You're unfit, unable. *"Come do(w)ng off de stage! It don('t) fit you!"* *[Call from audience to performer.]* [By shift of sense 'fitness, suitability for'. Cp *OED* 2 **fit** *vb* 1 5a. To be of the right measure (etc.) for [as in] "the cap fits"]

flat *adj* [AF] Lying face downwards on the ground. *Phrase* **get flat** *vb phr* (Jmca) [*Rastaf*] To quickly lie flat on the ground. (See cit.) *A dancehall term (about 1985) ... due to the heavy amount of gunfire at many reggae dances where one must be in a state of prepared-ness to get flat i.e. hit the floor out of the way of stray bullets.*—JJRW:21

fly *vb intr* (Guyn) [Esp of glass or porcelain] To split suddenly. [Housekeeper to] *Mistress A sorry. A put de glass bowl in de oven an(d) it fly'.*— [Cp *OED* **fly** *vb* 9.f To **fly** to pieces, or simply 'To fly' 'To break up suddenly, split up' + cits 1470–1881] □ **1.** Perh the EE usage has been retained at the folk level beyond 1881. **2.** No pa.t. form has been noted. Note monoform Cr.—pa.t. in cit.

fly-stick *n* (Bdos) A device for catching small birds. It is a flexible twig, one end stuck in the ground, the other bent over with a looped string attached, which would be triggered to 'fly' (hence the name) or close on the legs of a feeding bird.

fog *vb intr* (ECar) To spray designated locations that are infested with mosquitoes with a thin, drifting, fog-like mist which carries an insecticide in suspen-sion. [By extension] **fogging** *n.* The spraying of an area with the insecticide mist. *Fogging resumes: The Ministry of Health's Vector Control Unit resumes its fogging exercise at the Graeme Hall Swamp to control mosquito breeding in the swamp area from tomorrow May 2.*—AdV (2001.05.01, p.4) [*OED* **fog** *vb* 2 *trans* 'to envelope with or as with fog; to stifle with fog'. However the CE use is *intr*]

fog.ging ma.chine *n phr* (CarA) (A four-wheeled ve-hicle or tractor on which is mounted) a mechanical device used to spray or FOG an area with insectide. [< 'machine for fogging', as in 'washing machine', 'boil-ing house', 'burying ground', etc., without hyphen]

foop *vb* (Bdos, Guyn) [AF—Vul] To have sexual in-tercourse; to copulate. **a.** *In them days the old men didn('t) have any condoms to foop with. Was jus(t) al-ways a straight thing, y'know?*—(Bdos) **b.** *Oh yes, when I was a young boy at school, de fellows used to write foop, foop on the toilet walls. Now you can see f-u-c-k. Big. With drawings.*—(Bdos) [Cp (*SSE*) AmE **foop** 'to engage in homosexual practices'. Note also (*DARE*) Amer. dial Eng. **foop** *vb* To dance uninhibit-edly + cit (1928) "... you would go to the Congo (= a Black cabaret) and turn rioting loose ..., fooping and jig-jagging the night away"] □ This item remains in common use in intimate *AF/IF Bdos* talk.

for.eign *adv* [AF/IF] Overseas. *Phrases* **1. back from for.eign** *adv phr* (Jmca) Home from abroad. *She had seen him come back from foreign with his gun-foot pants, his straw hat and chain and seen him spending money.*—BJLSCH:107 **2. for for.eign** *adv phr* (Jmca) Going abroad. *How she can a do a thing like that after she leave for foreign all these years since I born, and she never come back or ever write.*—RHJSS:188 **3. go for. eign; leave for for.eign** *vb phr* (Jmca) To go abroad; to travel overseas. *Im a go foreign next week!*—Jmca.

fort.y night *n phr* (Gren) [Religion] A celebration of the fortieth night after a person's death, consisting of hymn-singing and feasting by relatives and friends to enable the soul's final release from earthly tempta-tions, as Jesus, after 40 days and nights, defeated the Devil's temptations. **a.** *I haven't tombed her yet, but I paid all the funeral expense. We had a Third Night for her, but no Nine Night, no Forty Night. And up to this I never make an offering for her, not yet.*—SDP:104 **b.** *Bongo II ... [A folk-music type] Music for dancing in the yard at a wake whilst hymns are sung in the house [at a] Nine or Forty Nights wake, carrying special com-mentary.*—ECDS:9 □ An act blending in folk culture, Christian and African religious beliefs, mostly in ru-ral areas and now rare. The number 40 played a part in OT chronology as equivalent to one generation.

four-"i" chapter; four-eye chap.ter *n phrs* (Bdos, Guyn) [AF—Joc] A short time or period of error or of some bungling. *Phrase* **fin(d) out in four-"i" chap-ter** *id phr* (Bdos, Guyn) To discover a painful truth after making foolish mistakes. **a.** *But when Prescod went 'cross to de Barbados Labour Party in de politri-cks o' inclusion, I did hear a ole Guyanese woman say 'e gine fin' out wuh 'e gine fin' out in four-eye chapter.*— NaT (2004.03.04, p.9A, Lickmout' Lou) **b.** *Dem dat runin(g) wid boys (in)stead o(f) studyin(g) de(ir) books goin(g) fin(d) out in four "i" chapter, I tell you.*— (Bdos) ["Chapter iiii" (four "i") an error of ignorance or folly, which embarrassing experience will correct, iv being the right representation] □ The variant 'four-eye', as in cit b is due to folk etym.

free black(s) *adj/n phr (pl)* (CarA) [Hist] See FREE-MAN, FREE COLOURED.

free col.oured(s) *adj/n phr (pl)* (CarA) [Hist] See cits; also FREEMAN **a.** *In discussing the characteristics of the free coloured population, it is important to note how the terms 'free coloured' and 'coloured' are used here. The former term lacks precision in the documen-tary bases used in this study. In the Barbadian situa-tion, the term was applied to persons of a wide genotype and phenotype. In the Levy (tax) Books, there are several instances of people being labelled as free co-loured (fc) in one year's assessment, free mulatto (fm) in another, and even free negro (fn) in yet another as-sessment. In this study however, the terms 'free co-loured' and coloured will be used as convenient labels to avoid the difficulties of identification which arise in the data base. In this usage the term will include all freedmen and women who might be further sub-classified* *as indicated above.*—P. Welch & R. Goodridge: "Red and Black Over White" (Bridgetown, Carib Research and Publications, 2000), pp.9, 10 **b.** *While the slave and white populations declined, the free coloured and free black (or 'freedman') population increased dramatically. Between 1810 and 1830 the freedman population grew by approximately 70 percent.*—HSPBC:76 □ IAE *free* "not enslaved" + CE *coloured* (a euphemism for) 'being of mixed race (African and European). See (*DCEU*) *coloured*.

freed.man *n* (CarA) [*Hist*] See cit. *The present work contains the names of some 888 Barbadians (about 166 females and 722 males) who are clearly identified as freedmen in primary historical sources. By freedmen we mean persons, whether male or female, who had some degree of African ancestry, and who were either born free or manumitted from enslavement during the period.*—HHWFB:i. [< IAE *freed* 'liberated, released' (in this case, 'from enslavement') + *man* 'human male']

free.hold.er *n* (CarA) [*Hist*] See cit. **a.** " *... a major law passed in 1721 ... modified procedures and qualifications concerning the eligibility to vote, hold elective office, and serve on juries. Those entitled to enfranchisement were required to be 'freeholders', twenty-one-year old males who were 'natural born' or naturalized British subjects, Christians, and who owned at least ten acres of land or a house having an annual taxable value of £10 island currency ... [This law] added the requirement that a 'freeholder' had to be white.*"—HTUP:67 **b.** *Although the law [of May 25, 1831] technically removed racial prerequisites from the definition of freeholder, even at this late date the Barbadian legislature could not bring itself to maximize the number of eligible freedmen.*—HTUP:102 □ The earlier cits from *Bdos* history represent the regionwide development of the restricted CE understanding of the term, although the dates of legalization would differ. The post-Emancipation defn aligned with the traditional BrE meaning "owner of landed property without encumbrance".

free.man *n* (CarA) [*Hist*] **1.** [During the era of plantation slavery.] A landless or small-holding white citizen of a colony. **a.** *Since they were not slaves, freedmen were legally subjects and could theoretically lay claim to the legal rights held by white freemen.*—HHWFB:i. **b.** *Property holders with less than ten acres are classified as freemen, meaning that they were not servants but that they could not vote. ... There were many small planters and freemen also ... living along the seacoast [of Barbados] where the soil is infertile and the rainfall light.*—DSAS:92 [< (*OED*) *Free* 1.1. 'Of persons': Not bound or subject as a slave is to his master' (+ cits from 888) + *man*, as originally a separate word as in 888 cit, but becoming a bound form in (*OED*) **Freeman** 1a 'one who is not a slave or serf' (+ cits from 1000)] □ '**Freeman**' but not '**Freedman**' became a common family name in Afric Caribbean and N. American social life. In 18C & ff. BrE **freeman** was given a fixed meaning in regard to blacks through the judgement of Sir William Blackstone in the famous Somersett case, as follows: "*And this spirit of liberty is so deeply implanted in our constitution, and*

rooted even in our very soil, that a slave or a negro, the moment he lands in England, falls under the protection of the laws, and with regard to all natural rights becomes eo instanti a freeman." In 18C and 19C AmE **freeman** long applied only to white citizens: '*Several of the [state] constitutions [of 1789] ... repeatedly use the word "freeman" or "freemen" when describing the electors, or other members of the state*'—The Unconstitutionality of Slavery (Ch 6)—Lysander Spooner, Boston (1845). However er the regular practice of freed blacks in the USA, whether escapees or liberated, was to call themselves freemen. e.g "*There is nothing very striking or peculiar about my career as a freeman, when viewed apart from my life as a slave*"—from Ch 22 'Life as a Freeman' in '*My Bondage and My Freedom*'—Frederick Douglas, 1881 **2.** [By extension] A black person born of freed (i.e. manumitted) parents A or of a freedwoman by a white father (also called **free black** or **free coloured**). **a.** *Freedwomen also participated in sexual relationships with whites, and these liaisons produced children who were not only "coloured" but also, because of their mother's status, free at birth.*—HTUP:21 **b.** *As a freeman, the freedman was a British subject and could theoretically lay claim to the legal rights held by white freemen; moreover, he shared with whites the obligations of citizenship, such as payment of taxes and service in the militia.*—HTUP:112 □ Caribbean historians do not appear to be absolutely clear together in the contradistinctive application of the terms "freeman" vs "freedman" in the CarA plantation era. See **freedman**. What is indisputable is that the term "**freedman**" never applied to whites in the CarA, even in sense 2, whereas "**freeman**" acquired extended legal recognition before emancipation for certain blacks, so coinciding with "**freedman**" in many contexts.

frig.gin(g) *adj* (Bdos) [*AF—Vul*] Blasted; damned. *Duh turn de friggin volume up again! Well, I kyan help it. I got to get out now!*—MMM:13 [BrE (Vul) *frig* **1.** To copulate. **2.** To masturbate] □ Barely short of social taboo in present casual *Bdos* speech.

froff.y *adj* (Bdos, Guyn) [*AF—Joc*] [Usu of a man] Poor and very shabby looking. *Drink made the family abandon him and you see him now a froffy old man walking the streets.*—(Guyn, Trin) [< IAE *frothy* 'worthless']

fruit *n* **Phrase all fruits ripe** *id phr* (Jmca) [*AF—Joc*] Everything is going fine. □ Made popular by a hit song from a local singer.

FTAA *abbr* (CarA) **F**ree **T**rade **A**rea of the **A**mericas, an economic grouping of 34 countries of the Western Hemisphere, agreed on at Santiago, Chile, in April 1998, covering the hemisphere's entire north-south length and including the 14 independent CARICOM countries. It is intended to create a major world mega-trading bloc. *The Heads of Government agreed on proposals ... submitted by the ... Sub-Committee on External Negotiations ... [and] reiterated the need to increase efforts to have the Region's interest and priorities included in FTAA negotiations.*—RNM Update no.0117, 2001.07.13

G

gal.e.ron [galerʌn] *n* (Trin) A ten-verse lyric set to music, accompanied by (Venezuelan) string-band instruments. *The following types of music are played during the celebration: Galerons, Malaguenas, Jotas ... which are accompanied by lyrics.*—SuG (1994.11.27, p.19) [Sp '(indoor) folk dance']

gal.ley *n* (Jmca) A large cooking pot on three legs. *The women would cook a huge galley full of goat meat ...*—RLTJWS:48 [Prob by shift of sense, fr 'large pot used in a ship's galley (cooking room)']

gan.ja [ganʤa > gyanʤa] *n* (CarA) // *herb* [Rastaf] // *indian hemp, marijuana, pot weed, wisdom weed* (Jmca) [IF] The popular folk-name for marijuana or cannabis (*Cannabis sativa, Cannabaceae*), a plant whose dried leaves are rolled and smoked for their narcotic effect, and (disputed) medicinal value; it is regarded as sacred by *RASTAFARIANS* (see *DCEU*). **a.** *Ganja (Wisdom Weed, Marijuana, Pot or Indian hemp), also called 'herb', was introduced into Jamaica by [East Indian] indentured farm labourers, but has become widely used in the society during the past 15 to 20 years, attracting more attention as its use spread through all classes and to all age groups ... It is illegal to grow ganja, trade in it or have ganja in your possession in Jamaica.*—RJH:26 **b.** *He also spoke of the United States refraining from issuing visas to Vincentians if it was concluded that government was supporting the illegal ganja trade. "The message is not that we want the right to smoke ganja," said J—— C—— at a meeting of marijuana planters at Georgetown last Saturday.*—NaT (1998.11.27, p.7) [< Hin *ganja*, name of the plant]

gar.ri.sons; gar.ri.son com.mun.i.ties *n (phr)* pl (Jmca) Areas (as originally in (West) Kingston, the capital) understood to be demarcated communities harbouring armed gangs wh are so violently loyal to one or other of the main political parties of *Jmca* that outsiders, including the police, are imperilled. See cits. **a.** *Political parties created Jamaica's street gangs in the 1970s, to rustle up votes. Since then, the gangs have turned to drug trafficking. But they remain staunchly and often violently loyal to their parties and live in politically divided, poor neighbourhoods called "garrisons". As a result, the line between drug-related and political violence is often blurred.*—AdV (2002.10.16, p.20) **b.** *In these areas the votes returned are close to 100% for the candidate representing the party it supports. A fair amount of intimidation goes on to prevent anyone voting otherwise. Clashes between opposing Garrison communities frequently end in mayhem and*

death.—DaG (2002.10.17, p.1) [< 'being garrisons', fr their closed nature and the use of armed look-outs]

gar.ri.son con.sti.tuen.cy *n phr* (Jmca) A political constituency dominated by a *GARRISON* whose party loyalty and intimidation ensure the exclusion of any opposing electoral opinion or vote. **a.** *West Kingston with its notorious Tivoli is the classic JLP GARRISON constituency where Seaga will win, and St. Andrew South Western may be regarded as a natural PNP garrison constituency which is a 'safe seat' for Portia Simpson.*—(Jmca, 2002) **b.** *Garrisons are political constituencies fiercely loyal to either the governing People's National Party or the opposition Jamaica Labour Party.*—DaG (2002.10.17, p.A1) [< GARRISON + (official political) *constituency*]

gar.ri.son pol.i.tics *n phr* (Jmca) The enlisting and ensuring of electoral support through the protective fostering of *GARRISON CONSTITUENCIES* in areas of Jamaica. *"I think one of the blights on this country is the continuation of garrison politics", Carter said. "This is a disgrace, in my opinion, to the essence of democracy to have certain neighbourhoods where freedom of speech is impossible and freedom of assembly is impossible."*—NaT (2002.10.16, p.12A) [See GARRISONS]

gas (ECar, Trin) [IF] *n* Propane gas, supplied in cylinders for home cooking. ***Phrase* cooking with gas** *id phr* (Trin) [AF—Joc] Advancing socially; seeing better prospects; moving up in life. *A see yo(ur) husband get a big work, so yo(u) cookin(g) wit(h) gas now.* — (Trin) [A ref to the installation of propane gas for use in domestic cooking, replacing kerosene stoves or in still poorer homes coal-pots, such a development being a social advancement at the time of the post-independence oil-boom in *Trin*]

gen.er.al *n* (Jmca) [Rastaf] A Rastafarian who is considered by his peers to be the very best at whatever he does. ☐ Restricted usage. Formerly reduced to **ginal** [Derog, see DCEU] this is a re-elevation in sense of the original word.

gi.ant Afric.an snail *n phr* (Bdos) A snail whose reddish brown shell is about 3 ins long, its outstretched body up to 6 ins long, the largest weighing up to 2 lb; it feeds on living plants esp vegetables and flowers, and is an identified agricultural pest; *Achatina fulica.Efforts to contain the giant African snail have been unsuccessful since its arrival here a year ago.*—NaT (2001.11.23, p.5)

gig *n* (Jmca) [*IF*] A child's top. *After recess, after you finished eating your mango, soursop, star-apple ... the bwoys used to mek and play with their gigs, or play marbles.*—RLTJWS:35 [*OED gig* (Obs) 'A whipping-top' + cits—1719 cit. See also *DJE*]

go *vb intr* **Phrases go school; went school** *vb phrs* (Bdos) [*IF*] To go to school; went to school. *And if she went scule widout lunch, yuh cud sen de drink an cutter later on.*—MMM:21 [By reduction of inter-syllabic consonant cluster /-cc-/, a common feature of *Bdos* pronunc. /tə-/ 'to' is lost before /s-/]

gone *Phrase* **gone over to the other side** *vb phr* (Bdos, Trin) [*IF*] [Of a man] To have become a homosexual. *When the mother understood that the son gone over to the other side, it nearly broke her heart.*— (Bdos,1960) [A euphemism for 'choosing the wrong biological side of sexual partnership']

grave.yard cold *n phr* (Bdos) [*AF—Joc*] A rattling chest-cold that is possibly leading to bronchitis. [Perh a euphemism for 'deadly']

groove¹ *n* [*AF—Joc*] The vagina. [Prob infl < AAVE usage. Cp *RHDAS* **groove 3**. Esp Black E. 'the vagina' + cits 1936–] □ Only occurs in CE in the phrases 'in the groove', 'grooving', without sexual association. *Phrase* **in the groove** *adj phr* (CarA) [*AF—Joc*] Happy; in a joyful state of mind; feeling very pleased. [Perh fr the suggestion of male sexual pleasure. Cp *RHDAS* **groove 5** Phr *in the groove* (Orig Jazz) 'doing exceptionally well; splendid' + cits 1932–]

groove² *vb intr* (CarA) **1.** To be in a happy state of mind; to display happiness. *A see yo(u) groovin in yo(ur) new car.*—(Bdos) [By functional n > vb shift of *groove¹*] □ Usu in the pres. part. form *grooving* 'doing well; being happy'. **2.** [By extension] To dance passionately. *Byron Lee and The Dragonnaries had the crowd groovin(g) long before midnight.*—(Jmca)

ground.at.ion; ground.a.tion day; ground.ings *n (phr)* (Jmca) [*Rastaf*] A Rastafarian assembly to 'reason', discuss policy, celebrate, and build community spirit through the ritual smoking of GANJA and open-ended discussion on any issue from a Rastafarian perspective. Designed to contrast with the uncertainty in the wider Jamaican society, "**Groundation Day**" marks the visit of Haile Selassie I to Jamaica in 1966 and offers hope and certainty to the Rasta brethren.'—MSMCDB:447 *Groundations are the Nyabingi celebrations of those who are gathered together in the sight on JAH, giving thanks and praises through chants and prayers.*—JJRW:21 [A blend < *ground*(ing,(s) 'sitting (s) on the ground' + (found)*ation*, 'fundamental soundness']

grow *vb* **Phrases 1. grow match** *id phr* (Guyn) (See cit.) *John and Gloria are grow match; they were both born in 1948.*—YRRC:20 [< *grow*(ing up) *match*(ed) together'] **2. grow (up)** *vb tr (phr)* (Jmca) [*IF*] To raise, bring up (children); raise the level, quality of. **a.** *"Grow them the way you should. Mothers spent more time growing up their children."*—Jmca, Speaker in radio interview 1997.07.30 **b.** *"Radio Mona, the station that grows your mind"*—Slogan for UWI Radio Station.

gua.va duff *n phr* (Baha) A guava-based fruit pudding boiled in a bag and covered in a rum-flavoured cream sauce. *Guava duff, you might say, is the national dessert of the Bahamas.* —(Baha) [< *guava*, the fruit + *duff*, as *OED* duff sb, 'a flour dumpling boiled in a bag'] □ Cp *DCEU* *duff* (Guyn)

gui.nea-hen weed *n phr* (Gren, Jmca) A weed with widely spaced, elliptical four-inch-long leaves, bearing a spike of tiny white flowers; it smells like garlic when crushed, is bitter tasting and favoured in folk medicinal use for skin disorders, inhaled for headaches, etc.; widely known in *CarA* by other names (see note); *Petiveria alliacea (Phytolaccaceae)* *She made me taste the guinea hen weed and the leaf of life, for better vision, she said.*—BJLSCH:76 □ See *DCEU* **gully root** (CarA) for other // //. See also *HCWP*:70.71 for more.

gui.nea-pep.per *n* (Gren) A hot red pepper, often with a pointed tip and a crenulated surface; *Capscium spp. She made me get a two-and-six coin and pieces of obi, break it in four; and guinea-pepper, cloves, milk and a open hole.*—SDP:86

gwaan *Cr vb intr* **Phrase A so yo(u) gwaan** *id phr* (Jmca) [*AF—Cr*] Behave; conduct yourself. *Me no like (h)ow im a gwaan. (I don't like how he's behaving)* —(Jmca) [Jmca Cr *gwaan* < 'go on' + intrusive labialization and /ɔ > a/ vowel opening]

H

Hail!; Hail-I! *excl* (Jmca) [*Rastaf*] A greeting of fraternity; a brotherly salutation. [< *Hail*, as in biblical salutations + (*Rastaf*) *I*, signalling brotherly embrace]

hair *n Phrase* **hair like gwenn kaka kabwit** *id phr* (Gren) [*AF—Derog*] Hair like (rolls of) goat shit. [From Fr Cr *gwenn kaka kabuit* 'rolls (of) goat shit'] □ Cp (*DCEU*) **black-pepper grains**.

half-a-mad.man *n* (Bdos) [*AF—Joc*] A congenital idiot. *And if it is, you are probably thinking that I could only be a piece-o-idiot, or half-a-madman to be in that part of the world where people are always involved in civil war and engaged in killing off each other.*—SuS (1989.06.25, p.9A)

hand *Phrases* **1. hand and foot** *n phr* (Jmca) [*AF*] All the vital support there is to depend on. **a.** *When dem gone, she call me. Yuh lickle wretch yuh! Ah know yuh do it. But ah cyaan say yuh do it in front a dem. Dem will kill yuh. And yuh a me hand and me foot.*—SSLG:97 **b.** *Martin was the Bridge Club's hand and foot, and when he died they soon folded.*—(Bdos) □ Cp *DCEU* **all and all** at **all** 1 *pron*, Phr 3.1, with similar sense. Note difference from IAE adv phr '(*tied to sb*) *hand and foot*'. **2. make a hand of (sb)** *vb phr* (Antg) [*IF*] To gain/get the upper hand. *When they come back with the reinforcement a riot broke out and they couldn't make a hand of the Point people. The massas call out the militia and when they come the riot really spread.*—SSHL:131 [Perh a dial BrE residue. Cp (*DNE*) Newfoundland Eng. *hand* n, 2 Phr '*make a hand* 'to have success' + cits 1924–1972] **3. shake yo(ur) hand** *vb phr* (CarA) [*AF—Joc*] Shake hands in agreement with (you); congratulate (you). *Bishop Brume, uh cud shake yuh hand! Guh long an talk yuh talk! Uh glad to hear yuh. Wunna Bajans, pay attenshun to dis man!*—MMSC:31

hand.sel [hansl] *n* (Bdos) A shopkeeper's first sale for the day or a first taking (preferably from the hand of a young person) in a fund-raising venture. *That ten-dollar donation you gave me for the sponsored walk was my handsel. You know we raised nearly nine hundred dollars?*—(Bdos) [*OED handsel* 3 ... 'The first money taken by a trader in the morning, a luck-penny; anything given or taken as an omen ... or pledge of what is to follow' + many cits going back to ME and 16C. However the spread of dial usage = 'an auspicious augury' is well attested in *EDD* **handsel** *sb* and *vt* in gen dial use in Sc., Irel., and Eng. + cits fr early 19C ... 'an auspicious beginning, a good omen' etc.]

hard *adj* (Jmca) [*Rastaf*] 'Tough, dependable, solid, long lasting, when describing a person, song, dance, etc. you can know that ... is something great.'—JJRW:23

Ha ya! *excl* (Guyn) "I am warning you". [Prob of W Afr. origin] □ An elder person's warning to a child that a blow may follow.

hay.fay (**hay-fay**) [hefe] *n* (Gren) [*AF—Joc*] See cit. *One of the words they influenced is hay-fay, which comes from the Spanish* **jefe**, *a chief. In Caribbean English, to call someone a hay-fay is to imply that he's pretending to be a big-shot.*—Suj no.17 (p.27, 1989/1990)

heart.i.cal *adj* (Jmca) [*Rastaf*] Recognizably RASTAFARIAN; sincere. See cits. **a.** *Heartical refers to emotions or feelings as an attachment to the rasta culture, especially expressed in the "ridim" drums.*—MSMCDB **b.** *HAILELUJAH is a more heartical way of saying halleluyah.*—(Jmca) JJRW:23 [< *heart* + *ical* for emotive effect as in 'musical'] □ In the cit *b*, the last syllable of the headword is 'Jah' [ja] (= God)

heat.ment *n* (Guyn) [*AF—Joc*] Great heat; intensity. *In the heatment o' the argument, they come to blows.*—Guyn. [< IAE *heat* = CE intensifier suff -MENT] □ Metaph usage only. See -MENT.

herb *n* (CarA) /// GANJA (Jmca)

he.self *pron* (ECar) [*AF—Cr*] Himself. **a.** *Someone else chimed in: "He won't stop and rest heself, even de American President does go every now and then somewhere and rest heself."*—AdV (1993.10.15, p.9) **b.** *No Bajan police never catch Hall the last two times that he was on the run. Hall catch heself.*—AdV (Eric Lewis, 1999.10.01, p.9) □ Belongs to the paradigm of *Cr* refl prons *me-* /yo(u)- /he- /she- /we- / *deyself*, based on the *CarA Cr* monoform pers pron system.

hi.bis.cus meal.y bug *n phr* (ECar) /// PINK MEALY BUG Alternative name of the PINK MEALY BUG of wh the hibiscus plant is the main host.

hick.ie *n* (Bdos) [*AF*] An imaginary crude, rough place, far away. [Cp *EDD* **Hickey** (Nottinghamshire) 'Name for the devil.' In *Bdos* 'the' is often added to place names of poor areas—'The Ivy, The Orleans', etc. (hence the foll phr)] *Phrase* **living in the hickie** *id phr* [*AF—Joc*] Living in a very poor area. *They now* come from livin(g) in the hickie yo(u) know—yo(u) can('t) mek them yo(ur) company.—(Bdos)

high bed *n phr* (Guyn) [*Hist*] A large four-poster bed (of the plantation era) standing about two feet off the floor and usu climbed into on a small step. It was the typical bed of the planter class. *All high bed na sof(t) i.e. "Those in high positions have their problems too".*—(Guyn (Prov))

Hin.du.nised/ized *vbl adj* (Guyn) (Be) practising the social and political habits of a Hindu neighbourhood without being a Hindu yourself. *He said that all Indo-Guyanese, even those who were Muslims and Christians, were Hindunised. Alexander stressed that once an Indo-Guyanese lived in those communities he came under the influence of the Hindu religion.*—NaT (2003.02.20, p.9) [< *Hindu* + suff *-ize*, 'to make or become like' (as in *Americanize*) with intrusive epenthetic *-n-*] The spelling *-ize* is preferred in modern usage.

hog.gish *adj* (Guyn, Jmca) [*IF—Derog*] Of rough manner, esp in speaking to others. **a.** *I wouldn('t) go an(d) as(k) him any favour—he's too hoggish.*—(Guyn) **b.** *Mrs M—— was a hoggish teacher.*—Jmca (Ms) [< *hog* 'a large pig bred for slaughter' + *ish* 'having the characteristics of'. Cp IAE *childish*]

home at (me/you) *adv* (CarA) [*IF*] At sb's home; at my/your (etc.) home. *So I assumin' dat you relaxin' home at you an' leffin de thousands o' idiots to go an' gi'*

Earl Spencer an' 'e fam'ly duh hard-earn coppers to get mo' rich offa.—NaT (1998.07.01, p.9A, Lickmout' Lou)

horn.ee *n* (Bdos) A man or woman whose spouse or partner is having a sexual relationship with another person; sb (usu the man) who has been horned. *One of the worst things about a horn, especially in this part of the world, is that the horner tends to enjoy some kind of hero status while the hornee becomes the brunt of ridicule, derision and mocksport.*—SuS (1999.05.23, p.9A) [< *DCEU horn*1 *vb* + noun-forming suff *-ee*, as in 'employee']

hot-mix *n* (Bdos) [*IF*] A hot mixture of bitumen and fine gravel used in surfacing roads. See cit. *Those offending craters should be dry, scraped clean of loose material as far as practicable, and then filled with bitumen [hot-mix, as it is sometimes called] then compacted with the use of road rollers [formerly known as «rock engines»] or the smaller, more convenient manually operated tampers.*—Action Mag (2004.06.13, p.1)

Hush! *excl* (Jmca) Never mind (darling); I'm sorry (that you're hurt). *The Bahamian visitor [to Kingston, Jamaica] was quite offended when a Jamaican stepped on her toe and promptly said "Oh hush!"*—(Jmca) [From the nursery rhyme "Hush-a-bye baby in the tree top"] □ Quite distinct from 'Hush up!' This common *Jmca* expression is an easy cause of misunderstanding in 'outsider' contact situations.

I

I *pron in attrib function* (Baha) [*Rastaf*] *They too identify with West Indian music and, interestingly, lace the new songs with I lyrics about the social problems they face in British society.*—NaG (1978.04.08, p.2) [*IF* borrowing of *Rastaf* idiom]

I an(d) dem *pron phr* (CarA) [*Rastaf*] People of our sort. *You no sight, dread. Sight how dem ballheads make I an dem walk down to dey office an put a sign to say 'No visitor'. Is pure jesterin, ah tell you.*—CrU:(1976.10.09, p.5) [(*Rastaf*) *I* with collective sense, reinforced by *Cr* post-posed **and dem** as collective pluralizer] □ See *DCEU dem²* Phr 2.1

In.di.an Ar.ri.val Day *n phr* (Trin) 1.(Trin) May 30th, celebrated annually in *Trin*, officially identified as of 1995, to commemorate the arrival in *Trin* of the first ship bringing East Indian immigrants to *Trin* plantation labour in 1945. **2.** (Guyn) An alternative name used in *Guyn* for ARRIVAL DAY (see), May 5th in *Guyn*.

In.di.an hemp *n phr* (Jmca) (A more formal name for) GANJA. [Fr its introduction by and association with Indian indentured labour introduced into *Jmca* in the latter half of the 19C]

in.vite list *n phr* (Bdos) [*IF*] A list of persons to be invited. *"Mirry was dragging her feet on everything—the invitations, the invite lists, her gown—everything. It's as if she knew she wouldn't be needing any of it."*—NSWOM, p.15 [By functional vb > n shift of IAE *invite*, whence the shift in sense to 'invitation']

in.vite.ment *n* (Bdos) [*AF—Joc*] *Golbourne was our star-boy ... Golbourne was never extended a invitation. Not a blasted invitememt! Never extended the courtesy, after a cricket game, to sit down in the verandah with the rest of the team, to drink a Bellfeels Special Stades White Rum.*—CPH:438 [< CE *invite* (n) + CE intensifier suff] □ See -MENT.

i.ron weed *n phr* (Guyn) One of about four varieties of a trailing leguminous vine, about four feet long; its green bifoliate leaves are dried and an infusion used as a folk-medicine for backpains and kidney problems; *Desmodium Spp*. *They call it iron weed because of the toughness of its stem, but it has no iron content.*—(pers info, C. Springer)

ites¹ [ɑɪts] *n pl* (Jmca, ECar) [*Rastaf*] **1.** (The colour) red. See cits. **a.** *[Ites] also means the red, which is the highest colour which the Rastafari flag of red, gold and green as flown by the Niabinghi Theocracy contains.*—PDT:51 **b.** *I see men tying ites, gold and green rope around Bussa's neck. That is disrespectful.*—AdV (2002.10.13, p.14A) [By characteristic *Jmca* folk-speech /h-/ loss from 'heights', symbolizing the high spirtuality of the Rastafari belief system] **2.** [By extension] *excl.* 'A greeting wishing the person greeted may arrive at the heights of spirtuality'.—PDT:51

ites² [ɑɪts] *vb intr* (Bdos) [*Rastaf*] To understand. *I-man (h)aits dat.*—(Bdos) (cit in PDT:50) [By functional n > vb shift of ITES¹, with the sense 'pick up'] □ PDT (p.51) suggests that this n > vb shift is peculiar to Bdos.

I.wer [aiwʊ] *n* (Trin) A type of marching dance, lifting the legs high, on the same spot, as often in dancing *soca*. *Some of the artistes did minister through their music but I was appalled at the behaviour of some "Christian" patrons. The Trinidadian artistes had a kaiso session and I saw people "wukking up" doing the "running man", "pepperseed", "The Iwer" and the "jump and wave"—rags included.*—SuS (1995.06.04, p.8A) [Named after *Trin* calypsonian Iwer George]

J

JA *abbr n, adj* (Jmca) [*IF*] Jamaica. **a.** *To help Employment: Another Loan for JA.*—Jan (March, 1982) **b.** *(adj) JA Art for US Tour.*—Jan. 23 & 28 (1982.03) [Journalistic headline abbr/Cp *Bim*, *SVG*]

Jah *n* (CarA) [*Rastaf*] See cit **a. a.** *JAH: The Rastafarian name for God. It often refers to Haile Selassie and, more often than not, to the Creator whose power (earthforce) pervades the universe.* —MSMCDB:5, 25 **b.** *That is I-and-I vision of the Great Return, / which Jah sent to you. For tongues of fire can dance on the hair of the least unknown, / and that crooked man who Babylon bend / Jah shall make straight.* —WOB:167 **c.** *I-Mar wrote Mbali a letter, introducing himself, expressing his interest in her work and her beliefs. He ended the letter with a prayer for Jah's guidance and protection as she moved forward in her life.* —NaT (1996.05.10, p.29) [As from (AVB) Psalm 68 v.4: *Sing unto God, Sing praises to his name, JAH, and rejoice before him*]

Ja.mai.can White *n phr* (Jmca) A Jamaican national who is visibly either wholly or mostly of European descent; a white Jamaican person. *People born in Jamaica today are simply 'Jamaican'. People of mixed ancestry and/or intermediate social status are referred to with a variety of color related terms such 'red', 'Jamaican white' [not foreign white!], 'brown' or 'browning'.*—(Jmca, Ms, P. Patrick)

jambust *vb tr* (Bdos) [*IF*] [In right-hand drive regulated traffic] To overtake a vehicle on the left, competing for front position in a single lane at a traffic roundabout. **a.** *... when a car jam-busts me on the roundabout after Bussa, ... I find myself transformed into a raving lunatic over whom I have no control.* —Nat (1998.03.27, p.9) **b.** *When people are jambusting me I can see in my rearview mirror what is their intention because they are driving along at a certain speed ...* —AdV (2000.05.20, p.9) [[*IF*] *jam*[1] 'jammed traffic' + *bust*[1] 'to break through, into; a word compound patterned on IAE n-vb tr formation such as fundraise, gate-crash, window-clean, etc.]

jam.bust.er[1], **the** *n* (Bdos) [*IF*] // *jambusting* (Bdos) The act of (permitted) overtaking on the left side of a vehicle (in right-hand-drive regulated traffic). **a.** *Since the jambuster was implemented in early November last year, 32 accidents were recorded up to the end of January at roundabouts on the ABC Highway ... . The Ministry of Public Works is expected to make a statement next week on the impact of the Jambuster after an in-*

terim period.—NaT (1998.03.14, p.5) **b.** *Over a year ago, the Government of Barbados introduced an experimental road traffic regulation that is familiarly known as "Jambusting".*—SuS (2000.01.16, p.12A) [JAMBUST + agential suff like IAE beater]

jam.bust.er[2] *n* (Bdos) [*IF*] The car wh or driver who JAMBUSTS.

jam.bust.ing *n* (Bdos) /// JAMBUSTER[1]

jeal.ous *vb tr* (StVn) [*AF*] To envy. *People talk because dey jealous me. More dey talk is less it bothers me.*—SVFS:20 [By functional shift] (adj 'envious' > vb 'be envious of')]

Jee.zan Peace! *excl* (Jmca) // *cheese on/an(d) bread!* (Bdos) [*AF*] (A euphemism for) Jesus Christ! *Jeezan Peace! If ever a word could start a fight quickly, it was a word of insult about a next person's mother.*—RLTJWS:36 □ See *DCEU* **cheese-on!**

Jen.kins *n* (Bdos) [*IF*] The government psychiatric hospital. *One [Rasta], I-pe, told of how a 'judge boy hear I word sound and send I to Jenkins saying that I mad'.*—(Bdos) [Fr its location on property in the Black Rock area of the suburban Parish of St Michael on land originally called 'Jenkinsville'] □ **1.** Also occasionally referred to as [*AF/IF*] **'Black Rock'** because of its location. **2.** See also *DCEU* **Berbice** Phr. 2.1, for a parallel *Guyn* usage.

join.er.y *n* (CarA) // *joiner-shop* (CarA) [By extended sense] A joiner's workshop, including provision for the sale of his craft; a cabinet-maker's shop. *I ordered a rocking-chair from Mr. Sealy's joinery.*—(Bdos) □ Sometimes coupled with 'upholstery' in similar usage in signs e.g. 'Joinery & Upholstery'. This extended sense is additional to, but in more frequent usage than the basic IAE senses '(a) craft or trade of a joiner, (b) work produced by a joiner'.

join.er-shop *n* (CarA) /// JOINERY (CarA)

jon.kon.nu *n* (Jmca) See *DCEU junkanoo* □ **1.** This is the preferred spelling currently in Jmca. See *SAZJ* p.84: *jonkonnu* (John Canoe). **2.** The rendering JOHN CANOE is still current.

jook-out *vb tr* (Bdos) To scrub clothes on a scrubbing-board wh stands diagonally in a tub of soapy water. *Anyhow, I gine hey an' jook-out dese clothes I* *got soakin', hear? So keep good an' God bless.* —NaT (2007.01.31, p.9A, Lickmout' Lou) [From the action of the scrubber who stands **jooking** downwards on the board] **1.** See *DCEU jook*¹ & foll, also **jooking-board**. **2.** Cp also **jook out sb's eye** as in DCEU *jook*¹ 7.3.2.

Juan Car.na.val; Juan.ci.to [huan karnaval; huansito] *n phr; n* (Belz) An effigy meant to represent people's sins, carried through the streets and ceremonially burnt to mark the end of the pre-Lenten Carnival celebration. See cit. *On the last day of Carnival, the Tuesday before Ash Wednesday, "el baile de Juan Carnaval" was held.* **Juan Carnaval**, *or* **Juancito** *as he was fondly called, was the character representing Carnival. He was made by stuffing a pair of trousers and shirt with dry banana leaves. His head was an empty calabash with his eyes, nose and ears painted on. With a sombrero on his head, he was intended to resemble a man. At dusk,* *around six p.m. everyone who partook in some way or the other in the Carnival celebrations would set off in procession form to an open spot where* **Juancito** *was to be burned ... When the group finally reached the pyre,* **Juan Carnaval** *would be burnt while all the people danced around the bonfire singing the song of* **Juan Carnaval.** *With the burning of* **Juan Carnaval,** *Carnival officially came to an end and the people then went home.*—Bes (vol.9, no.3, p.4) [< Sp, 'John Carnival', perh infl by *'John Canoe'*, another *Belz* folk figure. (See *DCEU*.)] □ Restricted usage. Northern Belize.

juice *Phrase* **get the juice** *vb phr* (Jmca) // **catch hell** *(See DCEU)* [AF] To have a bad time; to be brutalized. *Fe-him wife, Grace, used to get the juice.*—RLTJWS:86 [< *deuce* (by folk etym) as in *DJE*; orig. as *OED deuce*² a (in imprecations = 'devil, hell') + cits from 1657]

K

Ka.na.ri *n* (StLu) See cit. *To the north o Soufriere, still on the seashore, is the village of Canaries. Now, although it has been suggested that this unusual name may have been given by early French colonists on account of some resemblance between the mountains at the back of Canaries and those of the Canary Islands (Iles Canaries), it has also been suggested that the name has an Amerindian origin. It is certain that a clay cooking-pot, long since in use in St. Lucia, and which closely resembles Amerindian cooking-pots found there, is still called «Canari» or «Kanari» (pronounced: Kan-ah-ree).*—JASL:13–14

ka.pa.du.la *n* (Guyn) // *capadulla* (Guyn) A thick woody, greyish brown, forest vine that can be some 50 ft long, with large, veined green leaves and berry-like red fruit; it scrambles over trees reaching for the top; it yields a flowing sap, or the cut vine may be soaked, to be used as a folk medicine, and is prized by some as an aphrodisiac; *Doliocarpus dentatus (Dillenicaeae)*. *'Some men hide and use kapadula, yo(u) know, to get the stick up.*—(Guyn) [An Amerindian, perh Arawakan, name]

keep *Phrase* **keep the puppy tail out o(f) the ashes** *id phr* (Bdos) To keep poverty, want at bay; to manage to feed your family in spite of hardships. *After de husband dead she still manage to go about ironin(g) and mendin(g) to feed de children an(d) keep puppy tail out o(f) de ashes.*—(Joe Tudor, Talk Show Host, 1950s)

kiss Cassie an' bark at Lucas *vb phr* (Bdos) [AF—Joc/Vul] To go to hell; to kiss my arse [Vul]. *I know wuh I tellin' you 'cause de busylickums does mek my name snort when duh ready, too. It don' ever occur to dem dat wuh dem say 'bout certain people 'bout hey does be like water off a duck back. Leh duh kiss Cassie an' bark at Lucas, do! As far as I concern, I wish de Prime Minister an' 'e new wife all de bes'.*—NaT (2006.08.30, p.9A) [Euphemism of unknown origin, «Cassie and Lucas» prob being «folk characters» of identity currently lost]

(kitch.en) bitch *n phr* (Jmca) [AF] A small oil lamp made of tin. *The young man acted bravado before he got up and stumbled round to the back in the dark till smaddy called him and offered him a bitch lamp.*—RTJWS:131 □ See *DCEU* **slut-lamp** (Bdos)

km [khm] (Guyn, Grns) [AF] A very very small distance, 1/2 an inch or so. *Move it a km.*—(Bequia, Grens) [Perh of W Afr origin]

know *vb tr* **Phrase make sb know the ball dat shoot Nelson** *id phr* (Bdos) [AF—Joc] To speak bluntly in loud anger to sb; to give sb the length of your tongue. *She mout' en got nuh cover doh—an you know she too. ... an' girl, she en was'e nuh time to leh de Transport Board know de ball dat shoot Nelson after she an' nough mo' people get duh beak brek las' Sunduh in de bus-stan'.*—NaT (1998.03.18, p.9A, Lickmout' Lou) [The sense is 'to knock down sb.' A ref to the fateful single shot that killed the English naval hero, Lord Nelson in battle (1805). His statue stands in central Bridgetown, Bdos] □ This is a popular *Joc* catch-phrase in *Bdos* talk.

Ko.jo *n* (Jmca) A folk name associated with worthy resistance as characteristic of sb. **a.** *When pressure from the planters and soldiers grew too great, Kojo led his people to the cockpit country where he set up his main camp ... [and] waged guerilla warfare against the English settlers ... Kojo and his people were given 1500 acres of land ... and Kojo was made chief of his community for life.*—SAJZ:91 **b.** *Minister of State for Culture in the Office Of The Prime Minister, Ed. Bartlett, has said the long and distinguished life of Maroon leader, Kojo, "has left us a special legacy of unity and pride".*—JJRW:11 [(Ghana) Akan Day Name for 'child born on Monday'. The association of the name with toughness, though unexplained, is also found in *Guyn*] See note. □ **1.** See *DCEU* for *Guyn* ref. **2.** See also popular alternative spelling **Cudjoe.**

koo-koo *n* (Jmca) /// ACTOR-BOY (Jmca)

L

lab.ba-lab.ba *n; adj* (Jmca) [*AF—Joc*] Talkative. *No tell (h)im not(h)in(g); (h)im too labba-labba.*—(Jmca) [< IAE *blabber*. 'to talk indiscretely + excessively' + reduplication] □ Cp DJE **laba, laba-laba** (with many senses), + derivative **labrish** 'idle gossip'.—See DPJP:19

lame foot *n phr* (Jmca) [*IF*] A leg with a large incurable sore. *Hortense did have a lame foot that caused her to walk funny.*—RLTJWS:86 □ Cp *DCEU* **life sore**.

large off; larg.ing off *vb phr* (Bdos) [*IF*] To make/making a show of superior authority or social condition. **a.** *Every time I see Prime Minister E—— S——larging off—a classic Barbadianism beloved by the late Errol Barrow—on television, I have wondered how many others have, like me, been amused, dismayed or startled by the spectacle of a man apparently devoid of the gift of seeing himself as others see him.*—NaT (1990.09.07, p.8) **b.** *It was the age of the euphoria of socialism and our stage seemed really set for liberty, equality and fraternity to "large off".*—AdV (1998.06.28, p.12) [By characteristic *CarA* functional shift, adj > vb 'to become/make yourself large'. (Cp similarly 'SWEET', adj > vb). But note also *OED* **large** vb 3 Naut '(of the wind) to become [strong]'; + augmentative 'off' as in IAE 'show off']

lath-and-plast.er *n* (Bdos) [*IF*] A structure comprising thin strips of wood interlaced, as the base on which plaster is spread to make (usu inside) walls of a low-cost house; also called **wattle-and-daub** elsewhere.

laugh.in(g)-plas.ter *n* (Bdos) // **lath-and-plaster** [*X*] Properly LATH-AND-PLASTER. *By this time, the back of the building and a large portion of the west wing had been destroyed, with smoke billowing from the roof. Mayers said most of the smoke was because the structure, of what is called "laughing plaster", consisted of a plastered wooden frame which [made the flames] particularly difficult to extinguish.*—NaT (2002.10.07, p.3) [By folk etym. < lath-and-, with / θ > f / shift, common in *Bdos* folk speech]

leaf.hop.per *n* (ECar) One of several species of wedge-shaped bug, generally pale green in colour, and about 3 mm long; it sucks the sap of various types of plants, and also transmits various viruses, ultimately causing the plant to die; *Empoasca* Spp. *The leafhopper is thought to be the cause of the bunchy top disease that affects pawpaw trees.*—(Bdos, Ms)

limb.less *n phr* (Bdos) [*IF*] Astounded; limp with surprise. *Girl, de crime in Buhbayduss got muh limbless! Nuh joke, partly de same time yuh hear dat de crime rate gone down, yuh does be readin' dat somebody get kill, stab, shoot or lick-down.*—NaT (1998.02.25, p.9A) [*OED* **limbless** 'Having no limbs; deprived of a limb' + cits—1881; but not in metaphorical usage as here. However, note *EDD* (Dor, Som) 'all to pieces, utterly destroyed' + cit (Div) "I'll knock thee limbless"] □ Now *Obs* E. Not listed in *COD*.

Lind.bergh trou.sers [lɪnbʌrg trɒʊzɪz] *n phr* (Guyn) [*AF*] Nonsense; an absurdity. *Okay, so Linbergh trousers tie wid string! (i.e. 'so a millionaire's trousers have a string for a belt'.)*—(Guyn) [A ref to a popular jingle of the 1930s in Guyn: ('Ting-a-ling-a-ling / come hear dis ting / Lindbergh trousers tie wid string'. Charles A. Lindbergh, American aviator, became world-famous and wealthy after becoming the first man to fly across the Atlantic]

lin.gay [lɪnge] *adj* (Trin) // **slengere** (Guyn) [*AF—Joc*] **1.** Lanky; long or stretched out; limber and pliable. **a.** *"Yuh eh need no ladder to reach dem mango. Yuh done so lingay!"*—(From a Trin calendar, 1992) **b.** *He big just like you but younger, He lingay like you but harder.*—SuS (Cso (Sparrow, 1995), 1995.10.29, p.18) [Perh from a flawed pronunc of *lanky*] **2.** [By extension] Having an undeveloped mind; hard-headed.

Lis.bon yam *n* (ECar) /// **crop Lisbon** (Bdos)

lit.tle; (lickle; lil) *Phrases* **1. lick.le bit** [lɪklbɪt] *adj phr* (Jmca) [*AF—Joc*] Young and small-bodied. *One time when me was still 'lickle bit', a woman named Hannah Mitchell saw me coming from Redpan with a two-and-six pence pudding pan full o' water pon me head and she bawled out, 'Look Dead and Wake! ...*—RLTJWS:4 [< IAE *little*, by velarization + *bit*; compound with functional n > adj shift] □ /t > k/ velarization as in *miggle* < 'middle', etc. **1.1 lil (bit) mo(re)** *adv phr* (Guyn, Jmca) [*IF/AF*] **1.1.1** In a short while. *It was as well my buddy charmer and me had managed to get the place under such good control, for little more it wouldn't just be the two of us alone living there ...*—RLTJWS:98 [Prob a calque from W Afr languages. Cp (*DAFL*) Twi *kakerá* (adj) 'little'; (n) 'a little while' in similar contexts] **1.1.2** But for a little luck. *De rain save dem; lil bit more an(d) dey woulda-a los(t) de match.*—(Guyn) **2. lit.tle most** *adv phr* (Jmca) [*AF*] Almost; nearly. *Little most sickness caused me to die before time ... .*—

RLTJWS:5 [A redundant compound. Cp sense of **lil** in *Phr* 1.1 + *EDD most* 6. 'Almost, nearly' + many cits e.g. 'There's times she did go most crazy']

liv.e.ty [laɪvɪti] *n* (Bdos) [*Rastaf*] Way of life; manner of living. **a.** *In becoming and living the life of the true Rasta, the Barbadians have had to ... [accept] a new and rigid code of ethics in order to achieve their "upfull livety" ... Money ('Blindza') is an agent of "low livety" and has no place in their society.*—NaT (1977.02.13 p.14) **b.** *Asked whether she was influenced by her father she explained that she gives thanks, that through the power of the Most High, a seed was planted and brought forth. "Life is a livety. He doesn't fully understand my livety, but respects and honours me."* [A blend of *life* + suff -*ity* (as in 'dignity', 'quality') with intervocalic / f > v / voicing] □ Also used in *Jmca*, but pronounced [lɪvɪti]. Also refers to a lived experience.

look for (sb) *vb phr* (Bdos, Guyn, Jmca) [*AF*] To visit (sb) **a.** *Also "I remember one day I was about twelve Aunt Terry came to look for us".*—ObS (Mag) (2002.04.23.) **b.** *Now A get ol(d) de young ones don('t) come an(d) look for me no more.*—(Guyn) [Cp *OED* 2 *look* 15b 'To seek; to search for' + cit 1592. 'Caroline went to look for her a few hours afterwards']

los(t) [lɒ.s] *vb tr* [*AF*—*Cr*] To lose. [< *lost*, pa. t. of *lose* with Cr functional shift 'to loss', overcorrectly rendered in spelling as 'lost'. See Phr] □ *(To) loss,* '(to) lose', belongs to the group of CarA Cr vbs whose base-form derives from the pa.t. of the IAE original: / *brok* / 'break', / *lef* / 'leave', / *marid* / 'marry' etc. *Phrase* **lost (sb) away (in jail)** *vb phr* (Bdos) [*AF*—*Joc*]To send (sb) to jail for such a long number of years that they may be as good as lost to their relatives/ friends.. *[H]e ain't plan to stop thiefing. So I going to lost him away up Glendairy for enough years that when it is time to come out he can't even remember who he name.*—AdV (1998.11.27, p.10, Eric Lewis)

Lu.cian[1] [lušǝn] *adj* (StLu) [*IF*] Belonging or related to St Lucia. *Lucian Kaiso is an annual publication of the Folk Research Centre, Castries, St. Lucia.*—LuK (1995, p.4) [Familiar abbr of 'St Lucian' by aphaeretic suppression of initial syllable. Cp '*Bajan*' < Barbadian]

Lu.cian[2] [lušǝn] *n* (Bdos) [*IF*] A native of St Lucia. **a.** *The businessman who got hooked on a St. Lucian female dancer has moved out from his house ... Some people who are accustomed to seeing him at the night club said that since the Lucian turned his head, he has even travelled to her homeland.*—SaS (1999.05.22, p.11) **b.** *Lucians seem to like foreign artistes more than their own.*—(StLu) [By functional adj > n shift of LUCIAN[1]]

M

maas *n* (Jmca) /// **massa** *(CarA)* (See *DCEU*) [AF—
Cr] Master. *In those days pickney couldn't hold big talk
with their elders. You had to remember to call men
'maas' and 'sar'.*—RLTJWS:55 [< IAE *master* by apo-
cope, and vowel-opening]

make; mek *vb intr* **Phrases 1. A it mek** (Jmca) // *is da
mek (Guyn)* [AF—Cr] *That's why; it serves him/them
etc. right. Dem laas di match beca' dem too boasy. A it
mek (= They lost the match because they're too boast-
ful. That's why).*—Jmca *[Crab sell him head a market]
... A it make him have to carry him eye them ketch
down in him shoulder till now.*—(Text: V. Pollard, SCL
Series paper no.2, 2002, p.10) **2. make corn** *vb phr*
(Gren) [IF] To produce (corn, etc.) *Caribbean farmers will hope to "make a lot of corn" this harvest.* —Suj
no.17 (p.27, 1989/1980) **3. make (a) baby** [Prob infl by
IAE 'make sugar'] *vb phr* (ECar) [IF] To bear a
(child). *And even though 'faire' can be translated to
mean "bear" or "bring forth", women in the islands do
not bear or bring forth children. They "make babies".*—
Suj no.17 (p.27, 1989/1980) [Cp *KED* Krio *mek pikin*
'make child', with similar sense] **4. make/mek a dollar** *vb phr* (Bdos) [AF] To earn a little money to live
by. *It is really getting to be monotonous ... [E]very single time someone gets caught committing an unlawful
act the first uttered excuse is that they were only 'trying
to mek a dollar'.*—AdV (1993.08.07, p.20) **2. make
movements** *vb phr* (Gren) [AF—Joc] [Of a man] To
have /be in a sexual relationship. *Apparently this
smart fellow was making movements with someone
who was not his own. Unknown persons were calling
his partner to tell her about his other activities.*—NaT
(1998.08.05, p.9) □ See MOVEMENTATIONS

ma.li.cious *vb intr* (Bdos) [AF] To look inquisitively
at (sth); to meddle. *"Let me see it", said 'A', and 'B' pull
it out and showed it to her, all the time I want to look
round bad, bad, bad, but I ain't want the woman feel
that I maliciousing.*—AdV (1999.09.03, p.9, Eric Lewis) [By functional adj > vb shift of *DCEU malicious*
'inquisitive', 'meddlesome' (Bdos)]

mal yeux [mal yo] *n phr* (ECar) *Phrase* **put mal yeux
(on sb)** /// **bad-eye** (See *DCEU*) **1.** To bring an evil
spell to bear (on sb) by wish or believed magical influence. *If I have to gather cobwebs in a line, I try to lower
my stress by thinking, meditating, praying, making positive affirmations. Anything rather than cussing, or putting mal yeux on the stressed-out tellers who can almost
feel the silence or stage muttered vexations befouling the

air.*—NaT (2003.09.08, p.9) □ In commoner use as
maldjo in *Trin* Fr Cr. Spread by rare folk diffusion in
Bdos etc. **2.** [By extension] To look upon sb with ill will
or malice in mind.

ma.na.ger belly *n phr* (Guyn) [AF—Joc] // *corpora-
tion* (Baha) A man's huge belly. [Prob by assoc with the
portliness of men in executive positions usu on sugar
plantations, and also in large business institutions]

Man.din.ky *n* (Bdos) *Phrase* **kill a Mandinky
priest** *vb phr* [AF—Joc] // **kill priest** (Trin) See *DCEU*
To have done sth (perh unwittingly) to bring down
the wrath of God on you. *Girl I hope you prayin' fuh
Buhbayduss 'cause it look like we kill a Mandinky
pries'! Nuh joke, one t'ing after de nex' happenin' 'bout
hey all of a sudden, an' got we wonderin' ef de islan'
onder some spell or somet'ing.*—NaT (2007.09.05,
p.9A) [< 'Mandingo(~Malinke) priest', a prob ref to
the believed spiritual powers of the religious leaders
of the Mandingos, a widespread ethnic group of W
Afr. peoples who were enslaved. The killing of a
priest, in general CarA folk culture, was believed to
call down the wrath of God. For the *Trin* // see *DCEU
kill* Phr 3.5]

man.i.fest (on sb) *vb tr (phr)* (Gren) [IF] [Of spirit
possession] To possess, take hold of (a believer's
body). **a.** *A girl came and she did not want to dance,
she did not want any powers to manifest her.*—SDP:86
b. *And when they beat this drum for him, he start to
dance, Ogun manifest him.*—SDP:94 [In biblical
sense of revealing of divine power, as in (*AVB*) John
2.11 "This beginning of miracles did Jesus in Cana of
Galilee, and manifested forth his glory". Note also
OED **manifest** vb 6 Spiritualism '[of a ghost or spirit]
To make an appearance']

man.ners *n pl* (CarA) /// BROUGHTUPCY /// BROUGH-
TUPSY (CarA)

man.slayer *n* (Bdos) A person found guilty of
manslaughter. *Manslayer given 14 years.*—NaT (H)
(1995.10.17, p.5) [A back-formation < manslaughter]

ma.ri.jua.na *n* (CarA) /// GANJA (Jmca)

mar.ried name *n phr* (CarA) [IF] [Of a woman] Sur-
name as changed by marriage. *Her maiden name was
Byer, but her married name is Fraser. She was married
last week.*—(Bdos) [< married (woman's) name]

May Cross *n phr* (Trin) // ***cross wake*** (Trin) *Moreover, this composer was, for a particular period, a respectable interpreter and singer at May Cross or Cross Wakes, a cultural expression introduced by the coco panyol to the island.*—SuG (1994.11.27, p.19) [Fr the original month of celebration in Venezuela. See CROSS WAKE]

meal.y bug *n phr* (CarA) See PINK HIBISCUS MEALY BUG.

mek *vb* (CarA) See **make**

-ment *noun-forming suff* (CarA) [*AF—Joc*] A humorous intensifier suffix to nouns, i.e. one meant to signify added greatness, importance or intensity to the sense of the noun to wh it is affixed. Hence ***bashment, cussment, heatment, ingreasement, invitement*** etc. □ Cp IAE suff *-ment* 'forming nouns expressing the means or result of an action', hence usu added to verbs 'argument, curtailment' etc.

mes.ti.zo *n, adj* (CarA) **1.** [*Hist*] (Of or related to) a person of the Mayan Amerindian race. *A distinction might also be drawn between mestizo creole societies and mulatto creole societies ... Mestizo creole cultures involve [only] one group (the Amerindians) native to the New World, while in mulatto societies, both groups, European and African, are cultural strangers.*—BCSJ (Intro p.xvi) **2.** (Belz) (Of or related to) a person of part Mayan Indian race. **a.** *But native American Carnival came with the Mestizo and Indian refugees of the War of the Castes in the second half of the nineteenth century. As they settled in Northern Belize, they brought along with them part of their culture in the form of the Carnival fiesta. This celebration continued being a major feature of Mestizo and Indian culture for a century and satisfied important social, religious and economic needs.*—Bes (vol.9, no.3, p.2) **b.** *Long hair was and continues to be treasured in Mestizo society.* —Bes (vol.9, no.3, p.5) [Sp 'of mixed race']

mice-rat *n* (Jmca) [*X*] A mouse. *Look a mice-rat jus(t) run (a)cross de floor.*—(Jmca) [< IAE pl *mice* (Cp other IAE mutation pls functioning as Sg in CE, *lice* (= louse), *teeth* (= tooth) + redundant compound *rat*, as similarly, in CE *bull-dog* etc.)]

mi.di pan; mi.ni pan *n phr(s)* (Trin) Ornamental model steelpan(s), smaller than the standard size, for sale to tourists. See cit. *TTIL sells these types of pans of interest to the visitor: the 11-inch Mini Pan, which goes for between TT$200 and TT$300 (US$33–US$50) and comes complete with sticks for playing, an instruction booklet and a stand; the 18-inch Midi Pan, which costs TT$1,000 (US$166) painted or TT$1,400 (US$233) chromed comes with sticks ... and the 21-inch traditional Tenor Pan, priced at TT$1,700 (US$284) painted or TT$2,100 (US$350) chromed.*—CaB (97/7, p.56) [*midi-*, as *COD* 10, combining form 'medium sized'. *Mini-* = 'very small']

mi.ni.bus cult.ure *n phr* (Bdos) // ***ZR culture*** (Bdos) The ways of group behaviour of (usu secondary school) teenagers, including indulgence in sensual pleasures, and often involving the drivers and conductors of minibuses serving routes to and from school. □ By association with minibuses, the largest type of Private Service Vehicles (PSVs) wh are the preferred transportation to and from school for many teenagers in *Bdos*. Also called ZR CULTURE (*Bdos*).

min.ing pool *n phr* (Guyn) [Bauxite Ind] Mini-lakes which have resulted from excavating the overburden of clay and sand so as to expose, 40 to 100 feet below, the deeper deposits of rich bauxite ore, which is then calcined into aluminium oxide. These large areas filled by rainfall create catchment pools of variable size (up to 100 ha and depth up to 30 m). Recent worldwide advocacy of UNEP and WHO have urged that there should be environmental mitigation to restore riparian forests and natural conditions in such «open-pit» mining pools. *Perhaps this simple initial project can establish a similar legacy of sustainable fish supplies from these Linden mining pools, thus environmentally rehabilitating these areas for multi-purpose uses for food production and recreational benefits.*— (Ms) (2006.04.26, W.H. L. Allsopp)

miss *vb* **Phrase** **miss and** (+ *vb*) *vb phr* (Bdos) [*IF*] To make the mistake of (doing sth). ... *[P]lease don't miss and ask: "What pictures are you talking about?" If you do, your next few minutes are going to be filled with shocking details.*—SuS (2001.08.19, 9A, Al Gilkes)

mis.sion ground *n phr* (Jmca) // ***mourning ground*** (Gren, Trin) [Religion] See cit. *Members [of the Zion or Pukkumina group] reside at their private lodgings except for a few who reside at the "Seal ground" or "mission ground" where they all meet. The "seal ground" or "mission ground" is the site where the meetings organised by the "bands" are held. In Zion, a hut called a "mission house" for accommodating those who attend is built on this site, hence the term "mission ground".*—SRCJ:6 □ Restricted usage SPIRITUAL BAPTIST religion. See *DCEU* ***mourning ground*** (Jmca).

mis.sion house *n phr* (Jmca) See cit at MISSION GROUND.

mon.ey *n* **Phrase** **to have money to stone dog** *id phr* (Jmca) [*AF—Joc*] To have more money than you know what to do with, esp if suddenly acquired. *Man if yo can win dat lotto now, yo will have money to stone dog.*—(Jmca, 2001) [Pelting anything handy at foraging stray dogs is a common habit among the poor]

mon.key *n* **Phrase** **make monkey sport at** (**sb**) *vb phr* (Bdos) [*AF*] To mock (sb), to deride, taunt, or speak jokingly of (sb). *Don't laugh, those people back then used to make monkey sport at Noah and these prophets.*—AdV (2002.05.15, p.9, Opinion) □ Often also ***To make mock sport at*** (**sb**)

mo.tion *n* (CarA) Vigorous individual movement of the body, meant to be admired; a joyful display of the body's shape in dancing. *Moonlight poor man lantern*

/ *Moonlight, show me your motion* / *People come from far and near* / *Sound of music in de air* / *Come and mek your motion* / *An join in de moon light tay-lay-lay.*—SVFS:7, '*Moonlight*'. **2.** *Phrase* **2.1 show (me) your motion** *vb phr* (CarA) [IF] To display, show off, your skill in dancing [usu of a woman].

mourn.ing ground *n phr* (Gren, Trin) /// MISSION GROUND **a.** *If the Baptists have a love for you, they use some signs that when they put you on the Mourning Ground you will travel far from them, and you will see things in a better way.*—SDP:88 **b.** *She had newly baptised and she came from the Mourning Ground.*—SDP:96

mouth.er [mɒʊtʌ] *n* (Trin) /// MOUTHAR (see *DCEU*) [AF—*Joc*] See cit. *He had none of the dignity of the leader. He was a big talker: in Elvira they called him 'the mouther'.*—NSOE:3 [< CE *mouth*, often meaning 'tongue' + suff *-er*, as in IAE 'lover, performer'. This form (pronunced 'mout(h)a') prob developed into (*Guyn*) **mout(h)a(r)** (see *DCEU*)]

move.men.ta.tions *n pl* (Bdos) **1.** (Dancing with) vigorous, erotic hip movements. *'Breakdown' is super dance music. If you don't find your limbs galvanised into a few movementations when 'Breakdown' is played, your reflex system must be all shot.*—SaS (1993.08.08, p.11A) **2.** [By extension] Vigorous sexual intercourse. ... *[S]omeone taped Prince Charles and his outside woman planning movementations on the phone.*—AdV (1993.03.26, p.9) [< IAE *movement* + intensifier suff *-ation* denoting action. Cp IAE '*fomentation*', CE '**murderation**' etc.]

N

nat.u.ral hair *n phr* (CarA) A black woman's normal hair, chemically unprocessed, worn as a chosen hairstyle. *Natural hair is definitely a choice for many people. I think this is tied to the fact that women in particular are moving towards the natural hair because people are focusing very much on 'self' in terms of heritage. The whole question of ethnicity is prominent and is being acted out with the "natural hair", she said.*—AdV (1999.09.12, p.34)

need *vb tr* **Phrase** **it don('t) need** *id phr* (Bdos) [AF—Cr] There's no need for. *He turn and tell me "Cool down", it doan need all dat fuss.*—MMM:17 □ Cp Guyn *'It ain(t) got all o(f) dat in it'*, in similar context.

Neg.er.hol.lands *n* (CarA) [Hist] [Linguistics] The Creole language of predominatly Dutch lexicon developed in the Danish West Indian islands of St Thomas and St John in the late 17C and early 18C by enslaved Africans and their Dutch owners. *There is no direct reference to the creole until 1732, when Moravian missionaries arrived and began to learn Negerhollands in order to preach the Gospel to the slaves.*—HPC:326 [< Du *neger* 'black' + *hollands* 'Dutch']

ne.gro.crat *n* (Bdos) **1.** [In ameliorative sense] One who believes that authority to rule a community or nation-state of the African diaspora belongs by right to black people of high social status; a member of a self-appointed but locally recognized black elite class, esp in the Caribbean and the USA. See cits. **a.** *In a sense we would all be negrocrats on the strength of the contribution our ancestors made through enslavement to the development of the colonies that are now nation-states.*—(Bdos, Ms) **b.** *What is needed in Barbados is for us to come together as one, appreciating that once we put our heads together we can conquer the world. We should rid ourselves of Xenophobia and Crypto Racism, while seeing nothing wrong with being a Negrocrat for our country, as it is only an advancement from being a Negro. It is not the colour of a man's skin but where that man is going.*—AdV (2006.03.10, p.9) [By analogy < *Negro* 'black (person)' + suff *crat* a combining form denoting 'a supporter of a particular form of government or rule' (see *COD* 11) as in *democrat*, 'rule by the people'] **2.** [In pejorative sense, by extension] A person of African descent (an AFRIC) who expects deference in a community in the African diaspora by right of social status. See cits **a.** «*Garvey argued that the negrocrats, whatever, were not the intelligent ones, but sought positions of power and influence based strictly on biology and social positioning,*» *said Foster. "They*

thought they should have a leg up"—NaT (2006.12.03, p.23) **b.** *Prime Minister Owen Arthur, [said]* «*When I use the word negrocrat ... I'm not talking about the middle class,*» *... He said he was referring to* «*people who have aristocratic tendencies ... to people who felt they "must exercise an influence out of all proportion either to their lawful power or their competence because of who they are or where they have come from".*—NaT (2006.03.14, p.5) [A blend of *Negro* 'black (person)' + (aristo-/pluto-) *crat* < Gk *kratos* 'strength'] □ Cit **1b** illustrates the slipping of usage from a favourable sense to the unfavourable sense **2**, in which a *Derog* connotation is reinforced by emotive rejection of the idea of a black diasporan nobility.

ne.ma.kha.ram¹; ni.ma.kha.ran¹ [nimakaram/n] / 2´2 1 2 / *n* (Trin) [IF—*Derog*] [Indic] A despicable traitor. **a.** *The expression nimakharam is a terrible insult in Amity village. It is usually translated as "one who eats another man's food, then does him evil," but "ungrateful one" is a simpler and perhaps more pointed definition. The term reflects the delicate web of reciprocal behavior that forms between two non-related East Indians who are in constant association.*—M. Klass: 1961 'East Indians in Trinidad', p.199 **b.** *[Panday] had successfully stigmatised those Indian MPs who stayed with the NAR after the collapse of the coalition in 1988 as nemakharams, persons who had betrayed those who had struggled for the upliftment of the Indian community over the past decades.*—RPP:216 [Bhoj < Hindi *namak haraam* 'ungrateful one subsisting on others' earnings'] □ **1.** The term is generally used in political contexts by East Indians, to condemn others who support a political party in opposition to that wh has the mass of E. Indian electoral backing. It contrasts with **apan jaat** '[support] your own kind' wh is also popularly current. **2.** The variant pronunc is prob due to unfamiliarity with the orig. See next.

ne.ma.kar.an² *adj* (Trin) [AF] [Indic] Unworthy; foolish. *You are a most nemakaran, dotish girl.*—ExP (Mag, Vox) (1998.08.19) [By n > adj shift of **nemakharam¹**. See prec. note.]

Ny.a.bin.ghi [nayabɪŋgi] *n* (CarA) [*Rastaf*] **1.** A belief system developed out of spiritual resistance to foreign domination; it was introduced into Jamaica c.1940 from East Central Africa, and is becoming the fundamentalist faith of a major sect of RASTAFARIANS; it proclaims the inherent divinity of Ras Tafari, Emperor Haile Selassie I of Ethiopia, as direct descendant of the son of Solomon and the

Queen of Sheba (Ethiopia), and the promised Messiah. Its focus is ancestral, embracing all peoples of African descent, but aiming to free all life from oppression. **a.** *The purpose of Nyabinghi is to resurrect the people from darkness into light and to set all Black people free. Anyone can be a follower of Rastafari, but the order of Nyabinghi, exclusively, is intended to liberate all African people and set them in the ways of truth and light.*— (Statement by Nyabinghi Elders given to City Sun, June 15, 1988 (Internet)) **b.** *The false Rasta who uses drugs is an impostor. Nyabinghi is non-violent and non-abusive.*—(idem) **2.** (Bdos) [By extension] A member of the Nyanbinghi sect; (also) the collective membership. **a.** *Ras John was concerned that the Nyahbinghis were cutting off themselves and might be accused of being a Jim Jones cult.*—AdV (1990.05.05, p.5B) **b.** *The Nyabinghi believe that the herb [ganja] possesses important healing and other positive qualities necessary for long and healthy life.*—Jmca (Ms) **3.** (CarA) [By extension] The festive celebration with night-long drumming, dancing and singing to mark any time of religious significance to the NYABINGHI. *Grounding also takes place at a periodic movement-wide convention variously called "Nyabinghi" (or "Bingi" for short), "I-ssembly" (assembly), "Rasta convention," "Nyabinghi convention," and "Nyabinghi I-ssembly." By calling this gathering "Nyabinghi," Rastas are expressing their conviction that the activities at this gathering serve to unleash "earthforce," the cosmic energy that pervades the universe, against those who have historically oppressed African people. Nowadays, an I-ssembly can last anywhere from three to seven days and is marked by a festive atmosphere, intense activities, and ecstatic emotions.* — MSMCDB:356/357 [Said to be the cultist adoption of the name of a Ruandan princess: «The term NYAHBINGHI comes to us fr East Africa and refers to a religio-political cult that resisted colonial domination fr the last decade of the 19th century to about 1928» (see source at cit **1a**)]

O

obi *n* (Gren, Trin) Kola (Cola) nut; the seeds in the pod borne by the tree *Cola acuminata (Sterculiaceae)*. *She made me get a two-and-six coin, a two shillings, a sixpence; and she made me get pieces of obi (kolanut), two, and break it in four; and guinea-pepper, cloves, milk, honey and spice and open a hole; kill this fowl that belong to her, place the head and the foot inside the hole and put the money right around, and the four pieces of obi, and put the cloves and the guinea-pepper ...*—SDP:86 [< (*ADMY*) Yoruba *obi* (a) 'kolanuts and water are sometimes thrown away as an offering to Sonponnon (the god considered to cause smallpox.)] □ The tree was introduced to the *CarA* from W Africa, hence prob survival of the original name at the folk level.

o'clock *adv Phrase* **quick o'clock** *adv phr* (Jmca) [*IF*] Very quickly. *Quick o'clock, she came up to look for Gertel.*—RLTJWS:15 □ Cp **early o'clock** (Bdos). See *DCEU*.

often.times *adv* (ECar) Often; many times. *Of course, she came home oftentimes, she used to sleep home, but I never touched her or anything.*—SDP:90 [Influence of biblical E. usage, e.g. 'for oftentimes [the unclean spirit] had caught him.'—Luke 8:29] □ *COD* 'archaic or N. Amer'. In the *CarA*, more likely in the speech of older folk.

On.der.neem.ing boy *n phr* (Guyn) [*Hist*] A delinquent or one-time delinquent youngster who is/was detained at the government's reform, industrial school in Br. Guiana (now re-named "The New Opportunity Corps", under the control of the Guyana Defence Force.) *Or an Onderneeming boy, reporting as he was bound to do after his discharge, might be followed by a doubtful tale of bad luck.*—CDID:12 [< **Onderneeming**, name of the site of the reform school for delinquent boys, on the W. coast of Essequebo, Guyn] □ Obsolescent.

one pot *n phr* (Bdos) A meal of vegetables and meat boiled together; see *DCEU* **all-in-one**. *I got a little yam and a little potato and some plantain and cook up a one pot.*—AdV (1998.03.21, p.17)

on.fair [õfe.r] /1´2/ *adj* (Bdos) [*AF—Cr*] Unjust; not showing fairness. **a.** *E accusin' de party o' bein' onfair, dat certain people does get treat wif respeck an' others wif disdain.*—NaT (2004.03.24, p.9A) **b.** *I en know whey de BBC woulda get dah from, doh ... but it onfair to de young boy, dis bein' 'e firs' time out as a tes' player.*

An' I only hope dah report don' affeck 'e an' dat 'e show dem English batsmen de ball dat shoot Nelson!—NaT (2004.03.10, p.9A) [A variant dial spelling of *unfair*, reflecting *Bdos* pronunc]

on.gl.e [õgl] *adv* (Jmca) [*AF—Cr*] Only. **a.** *Anyhow, Tyson buy on trouble pon imself dis time. Im lucky a ongle suspend dem suspend im.*—Outlook Magazine **b.** *Smaddy seh Mutty Perkins ongle a tek I mek poppyshow: one nother holiday fi idle black people sit down do notn.*—ObS (1996.10.18, p.7, Wuman Tongue) [< *only* by dial / n > ŋ / velarization]

on.lest *adv* (Baha) Only. Bahamian style. GMMTB:74 [A variant of *CarA* dial **onliest** wh is an E dial survival in CE. See *DCEU*]

on.pick *vb tr Phrase* **en on.pick.in yo(ur) teet(h)** [ɛn õpɪkɪn] (Bdos) Not uttering a word; remaining silent. *I suppose one or two may not be aware Duh forefathers was "indiscreet" ... But de ones dat know en sharin' dat info. No way ... dem en onpickin duh teet'!*—SuS (2004.04.11, p.9A) [A spelling representing *Bdos* pronunc of dial **unpick**. See *DCEU*]

o.ra.ture *n* Orature is the body of a people's essentially spoken folklore. It comprises tales and stories told to children from earliest times, riddles, proverbs, ballads and folksongs, legends etc. Facial and other forms of gesture, singing and mime are regular and important decorative performance components, occasionally together with key words and phrases. *In the Caribbean orature comprises riddles, nancy stories, contes, jumbie and duppy stories, talk shows, pantomime, calypsoes, teasing songs, Comedy shows, etc.*—SRRA (Ms, 2006) [*Ora*(l) + (litera) *ture* by analogy with *literature, scripture*] For an earlier introduction of the term (in a 2002 Ms text) see *BACP* p. xiv.

O.ri.sha [oriša] *n; adj* (Trin) (Of or pertaining to) a W African religion brought to the New World (during slavery) in wh there is worship of deified ancestors of the Yoruba people of Nigeria; some of these deities have Catholic saints as their counterparts. *Tanker discovered African music "by opening myself up, being among drummers—the music is mainly drums and voices working with them—going to Orisha ceremonies, reading". He studied the Orisha faith, "mainly at the level of a musician trying to understand where the music came from, the folk elements".*—Cab (July/August, 1997, p.22)

or not *conj phr* (Bdos) [*IF—AF*] Or else; if not. *I stoppin' whey I is fuh now, soul, 'cause a answer I might gi' to some immigration official is one 'e might interpret wrong, an' nex' t'ing yuh know, I get grabble-up at some international airport! Or not, I might fin' myself somewhey jes' at de time a bomb decide to go off, an' I gone to glory.*—NaT (2004.05.05, p.9A, Lickmout' Lou)

out-and-out *n* (Jmca) [*AF*] A person (esp a woman) who dosen't care about their reputation. *Single woman dem used to call 'out-and-out'. Dem used to say, 'If yuh single, yuh wanton. Yuh a warrior.' Dat was di system.*—SSLG:162

out-out *vb tr* (Baha) [*X*] To extinguish, put out (a fire). *A teacher can 'out something out' off the chalkboard with an eraser. You also can 'out-out' a fire, if you so choose.*—GMMTB:74 [By functional shift and reduplication of adv '*out*'] □ Cp also [*IF*] '**to out a fire, a batsman**'.

out school *vb phr* (Jmca) [*X*] To leave school (when the age limit is reached). *... [W]hen we outed school we could think about learning a trade.* —RLTJWS:37

over *vb* (Trin) [*X*] To be in a higher position than generally accepted; to move up to a higher level; to acquire a new, better trend of thinking. *He overs that* = *he's gone beyond that.* [By functional prep >vb shift of prep form '*over*', and assuming the 3rd pers sing. pres tense form of a regular verb by analogy]

over-in-away *n* (Bdos) [*AF*] Foreign countries. *Bajan brown sugar en fuh nutten like we, / It fuh big-ups an' fuh over-in away; ...*—AdV (1993.05.28, J. Layne-Clark) [By functional /adv> n/ shift of dial adv phr '*over (and/in) away*'. See *DCEU*] □ Note need for hyphentated form in this function.

P

pa.ki *n* (Jmca) A calabash; the cut and dried half of the fruit of the calabash tree used as a bowl. ... *[A]nd they would run with their paki go get it full up of peas soup with corn dumplings ...*—RLTJWS:20 [< (*DAFL*) Twi *apakyi* 'a broad calabash with a cover'] □ An original folk name: note the collective singular form in cit. See *DJE* for other spellings, **packy** etc.

pa mélé *adj phr* (StLu) /// DON('T) CARISH *From time to time (like when listening to a really terrible calypso), a cynical voice inside of me asks: What's the big deal about Kaiso in St. Lucia? A set of happy go lucky pa mele fellars and women too, more and more make their appearance early in the year and either sing a stock of whine whine, grind grind, hand in the air stupidness or take some cheap shots at easy targets like politicians, calypso judges, businessmen, anybody they envy. What's the big deal? What purpose all that serving? You really see anything in that pappy show?*—LuK (1995, p.21) [Fr Cr > *pas mêler* 'not (to) meddle']

Pa.na.ma mon.ey *n phr* (Bdos) [*Hist*] See cit and note. *The remittances from the Isthmus of Panama, often referred to as 'Panama money', provided the means whereby many labourers acquired land and became small farmers.*—NTSM:106 □ Some 48,000 Barbadian labourers were recruited in the building of the Panama Canal (1909–1914). They sent funds back home (hence the phrase) and saved substantially from their earnings.

pan jam *n phr* (Trin) Festive street dancing to the accompaniment of steelbands. *Other events will be pan jams on Broadway, Port of Spain and Arima, a book exhibition and youth rally.*—ExP (1993.08.22, p.5) [< *DCEU* pan 3 + functional vb > n shift of *jam*¹ 4]

pan.nist *n* (Trin) One who plays a steel pan. *Pan Trinbago plans to form a youth arm ... consisting of pannists from school steelbands and Police youth club bands.*—ExP (1993.08.22, p.5) □ The earlier meaning, 'the professional soloist' (see *DCEU*), is now extended (*ECar*) to include steelband players in general.

par.ty par.a.mount.cy *n phr* (Guyn) **1.** The precedence of the rules and interests of a political party over the wishes or interests of any of its subdivisions or members. *The practice of party paramountcy was used by the ruling party to expand its control of as much political space as possible. Human rights abnormalities became a central aspect of the control process.*—FSCD:291 **2.** [By extension] The control of all public administration, organizations and movements according to directives or wishes indicated by the leadership of the governing political party. *It was also decided that the Party should assume unapologetically its paramountcy over the Government which is merely one of its executive arms. The comrades demanded that the country be given practical leadership at all levels—political, economic, social and cultural—by the P.N.C. which had become the major national institution. The central doctrinal departure related to the issue of party paramountcy.*—FSCD:157–58 [= The paramountcy of the Party; < paramount 'supreme' + suff -cy 'state of being']

pas.sa-pas.sa *n* **1.** (Jmca) Scandalous behaviour; gossip. *Stop with the passa-passa (= Stop the noisy behaviour).*—(Jmca) **2.** Rowdy, open-air dancing characterised by erotic individual displays (esp at night fêtes.) *In Barbados no stand has been taken at a national level even though passa passa events are advertised on at least two popular radio stations weekly. And I expect nothing will be said officially until some event gets totally out of hand or violence occurs. While I cannot help but compare passa passa somewhat to carnivals and Crop-Over—where similarly lewd soca songs, skimpy modes of dress and vulgar dances abound—dancehall shows have tended to incite far more negativity and violence.*—NaT (Groove 2006.03.12, p.5) [**1.** Maybe a devoiced rendering of (*ECar*) *bassa-bassa* 'noisy behaviour', 'row', of W Afr origin. (See *DCEU*.) **2.** Poss an extension of Sense **1.** into the domain of Entertainment. Cp a similar shift in sense of (*Bdos*) **kadooment** (see *DCEU*). May also be reinforced by dial Sp < 'pasar' > pasa-pasa, 'a happening']

pa.ta.ki *n* (Belz) A wicker-work basket of straw material, tightly woven; it is about 2 ft by 1 ft by 3 ft and sometimes fitted with a rope handle for travelling. See cit. *Their luggage consisted of two huge rectangular baskets of the type called 'pataki'. Tightly woven, crafted of the strongest wicker-work and straw, they were so waterproof that they could survive for weeks in the sea without sinking, or wetting, even slightly, the clothes, cassava bread and other stuff packed within.*—YPF:63 [Miskito, 'a basket' (*DMEI*, p.184)]

pay *vb Phrase* **en payin' taxes fuh muh mout(h)** *neg id phr* (Bdos) (= Ain't paying taxes for my mouth) not bridling my tongue; not restraining myself from speaking out. *I hope dis letter fin' yuh enyoyin' good healf an' abidin' in de faif. I awright—poor, peaceable an' presumptious ... an' I still en paying' nuh taxes fuh* *muh mout'.*—NaT (Lickmout' Lou, 1998.10.07, p.9A) [A *Joc* ref to tax restraint imposed on oneself by avoiding excessive display of one's holdings (i.e. information acquired of what one knows about a person or happening.)]

peas *n pl* **Phrase peas and rice boon(g).gy** *n phr* See BOONG(G)Y.

pen.e.trate *vb tr* (Jmca) [*Rastaf*] To think about and understand; to give full attention to, get the full meaning of (sth). **a.** *I explained to the doctor what the problem was but I never knew she was penetrating me so deep.*—General Trees (DJ) quoted in Daily Gleaner, Monday, Jan. 11, 1988 (cited PDT:77) **b.** *"The car just broke in two. The first thing was to try and help, so me stop penetrate the car and was about to try and help the man ..."*—Eyewitness report of car crash, Daily Gleaner, Friday, Mar. 3, 1989. (cited PDT:78) [By metaphorical shift of sense of IAE *penetrate* 'to get into, through sth] □ Restricted *Rastaf* lexicon spreading into more general usage. (See *PDT* Ch 5)

peo.ple *n pl* (Bdos, Guyn) [*AF*] **1.** White people as colonial owners. **a.** *Till den, you behave yuhself in de people country an' remember Lou in yuh prayers.*—NaT (1998.02.04, p.9A) **b.** *Yo(u) better go an(d) do de people wo(r)k befo(re) yo(u) don('t) get pay.*—(Guyn) □ Cp African-American Vernacular English 'The man'. **2.** *Phrases* **2. 1. bit-'na half people** *n phr* (Guyn) [*AF—Joc*] People (usu a family) who exist just above the poverty line, often of the artisan class [post WWI]. *They are only bit 'na half people, but since the son gone to England to come back a lawyer they putting they nose in the air.*—(Guyn, 1949) [In Colonial (Br. Guiana) currency, a *bit* was a silver coin valued 8 cents (four pence), so that **a bit and a half** would have been equivalent to the Br sixpence, half a shilling or 12 cents. '**Bit 'na half**' was a popular retail food-price marker esp in markets. Cp next Phr] **2.2. three-cents people** *n phr* (Guyn) [*AF—Joc*] Poor people (usu of a family) of low social standing; a family/families of no financial worth [post WWI]. *There are a lot of three-cents people in the whole of the area that they can bribe to vote for them.*—(Guyn) [When the (colonial) Br Guiana dollar was based on the British pound sterling, 'three-cents' was the equivalent of 'penny-ha' penny', and used to indicate cheapness, related here to social worth. The term survives currently as a metaphorical relic]

perch *n* [*Obs*] *Then there was another piece of two acres, I bought that. It come to eight acres and seventeen perches.*—SDP:103 [As for sense **b** of (*OED*) *perch* sb2 III.5. A rod of definite length for measuring land, etc. a ... in standard Measure equal to 5.5 yards or 16.5 ft, but varying greatly locally: + cits—1850. **b.** A measure of land equal area to a square of which the side is a lineal perch (normally 1/160 of an acre) + cits—1863]

pick *vb* **Phrase pick pond grass** *id phr* (Bdos) [*AF*] To clear damp plantation land of creeping POND GRASS, by hand. **a.** *If Tony didn't get the C.E.O. job he could not go back to deputy 'cause somebody else had the job. Therefore he would have had to go home and cut cane or pick pond grass.*—AdV (1994.06.10, p.9 Eric Lewis) **b.** *Mr—would not want to see a young black-skinned woman with kinky hair in Parliament ... He must no doubt feel that women who look like [her] should be picking his pond grass preferably without pay and without even bus fare or lunch money.*—SuS (1996.06.23) □ This was a low-paid task usu assigned to black children, esp. in the plantation era. See POND GRASS.

pi.co.plat [pikoplat] *n* (Trin) // **ring neck** (Trin) A gray or dark brown cage-bird about 4 1/2 ins long; it has a pinkish bill and whitish band across the throat (hence also known as *ring-neck*), and is famous for its whistles and chirps; *Sporophila intermedia*. (See FGBTT:428) *A whistling sensation, 'silver-beak and nun' types. Venezuelan picoplat with pink legs called "Ah Veni".*—HTTD:32

piece-o-id.i.ot *n phr* (Bdos) [*AF—Joc*] A real fool; a damned idiot. *And if it is, you are probably thinking that I could only be a piece-o-idiot, or half-a-madman to be in that part of the world where people are always involved in civil war and engaged in killing off each other.*—SuS (1989.06.25, p.9A) [*piece of*, used as a *Joc* or pejorative qualifier. For many exs fr BrE slang, see *DSUE* 2 e.g. piece of stuff 'a woman' etc.]

pink (hi.bis.cus) meal.y.bug *n phr* (ECar) // **hibiscus mealybug** A small, oval-shaped insect with a segmented body covered in wax, turning pink when mature; it feeds on plant juices causing stunting and death of the plant; *Maconellicoccus hirsutus*. **a.** *The government here lists the Pink Mealy Bug as a notifiable pest, compelling citizens to report sightings.*—AdV (1995.09.24, p.14) **b.** *The Grenada experience was ample evidence that the pink mealy bug is an insect that is capable of causing enormous economic losses in the non-traditional agricultural sector.*—Gyr (1999.04, p.42)

pipe gun *n phr* (ECar) A home-made weapon using a length of half-inch bore metal pipe as a barrel, on to which the trigger mechanism of a normal gun and a wooden butt are fitted. *Dese minibus men does carry big stick / an cutlass an pipe gun; and real guns, too, yuh hear?*—MMM:12

Pitch.y Patch.y *n phr* (Jmca) A costumed dancer in the annual JONKONNU Festival of *Jmca*. See cit. *The most flamboyant and athletic of the performers is "Pitchy Patchy", who dances with rapid, small jumps, forming large circular patterns. The shoulder movement, in combination with sweeping arm extensions, is accentuated by Pitchy Patchy's costume which is made of layered strips of brightly coloured fabric ... . Some research has shown that contemporary oral tradition claims that Pitchy Patchy's costume is based on the leafy costumes employed as camouflage by the Maroons during guerrilla warfare.*—JJRW:9

play-play *adj* [*AF—Vul*] **1.** Imaginary, as in child's play. *"We are talking about a man [who] was homeless, another who was a drug addict and two others. They are what we used to call in Barbados 'play-play' terrorists who didn't have two pennies to rub together. But after 9/11 the authorities couldn't play around with them."* **2.** [Child talk] (Guyn) [Initiating a game] "Let us suppose ... "; Let us play / imagine that ...

Poco [pˑkˑ] *n* (Jmca) [*AF*] One who practises the Pocomania or Pukumina folk religion. *Dem deh parson just a tek advantage of dem member. Me say me no waan nobody downgrade me say me a Poco. Me decide seh me nah go back a Sammy Joker.*—SSLG:68 [An abbr of *Pocomanian*. See *DJE* **poco¹**; also *DCEU* **Pocomania**]

pol.i.tricks *n* (CarA) [*AF—Joc*] The trickiness of politics. *I wun tell yuh a lie, I really t'ought we was in fuh a close finish wid de Bees nippin de Dems by a nose. But it jes' go to show—duh en neffin predictable 'bout politricks, girl.*—NaT (1999.01.27, p.9A, Lickmout' Lou) [Blend < 'politics' + 'tricks'] □ A popular pun.

pol.lard *n* (Bdos) Coarse wheat siftings sold in bags, once imported for duck feed. *The time mummy caught me on top of a trainee-maid from Forty Acre on a bag of pollard.*—NaT (1998.09.14, p.9) [*OED* Pollard sb2 I.3 short for *pollard wheat* II.4 Bran sifted fr flour + cits 1573–1688; also cits 1577–1846 (... fine pollard, coarse pollard ...)]

pond grass *n phr* (Bdos) A succulent creeping grass that flourishes in damp ground, esp. around ponds (hence the name), and has to be weeded out by hand on cultivated ground; *Commelina diffusa* (*Commelinaceae*). See *DCEU* **water-grass** for CarA // //. **a.** *If Tony didn't get the C.E.O. job he could not go back to deputy 'cause somebody else had the job. Therefore he would have had to go home and cut cane or pick pond grass.*—AdV (1994.06.10, p.9 Eric Lewis) **b.** *You had to go into the plantation at 13 and work. I stay around a little. They had gangs that was picking pond grass. First, second and third class. They had a supervisor to see after them.*—ADV (1998.05.03, p.16)

pooch back *vb phr* [*AF—Vul*] (Bdos) /// DO THE DOG (Bdos) [Of a woman] See cit. **a.** *This group also follow through with Madd's dance instructions of "Bend down, touch ya toes, pooch back and let yo bamsy roll," which are frequently echoed in the* **Madd Revival Song.**—SuS (1993.07.25, p.13A) **b.** *Or do they feel our culture has now reached an acceptable zenity (sic, = nadir) when 90 percent of party songs encourage our young ladies to pooch back so men simulate sexual movements on their backsides?*—NaT (2005.07.29, p.7) [< push back the pooch [*AF—Joc*] = 'backside']

poo(l).shark *vb intr* (Bdos) [*AF—Joc*] To dawdle, waste time over work to be done; to do an assignment without serious attention. **a.** *Poor fishermen still out to sea / No agreement with T & T / De reason for all the pool sharking / It's de poor man who is netting / So*

ah know that yuh seeing red.—Cso, RPB, 2002 **b.** *Eversince I ask you to do this letter, an(d) yo(u) only siddung de(re) poolsharkin(g).*—(Bdos) [By functional n > vb shift of **pool shark**, an aquarium shark idling on display in a pool'. From the notion of idling while appearing to be active, like such — shark] □ Perh by transfer from USA via tourism.

pooma; puma *n* (Bdos) A small old car. *Soul, I get there after 7:30 and realized that the place was ram off with cars ... but I saw a li'l opening and stick my puma in it.*—SaS (2006.05.13, p.11) □ Note **pooma** (*CGBD*)

poor-ra.key *adj* (Bdos) [*AF—Joc*] Scrawny and poorly dressed; looking in need of kindly help. **a.** *But Ness, dem two in de same bee-hive, so far be it from a li'l po'-rakey body like me to comment 'pon dat. Dem is political matties, soul, so I leffin' dem to deal wid one anedduh.*—NaT (2006.04.12 p.9A.) **b.** *And so my suggestion to the honourable Mr. Jackman is to tell 'Venezuela' not to be greedy: it aleady has untold billions of barrels of oil reserves, and 'nuff' gold and diamonds and minerals on its side of the present border, while poor-rakey Guyana desperately needs whatever wealth can be dug or drilled or scratched out of the disputed region.*—(AdV (1999.11.07, p.9) [< IAE poor 2 + rake (as OED rake sb5 = a man or woman of destitute and deteriorated character); + suff -y' (as COD 10) with deprecatory ref. Cp **shakey**, **nosy** etc. Cp also *EDD* poor ..., poor's a rake]

pop *vb tr* (CarA) [*AF—Joc*] **1.** To burst or break (usu violently) **2.** *Phrases* **2.1. kite pop** *id phr* (Guyn) The kite string has burst (and your kite has been blown away). **2.2** [By metaph extension] Your effort has failed. Your plan has collapsed. **3.** (esp. Jmca) **pop your tail (to do sth)** To put yourself to the greatest trouble to 'break your neck' (to get sth done) □ **tail** = backside, hence *Joc/Vul* 'break/burst your ass' (to achieve sth, risking failure)

por.ong *n* (Belz) A pitcher made of porous brown clay, used for keeping water cool. [< Sp *porrón* 'a wine jar with a long spout'] □ Cp *DCEU* **goblet** (Guyn), **monkey** (Bdos) names for items in similar use.

pot-cover *n* (Jmca) // **wicker** (Bdos) See *DCEU*. [*AF—Joc*] A lesbian. *"Yo ever see two pot-cover shut yet!"*—Xnews Jmca (1997.07.28, p.3) [Perh a metaph ref to the 'sweating' unproductive function of a pot cover while the pot boils]

pot-starv.er *n* [*AF—Joc*] (Bdos) A starving stray mongrel. *Navy Gardens, where the white or whitish people lived, was more profitable but less comfortable and the Navy Gardens' dogs were more serious than the pot-starvers and salmon-tot retrievers of the Bay Land and Brittons Hill.*—AdV (2003.12.25, p.24) [Starved of leavings of cooked food, such as mongrels survive on]

pot weed *n phr* (Jmca) /// GANJA (Jmca)

pound cake *n phr* (Bdos, Guyn) A rich fruit cake made from ingredients including one pound each of flour and chosen fruits, hence the name. (See cit a.) **a.** *"You make up your mind if you doing a pound or a half-pound. If it is a pound, you will need a pound of raisins, the same of currants, a pound of prunes, half-bottle of mixed peel, one bottle of stout, falernum, a little wine, a little rum, half-pound of flour, half-pound butter, four to six eggs, three-quarters pound of sugar, a six-clove, spice and a piece of nutmeg; oh, and some colouring."*—AdV (1998.12.20, p.20) **b.** *Pound cake sells better than plain cake at fairs.*—(Guyn)

Pow.er(s) *n pl* (Gren) [Often pl] The spiritualistic influence, believed to be of original African source, invoked by leading worshippers in Baptist folk ceremonies. *And she tell me to put a bandage on my hand, that would help me to travel farther. But the Powers told me not to do that, she wanted to get me to the madhouse.*—SDP:93 □ Usu cap. **Phrase be in Powers** *vb phr* (Gren) To be possessed by spiritual forces. *This is why on Friday, on St. John's feast, when you offer the sheep, everybody in camp does be in Powers.*—SDP:93

prick.le *n* (Bdos) [AF] A ne'er-do-well who is caught up in the drug culture; a paro; a narco; one who is reduced to beggary or crime through dependence on drugs. *I turn and say "you mean you tief from you brother?" He say "well Lil' Rick I is a prickle forever, And when I want drugs I don't care 'bout a fella".*—AdV (1990.06.06, p.7B) [By metonymic shift of sense < **skin prickle(s),** 'goose pimples wh are said to be one of the effects of taking crack cocaine]

prime *adj* (Jmca) [AF] Rude; impudent. *She must have told him to go check the thing himself for he wasn't her pupa. George took exception and simply told her, "Yes, Miss Elizabeth, see how yu prime ... ."*—RLTJWS:176 [Perh a survival fr EE, with functional

shift. Cp *OED prime* vb.2 'to domineer; to lord it (over sb)' + cits fr 1756] □ Used of a child behaving as if equal to an adult.

prop *vb tr* (ECar) *Phrase* **prop sorrow** *vb phr* (ECar) To sit looking dejected, with your arm propping up your jaw. *You are the leaders of tomorrow / Don't want you propping no sorrow / So stay in school and learn like crazy / Before your brain gets quaily, quaily.*—Cso, David Rudder, 1992 [Cp *OED* 2 (prop) vb tr 1b. In various and ironic phrases, 'prop up a wall, a bar etc.': + *sorrow* sb 4. 'The outward expression of grief']

pud.ding pan *n phr* (Jmca) A round pan, made of tin, about 12 ins in diameter and about 5 ins deep. *One time when me was still 'lickle bit', a woman named Hannah Mitchell saw me coming from Redpan with a two-and-six pence pudding pan full o' water pon me head and she bawled out, 'Look Dead and Wake! ...*—RLTJWS:4

push-up *adj* (Jmca) [AF] Pushy. *You know, Papa was very much a man of his time; he minded his own business, he wasn't push-up.*—RLTJWS:182 [< IAE push + CarA Cr intensifier *up* as in BEAT UP (vb intr) BIG UP, etc.]

py.ro.clas.tic (flow) / (surge) *n phr(s)* (Mrat) The (flow of) molten lava from a volcano. See cit. *Pyroclastic density currents are gravity-driven, rapidly moving, ground-hugging mixtures of rock fragments and hot gases. High concentration density flows are called pyroclastic flows and low concentration density flows are called pyroclastic surges which can expand over hill and valley like hurricanes. Temperatures may be as hot as 900° celsius and the velocities range between 10 to 300 metres per second.*—NaT (1997.07.03, p.17A) [< Gk *pyro* 'formed by fire/heat' + *clastos* 'broken pieces (of rock)'] □ This international item from IAE became common CE vocab after the volcanic eruption in Mrat, 1991.

Q

quad pans *n phr*; **quads** *n pl* [*IF*]; **quad.ra.phon.ic** *n* (ECar) [Steelband] **1.** A set of four drums (pans), two or all of wh may be mounted horizontally, different notes being distributed among them. **2.** [By extension [*AF*]] Any set of four pans in the steelband having the notes distributed to render guitar-like tones. RC: *What are you experimenting with now? I noticed that you are building Quad pans and elevated bass pans.* CA: *If you watch the video tapes from Trinidad, there they use 12 bass and 8 bass and quadraphonic, which is 4 drums; here we just started to do that to keep up with what goes on in Trinidad.*—Inflight Mag (1996, p.51) [An adaptation of the term first used in the American market in sound systems about the 1960s–70s, to indicate 4 channels of sound 'surrounding' the listener. The *Trin* adaptation, however, suggested the booming effect obtained by raising the set (or some of them) horizontally]

quail.y [kweli] *adj* (Trin) [*AF/IF*] Limp from age or loss of quality; dull. *You are the leaders of tomorrow / Don't want you propping no sorrow / So stay in school and learn like crazy / Before your brain gets quaily, quaily.*—Cso, David Rudder, 1992 [By functional *vb* > *adj* shift of IAE *quail* vb¹ (*OED*) '[Of ... persons, plants, etc.] to decline fr a flourishing condition' + *suff -y* (*COD*) 'inclined to'. The use of *quail* as adj is characteristic CE functional shift]

Qua.ka; qua.ka *n* (Belz) [*AF—Derog*] A black person of low social status. *"Black is for quaka and quashy and kofi, not for you,"* Isabella had pronounced, much *to the profound mystification of the clerk who, city reared, had never heard such terms before. Then there had been arguments over brown, light brown, moderately light brown, dark brown, fairly dark brown and quite a few more, including 'Latin' and 'Hispanic'. In the end it was decided to print 'dark' in spite of a pronounced pout the word occasioned from Isabella.—* YPF:31 [Cp African day-name (*DAFL* Twi) *Kwakú* 'of a male person born on a Wednesday'] □ W African Day Names have (in CarA culture) come, through the stigma of slavery, to be widely derogatory. Cp Cuffy < Kofi (Guyn), Cudjoe < Kojo etc. (CarA)

quar.rel-mis.sy *n* (Guyn) [*AF—Joc*] A cantankerous woman, who is sometimes noisily quarrelsome. *You come up in Sunday school, you en able wid she, she is a real quarrel-missy.*—(Guyn) [< *quarrel*(some) + *missy, [Derog]* as in 'sissy']

quinge up *vb phr* (Jmca) [*AF—Cr*] To sit or squeeze closely packed, as on the seat of a bus. [Shift of sense > IAE *cringe* + intensifier *up*]

R

raas klaat *excl>adj phr* (Jmca) [*AF—Vul*] *Any police-man com yah will get some righteous raas klaat licks, yea man, whole heap a licks'.*—JMRF:10 [< *rass/raas/*'arse' + '*cloth*', pronunc /klaat/, 'cloth used to wipe the anus'; hence a conveniently obscene excl developing here as an expletive qualifier. See *DCEU* ***rass-clate*** n]

rad.i.o DJ *n phr* (Jamca) // DEEJAY (*Jmca*) *After winning the Teeny Talent show at eight years old, radio DJ Barry G introduced him to King Jammy's Volcano and other sound systems ... His popularity inspired Bunny Lee to invite him into the studio, resulting in the release of "The Ten Year Old DJ Wonder".*—NaT (Hott Mag, 2002.12.27, p.25)

rag.ga rag.ga *n phr* (Bdos) A genre of dance music originating from a popular song of the same name by the Barbadian calypsonian 'Red Plastic Bag', in the 1990s. [The term is an *AF—Joc* representation of confused wording as typical of some lyrics of the time]

rag.ga so.ca *n phr* (Bdos) A genre of dance-music combining RAGGA RAGGA and **soca**. See *DCEU. For your information, Sir, Byron Lee and Arrow were kicking back on ragga soca long before those two songs, and if you want to say those two songs started something, sorry, because even if it came in late, the one song that created the boom in ragga soca is Ragga Ragga by RPB.*—NaT (1994.11.24, p.7) [Derived fr *ragga* (*ragga*) + **soca**. See *DCEU*]

raise up *vb intr* (Jmca) [*AF*] Grow up. *"Raising up as children under the faith of Rastafari, we all didn't have dreadlocks at one point."*—Sky Writings (inflight mag, Jmca) (2001.06, p.35)

Ram *n* (Trin) [*AF—Joc*] **1.** (A common folk-name for) any male East Indian. **2.** [By extension] East Indians collectively. [< *Ram-*, a frequent prefix to Hindu family names. By extension 'any East Indian man'] **2. Phrase every Ram and Sam** *n phr* (Trin) [*AF—Joc*] Any and everybody; every Tom, Dick and Harry. *Long time we use to sarriaaway—shame about we curry, hide and eat we roti. Now, every Ram and Sam standing in line by Patraj. Look, Doc, it is curry that unites.*—SuG (1999.04.18, 'For a Healthy Currybean'.) [< *Ram* (as above) + *Sam* 'any Afric man'] □ The heading of the column *Currybean* (= Caribbean) confirms the *Joc* usage, a characteristic of *Trin* talk.

ram off *vb phr* [*AF—Joc*] (Bdos) To pack/be packed, jam or be jammed (with people or vehicles). **a.** *Soul, I get there after 7:30 and realised that the place was ram off with cars ... but I saw a li'l opening and stick my puma in it.*—SaS (2006.05.13, p.11) **b.** *You ever was in a position to be driving and see a ZR van or minibus ram off, with the driver doing bare junk 'pon the road, and you thought that the lives of the passengers were in danger?*—SaS (2006.05.20, p.11) [IAE '*rammed tight*' + intensifier adv '*off* ']

rant!, (O) *excl* (Guyn) (A euphemism for) O rass! *O rant boy! Look da kite bu(r)s(t) away!*—Guyn □ Once common among schoolboys, and considered generally acceptable. (See **rass**) (*DCEU*)

rap.so *n* (CarA) A genre of dance music combining 'rapping' and **soca**. *And a whole host of ragga soca music which combines reggae, rap and soca in one smooth blend. Keyboards by Junior I.B.O. Joseph and Kenny Phillips on guitar, background vocals by Shades of Black, Major Ranks rapping and Oscar B chanting, and rapso by Barcum.*—Cab (Winter 1994/95, p.12) [Blend < *rap(ping)* + so(ca)]

ras.ta.ry [rastari] /1´1 2/ *adj* (Bdos) [*AF—Joc*] Seeming typical of the Rastafarian life-style. *I ain('t) like anything with them red and yellow colour, wid black an(d) all—those colours too rastary.*—(Bdos) [< *Rasta(farian)* + IAE adj. suff -y 'having the quality of', as in 'messy', with intrusive intervocalic / -r- /]

reason *vb intr* [*Rastaf*] (Jmca) To explain Rastafarian culture and way of life by discussion among its members. See cit. *Reason—The Rastafari form of expounding and clarifying I and I culture and doctrine in and of itself, as well as in relation to Africa and the rest of the world. Historical, Current and Biblical futuristic revelations are all brought to the forefront of Rastafari thought.*—JJRW:42

re.con [rikɑn] *n* (Bdos) // ***deportee*** (*Jmca*) // ***roll-on roll off*** (*Trin*) [*AF—IF*] A used car imported (usu from Japan) for resale in Bdos. *The recons you get are generally always white, and of course Toyota Coralla recons are the most popular.*—(Bdos) [Reduced form of "reconditioned car", in ref to the mechanical renovation of the used vehicle before it is exported]

re.mous [rəmu] *n* (Trin) See cits. **a.** *The Solitary Internal Waves (SIWs) appear to be generated at the turn-of-the-tide at about low water (or just before) in* the *Boca de Monos. The sudden, relatively strong current speeds and sea surface banding associated with the events are referred to locally as the remous.*—Caribbean Marine Studies vol.4, 1995, p.18 **b.** *The dangers posed by the sudden and strong nature of these currents (remous) are evident from the large number of small vessels that have reported difficulties (that in some cases led to wrecks) while transiting the strait.*—(idem) [Fr 'swirl, eddy'] □ Restricted usage. South Trinidad boatmen.

re.vi.val.ism *n* (Jmca) See cits. **a.** *Revivalism is the cult form which has persisted as the main heir of the Great Revival in so far as Afro-Christian religious sects are concerned, and two major groups exist, Pukkumina and Zion ... . It is perhaps more closely linked semantically with Kumina, surviving as a purely African Religious cult which absorbed Myalism and became prominent in the second half of the last century, after introduction, it is said, by post-emancipation African migrants to the St. Thomas area in the 1850's. More strength is given to this interpretation by the fact that the Great Revival, the forerunner in inspiration of the Revival cult, took place at around the same time.*—SRCJ:4 **b.** *Revivalism: The spirit of or movement toward religious reform and renewal through subjective internal experience; may be characterized by prophetic utterances, unintelligible linguistic expression, shouting, spirit possession, or ideological and mental renewal.*—MSMCDB (Glossary): 4, 149 [IAE *Revival* + suff-*ism* as denoting a system, such as 'Anglicanism']

re.vi.val.ist *n* (Jmca) An adherent of the cult of REVIVALISM. *Revivalists are mostly outside the socio-economic framework of the middle-class; membership is drawn primarily from the working class. The Christian middle-class widely holds particular views of Revivalists: pagan, superstitious, comical in ritual behaviour, tolerant of dishonesty.*—SRCJ:5 [IAE *revival* + suff -*ist*, adherent of or believer in a particilar system]

rhum.ba box *n phr* (Jmca) A wooden box with a hole, to which strips of metal of varying lengths are attached; the player sits on it and thrums to produce a bass effect. *There are many persons who don't even know which instruments mento bands use. The music is played using the guitar, banjo, a rhumba box—something like a box with guitar strings, a maracas, a harmonica and a saxophone. All the instruments with the exception of the rhumba box which is made by local carpenters are bought at music stores.*—DaG (2001.06.10, p.E1) [From *rhumba*, a type of Cuban music + *box*]

rid.dim *n* (Jmca) [*AF*] Electronic rhythm track used in DANCEHALL and other types of local music. *RIDDIM—the rhythm and melody of reggae music sustained primarily by drums and bass.*—JJRW:44 [< SE *rhythm* but undergoing semantic extension to apply to the particular rhythm of REGGAE and DANCEHALL music. □ Folk pronunc with voicing of /θ/ > /d/, the spelling reflecting the pronunciation.

right.ed *adj* (Jmca) [*AF*] Sane; mentally normal. *[L] ightning struck him and he lived. Folks expected that after the first time he wouldn't be too righted, much less live to tell the tale.*—RLTJWS:152 [Perh from 'right (-h)ead', 'right in the head'; or by paragoge: Cp **lated**; (see *DCEU*)]

rinch *vb* (Jmca) **1.** wrench (?) [Perh a dial variant of IAE *wrench*] **2.** *Phrase* **rinch up yo(ur) face** *vb phr* (Jmca) [*AF*] To assume a very serious facial expression. —DPJP:33 [Perh related to E dial *rinch* a variant of *ranch* < *'wrench'*. See EDD **ranch** vb² n. Yks]

ring.bang *n* (Bdos) See cit. *Ringbang is clearly a fusion of traditional Bajan tuk and calypso, tuk band music with modern and commercial tones to spice it up. That concept was originated by* **Poonka**.—NaT (1994.11.24, p.7)

ring-neck *n* (Trin) /// PICOPLAT

RNM *abbr* (CarA) The Caribbean **R**egional **N**egotiating **M**achinery (RNM) was established on April 1, 1997 as a creation of CARICOM governments to develop and execute a cohesive negotiating strategy for various trade-related negotiations in which the region is involved. Its Headquarters are in Jamaica, with a sub-office in Barbados, and «presences» regionally. *The Caribbean Regional Negotiating Machinery (RNM) says it has a top-notch team of negotiators defending the interests of the Caribbean as intense trade talks begin this week in Barbados with the European Union.*—NaT (2006.03.27, p.3)

rob *vb tr* (CarA) *Phrase* **rob (sb) blind** *vb phr* (Antg, Guyn) [*IF*—*Joc*] To rob somebody unconsciously. *The bakkra kept on robbing the small farmer blind. In most cases you would just be working the land for the estate.*—SSHL:129

rock en.gine *n phr* (Bdos) [*AF*] A steam-roller used in road construction. *Those offending craters should be dry, scraped clean of loose material as far as practicable, and then filled with bitumen [hot-mix, as it is sometimes called] then compacted with the use of road rollers [formerly known as «rock-engines»] or the smaller, more convenient manually operated tampers.*—Action Mag (2004.06.13, p.1) [*rock* + *engine*, 'an engine for crushing rocks' compound like IAE wallpaper, etc.]

rod *n* (Gren, Guyn) [*Obs*] A land measure, about 12 ft *She was outside, about seven rods from the house.*—SDP:96 □ Still *Hist* in Guyn land surveying.

roll-on-roll off *adj* (Trin) [*AF*—*Joc*] /// DEPORTEE (Jmca) **a.** *Criminal Investigation officers who have been liaising with officials in Japan, confirmed they have unearthed evidence to prove that many used cars on the roads in T&T were stolen in Japan and shipped to T&T, either as completely-knocked-down or roll-on-roll-off.*—TrG (2003.11.17 p.7) **b.** *Police seized seven roll on/roll off cars as they were being driven along the*

Churchill-Roosevelt Highway, Macoya, yesterday. ... "The cars belonged to Japan Motors and have been impounded at the Tunapuna Police Station."—TrG (2003.12.10, p.5) [A *Joc* ref to the unofficial way in wh such cars are obtained, by being rolled on at the sender's end and rolled off at the receiver's, without due processes being observed] □ The compound also occurs in talk as a noun.

RSS *abbr* (CarA) *R*egional *S*ecurity *S*ystem: A regional mutual defence force comprising the Police and defence forces of seven Eastern Caribbean independent states—Antigua & Barbuda, Barbados, Dominica, Grenada, St Kitts & Nevis, St Lucia, and St Vincent & the Grenadines—and responsible for assistance and military protection of any member state, in any danger, maritime policing problems, national emergency or threat to national security. The system is recognized by the US Department of State. *Attorney-General Mia*

Mottley has said that Government is pushing for nations within the Regional Security System (RSS) to sign a treaty with non-RSS Caribbean Nations. Mottley made her comments yesterday during a thank-you ceremony for officers of the RSS who came to Barbados to assist in the aftermath of the March 29 fire and riot at Glendairy Prison.—NaT (2005.08.03)

run.ning man *n phr* (CarA) Dancing with a running action while remaining on the spot, with a forward movement of the head (as in running). *I attended Gospelfest '95 on Sunday night with the expectation of a spiritual upliftment but I was appalled at the behaviour of some "Christian" patrons. The Trinidadian artistes had a kaiso session and I saw people "wukking up" doing the "running man", "pepperseed", "the liver" and the "jump and wave"—rags included.*—SuS (1995.06.04, p.8A)

S

salt *n* (Trin) // **cutter** (Bdos) See *DCEU*. [*AF—Joc*]
1. Salt bread, esp a small breakfast loaf of white bread
(usu in foll phr). **2.** *Phrase* **pass a little salt in your
mouth** *id phr* (Trin) [*AF—Joc*] To eat a light snack of
sliced salt-bread and ham (in order to restrict the ef-
fects of alcohol in continued drinking). *"And Sammo,
A could pass a lil salt in me mout" he called as they
ordered another drink.*—(Trin, short story, Ms)

salt.fish *n* ECar [*AF—Joc/Vul*] The unwashed pu-
denda of a mature woman. □ **1.** [From its alleged
smell] The item consequently occurs in popular eu-
phemistic use in calypsoes. □ **2.** Cp similarly CRABBIE
(Baha), also (*DCEU*) **bacalao** (Trin)

sa.pote [sapoˑt] *n* (Gren) An edible brown fruit
borne on a large tree of the same name; *Pouteria
sapota (Sapotaceae)*. See *DCEU* **mammee-sapote**
(CarA). *The large seed of the sapote has three sides.
Two of them look like old polished mahogany, while the
third is a lighter brown, and rough. The kernel is
creamy white and has an almond flavour and is grated
and used in cakes, pies, etc.*—SGIS:103 [< Sp *zapote* <
Aztec *tzapotl* 'sapodilla', although here it evid applies
to a different variety of fruit]

say; seh [se ~sɛ] *vb intr* **Phrases 1. Me seh!** *excl* (Jmca)
[*AF*] I tell you!; I say! *Me seh! The day came a week later
and Peter arrived carrying a bottle of rum.* —RLTJWS:65
[< IAE I say!] **2. say hi to (sb)** [se/sɛ haɪ tʊ] *vb phr*
(CarA) [*IF*] To greet (sb). *After saying hi to me, she went
to speak to him.*—ObS (2001.04.23) □ A familiar phrase
widely used within young peer groups. **3. say this to say
that** *id phr* (Bdos) [*IF*] [Introducing a sequential state-
ment] (And) I must also say; but it must also be noted.
*But wen yuh done say dis, say dat: I lucky ... Duh got
some oder bosses does fire yuh tail just so.*—MMM:16
□ A common 'linking' phr in Bdos *IF* speech.

se.cond-day *n phr* (Bdos) // **second sunday** (Guyn)
The first (*Bdos*) or second (*Guyn*) Sunday following a
wedding day, when a special home celebration with
friends is held for the newlyweds,. □ A folk custom.
When the wedding day is held on a mid-week day,
the first Sunday following is chosen (Bdos); when on
a Saturday, as often (Guyn), the second Sunday following is chosen, the couple, esp. in former times, not
being likely to be absent abroad on honeymoon.

se.dan porch *n phr* (Gren) [Hist] A brickwork porch
built to facilitate the use of sedan chairs. (See cit.) It
remains still a feature of *Gren* architecture. *Some very*
*old buildings stand on Church Street, and there are still
three excellent examples of sedan porches, used in the
seventeenth and eighteenth centuries to shelter passengers from the elements when embarking or disembark-
ing from sedan chairs.*—SGIS:40

see *vb* **Phrase see deh now** *id phr* (Jmca) [*AF—Cr*]
There it is; Look/see now. *Yuh turn big woman now.
Dis is yuh period. If yuh have anyting fi do wid a man,
yuh wi get pregnant. See deh now', me say inna me
mind, 'me a breed!'*—SSLG:49 [= See there now]

seed-un.der-leaf *n* (ECar) // **gwenn-anba-fèy** (ECar)
(See *DCEU*) A green weed used in folk-medicine;
Phyllanthus amarus (Euphorbiaceae). (See *DCEU*) *As
they walked around the perimeters of his gardens he
pointed out castor oil and seed-under-leaf among others, growing wild.* —SuS (Mag) (2001.07.22, p.8)
[From the bearing of its seeds on the underside of the
leaves]

sei.tu; sit.(t)oo *n* (Bdos) [*AF*] A session of **stick-
licking** (see *DCEU*) contests. **a.** *Abraham «Dynamite»
Rock was a boss stick-licker. A big sitoo was coming up
and he and «Lightning» Vaughns was to represent
St. Thomas.*—Nat (The Lowdown, 1996.01.12, p.9)
b. [*Stick fighting*] *contests, called seitous, were very
popular, and were held on Saturdays or on bank holidays.*—FAZBH:175 [(*Sitoo*) (noun) properly 'set to', a
stick-licking tournament. — CGBD6:97]

se.mi-con.tract *n* (Jmca) /// APASOTE (Belz)

set-up *n* (Jmca) An open-air all-night wake at the
house or yard of a deceased person, with hymn-singing, eating and drinking. *What drew momma to
dead-yards was the nightly singing of hymns and the
gossip groups. Her voice was in much demand at every
'set-up' (big feast on the night before burial) ...*—
JTGDD:10 [Pronunc of *sit up* (late into the night)]

shack.le *vb intr* (Bdos) [*IF*] To fall apart; to come un-
done. **a.** *The book is shackling out, the leaves are
loose.*—(Bdos) **b.** *The old door begin to shackle.*—
(Bdos) [Cp *EDD* in gen. dial. use in Sc, Eng and
Amer. *Shackle* vb2 **1.** 'To shake, to joggle; to rattle
from looseness'. Perh related to 'ramshackle'. Cp *OED
shackly* adj US and dial, 'shaky', 'rickety']

shake *Phrase* **shake yo(ur) hand** *vb phr* (CarA)
[*AF—Joc*] Shake hands with (you); congratulate
(you). *Bishop Brume, uh cud shake yuh hand! / Guh*

long an talk yuh talk! Uh glad to hear yuh. / Wunna Bajans, / Pay attenshun to dis man! —MMSC:31

Shan.go feast *n phr* (Gren) [Religion] A religious feast of many hours of singing and eating, that may be accompanied by spirit possession. See cit. *He would not oppose me if it was an African feast, but if it is Shango I would not carry it in. He brought the log-book, he showed me that a Shango feast is for people that used chalkmark, and they invoke the evil spirit and they will throw somebody down and they will beat up themselves, some of them will even dead. This is what they call Shango.*—SDP:98 [Of W Afr. origin. See (*DCEU*) **Shango**]

she.self [ʃɪsɛlf] *pron* (CarA) [*AF—Cr*] Herself. **a.** *They call me and say "Look, she have nail in the head, she cross sheself with steel and she say she didn't want to dance!"*—SDP:86 **b.** *Nobody ain't searching me, so if Mia want me search let she come and search me sheself ...*—AdV (1996.08.23, p.12 Eric Lewis) [A reflexive form based on the Cr monoform 3rd pers sg fem pron *she*, and patterning with other Cr refl forms *meself, yo(u)self, heself, weself, deyself*] □ Such forms are common in middle and lower level familiar folk speech, but are not normally found in writing except in representative dialogue.

she-she *n* (Bdos) // *shi-shi man (Jmca)* [*AF—Joc*] A homosexual male (usu the one performing the female role). *In Barbados they only laugh at a she-she, but in Jamaica they beat sometimes kill them.*—(Bdos, 1990) [By *Derog* reduplication. Cp *DCEU* **boo-boo**, *pya-pya* etc.]

Ship.rid.er Agree.ment *n phr* (CarA) An agreement signed in 1996 between CARICOM states and the USA, giving conditioal permission to the US Intelligence and Coast Guard authorities to pursue and take into custody, in vessels or aircraft registered or in the territorial air and sea-space of the CARICOM states, any agents suspected of drug-trafficking or related operations; the condition relating to Barbados and Jamaica allowed for reciprocity of permission with the US.—CDB Library 17–25/09/07

shit-work *n* (UniK/CarA) [*AF—Vul*] Any work that might be considered menial or degrading, esp. cleaning away dirt of any kind; also called *'slave labour'. But the hustler-ponce wants his rewards now without any of the indignities and hardships associated with "shit-work" and without having to defer the present gratification of the self to a later date.*—Ken Pryce, "West Indians in Brixton"—'The Black Experience in Britain'.—ISER, UWI, Trin.

shop.a.hol.ic *n* (Bdos) [*AF—Joc*] See -AHOLIC *Barbados is fast becoming a nation of Internet "shopaholics". / And in Barbadians' drive for price savings, wider variety and assortment and convenience, they are going online in an effort to save money even when high shipping costs, duties and taxes are included.*—NaT (2007.07.23, p.1)

Shout.er Baptist Lib.er.a.tion Day *n phr* (Trin) March 30, celebrated as a public holiday in Trinidad and Tobago in official recognition of the Spiritual/ Shouter Baptist religion. *Spiritual Baptist/Shouter Liberation Day commemorates the repeal on March 30, 1951 of the 1917 Shouter Prohibition Ordinance that prohibited the activities of the Shouter or Spiritual Baptist faith.*—Wikipedia, 2006.

Shout.ers *n pl* (ECar) See cit. *The Shouter Baptist Community is a body of people who share a common set of religious beliefs. The members of this religious body claim their spiritual lineage from the Biblical figure, John The Baptist. They are also [called] Shouters, or Spiritual Baptists or simply Baptists.*—JJCM:1

sick *vb* (Guyn) /// SOOK (Trin)

sing-bar *n* (Trin) The bar put across a bird-cage, on wh a cage-bird perches and warbles or 'sings'. [= 'bar for singing'. A rarer type of IAE agential noun-compounds, 'base-vb + n'. Cp IAE *play-room, runway*]

sist.ren *n* (Jmca) See cit. **a.** *Sistren is an independent women's organisation, which works at advancing the awareness of its audiences on questions affecting Caribbean women. Sistren, which means 'sisters', is a collective. It has developed from the initiative of working-class women in 1977, and is best known for its theatre work.*—SSLG (Foreword) **b.** *This glossary ... is a guide for Rastafarians not of Jamaican descent to help in understanding the reasoning of brethren and sistren.*—JJRW:1 [By analogy with the IAE plurals *brethren, children*] □ The term **sistren**, perh influenced by or originating in *Rastaf* 'Dread Talk', has gained steadily in status in the wider *CarA*.

sit.too *n* (Bdos) See SEITOU.

six *n Phrases* **1. give sb a six for a nine** *id phr* (B'dos, Guyn, Jmca) [*IF*] To fool, cheat or trick sb. *The contractor used pine instead of the greenheart he promised them, and when it was painted they couldn't tell—he gave them a clear six for a nine.*—(Guyn) [The number 6 turned upside down becomes 9, hence misleading as a figure] **2. take a six for a nine** *id phr* (Bdos) To make a big mistake; to fool yourself; to be fooled. *"The organised representatives of the workers at the Port have got to be respected, and until that happens I'm afraid that somebody may be taking a six for a nine."*—AdV (1996.05.20, p.8)

skeet [skit] *n* (Bdos) **1.** (Popular name for) any species of sting-ray; *Dasyatis americana*, family *Dasyatidae*. [< IAE *skate* 'a marine fish of the ray family'] **2.** *Phrase* **wuk up like a skeet** *id phr* (Bdos) [*AF—Joc*] To dance wriggling vigorously from the waist down. *Anyhow, dah is dem business, It look like de onlies' interes' nough Bajan women got in Crop-Over dese days is descendin' to de depths o' vulgarity, wukkin'-up like skeets 'pon de men an' pon one aneddah in de name o' "enjoyment".*—NaT (2003.08.06, p.9A, Lickmout' Lou) [Ref to the wriggling motion of the tail of a sting-ray as it makes its way]

Ske.pi Dutch [skepi dʌč] *n phr* (Guyn) [Hist] [Linguistics] The Dutch-based creole language developed between enslaved Africans and their white Dutch masters in Essequibo (Guyana) in the early 17C; it was evid strongly influenced by the Ijo language (of E. Nigeria); it is currently all but extinct. *The fact that Guyana is now a single entity should not blur the fact that Berbice Dutch and Skepi Dutch developed in what were two separate colonies i.e. Berbice and Essequibo ... . The lack of mutual intelligibility between present day versions of Berbice and Skepi Dutch may be accounted for in several ways.*—I. Robertson 'Berbice and Skepi Dutch' in Taalkunde,105.1 (1989) p.5 [**Yskepi** is the early Dutch spelling of the name of the Essequibo (River), a name which has been retained only in the name of the language discussed in this article, Skepi Dutch: I. Robertson, op. cit., n.1, p.20] □ See also **Berbice Dutch** in *DCEU*. Both, now all but extinct creoles, are the subject of current scholarly investigation.

skin *n Phrases* **1. all out of my skin** *adj phr* (Bdos) [*AF*] (Scared) to death. *To say that I frighten is putting it mildly, to say that I would be scared all out of my skin would be an understatement.*—AdV (1996.01.12, p.11) **2. skin the cat** *vb phr* (Baha) /// TURN CATGUT (Baha) **3. skin cuffins** *vb phr* (Bdos) /// TURN CATGUT (Baha)

skin prick.le(s) *n phr* (Bdos) Goose bumps; goose pimples. *I don't like too much air-conditioning. It sometimes gives me skin prickles.*—Bdos. [Adapted fr IAE *prickly heat* 'an itchy skin rash experienced in hot weather/climates']

sleng.e.re [slɛŋgɛrɛ] *adj* [Guyn] [*AF—Cr*] /// LINGAY (Trin)

smad.dy *n* (Jmca) [*AF—Cr*] Somebody. *The young man acted bravado before he got up and stumbled round to the back in the dark till smaddy called him and offered him a bitch lamp.*—RLTJWS:131 [< IAE *somebody*, by syncopic reduction of /mb / > / m / and Cr vowel opening / o > a /]

small *n* (Bdos, Jmca) [*AF/IF*] Very early youth. *Phrase* **from small** *adv phr* (Bdos, Jmca) From (your) early youth *Y'see, I is a proud Bahbajan. Good sugar I know from small.* —AdV (1993.05.28) [By functional adj > n shift of IAE small (adj) as in 'small child', or reduction of a fuller IF phrase *from I was small*, often heard]

small man, the *n phr* [*IF*] (ECar) Any small-scale entrepreneur or artisan. *If you require the beach vendor to have his own facilities you will drive him off the beach. How is the small man to make his dollar? —*(Bdos,1991)

small one *n phr* (Jnca) // *cut-down* (Bdos) See cit // *done-grow* (Baha) *A very short man.*—YRRC2:19

smell *vb tr* (Bdos) [*IF*] **1.** [*Restricted use.*] To perfume (with sth). *Christmas Eve night, you would hang up the curtain on tacks, not rods. And if you got a little*

perfume you smell it all over the house. Christmas morning, you go to five o'clock.—AdV (1998.12.20, p.9) **2. Phrase 2.1. smell up** *vb tr phr* (ECar) To cause (a place) to smell of. *Curry always smells up your house.*—(Guyn)

so.ca.hol.ic *n* (Bdos) [*AF—IF/Joc*] A participant in festive outdoor dancing in wh individualistic, semi-erotic, personal displays are encouraged, sometimes involving competition. *There are major prize gains to be derived from being a "socaholic".*—NaT (2005.06.15, p.22A) [Physical blend of *soca* + -AHOLIC a dance-style (see *DCEU*)] Popularized from about 2002 in the **Crop-Over** festival in *Bdos*.

solder-man *n* (Antg) [*Obs*] See cit. *They also learnt how to fit pipes and weld. And it was because of the factory that the solder-man or tinsmith came on the scene ... . Those tinsmiths use to travel from village to village and from estate to estate with them coal, coal-pot and solder iron. "Solder man in town!", that was the cry ... The solder-man could put handle on tin cups, make saucepans, graters, food carriers and frying pans.*—SSHL:128

some.thing *n* (Jmca) [*AF—Derog*] Thing. *You a tall, long foot naked somet'ing, eyes hangin' out of a thick nonsense 'ead. You an' you slow ways make me sick for true.*—SAS:14 [Dialectal personalization of the pron for *Derog* effect. Also sometimes '*sinting*' in such contexts. See DJE **something** for more] □ For similar Derog usage, cp IAE slang, as (*DSUE* 8) 'like something the cat's brought in'.

so.much.y *adj; pron* (Bdos) [*AF—Cr*] So much; so many (of). *Boy dem got so many doors, doors an' doors an' doors fo' so ... /Yo cyan' imagine somuchy doors.*—Poetry Chap-Book no.1, 1982, B. St John, p.6 [IAE so-much + paragogic / -i /] □ Now rare. Surviving evidence of early CarA Cr in Bdos. See and Cp **toomuchy**.

sook *excl; vb tr* (Trin) // *sick* (Guyn) **1.** (excl) [To a dog] At that person! (Or thing). *Sook! Sook im!*—(Trin) [A variant of (*COD* 10) dial Br E **sick** 2 'set (a dog) upon'] **2.** (vb tr) To set a dog after sb or sth. *They would even sook the dog on a beggar.*—(Trin)

speak.ey-spok.ey [spiki-spoki] /1΄122/ *n* (Jmca) [*AF—Derog*] Comically affected in speech; pretentiously imitating the speech of native English people, with noticeable faults of pronunciation and grammar. **a.** *Those teachers used to affect the speech of blue-blooded English aristocrats! Speakey-spokey we called them.*—RLTJWS:33 **b.** *This time hear the speakey-spokey, man: "Ave you hever went to Landan?"*—(Jmca) [By Derog reduplication. Cp IAE *shilly-shally*]

Spir.i.tu.al Bap.tist *n phr; adj phr* (Bdos, Gren, Guyn, StVn, Trin) A member of (or belonging to) a denomination of the Christian religion which originated in St Vincent about the turn of the 19C; it is characterized by marked manifestation of (West) African spiritual emotion blending with a belief in the inerrancy of the Bible, particularly the New Testament; its practices include baptism by immersion in the sea or river, invoking of spirit possession, SHOUTING, MOURNING, and the wearing of congregational robes and head-ties; and its organizational structure broadly follows that of the British protestant church, under territorial Archbishops. (See cit.) *The Spiritual Baptists are an international religious movement. I have visited congregations in St. Vincent (where some Baptists claim the faith originated), Trinidad and Tobago and Grenada, Guyana, Venezuela, Toronto (Canada), Los Angeles, and New York City. There are a number of religious groups on other islands whose rituals are similar to those of the Baptists (e.g. the "Tieheads" of Barbados and the so-called "Spirit Baptists" of Jamaica), but Trinidad Baptists do not consider these others to be part of their religion and do not participate in joint worship, pilgrimages, missions and other services with members of these other groups.*—KACR I:108 [*Spiritual,* from the belief in the visitation of the Holy Spirit during worship + *Baptist,* as acknowledging the biblical manner of baptism by immersion as ritualized by John The Baptist (*NT*)] □ See also MOURNING, SHAKERS, SHOUTERS TIE-HEADS.

spon.sor.ed walk *n phr* (Bdos) A walk by a large group of (usu young) persons along some miles of a public road, as a show of support for a charitable cause or institution, for which money has been collected from invited persons, called 'sponsors', beforehand. *These Sunday morning sponsored walks can be a nuisance as their lines block crossroads, and cause irritating traffic delays.*—(Bdos)

sprad.dle out (sb) *vb phr* (Bdos) [*AF—Joc*] To knock down and send (sb) sprawling. *It was a glarin' obstruction an' Campbell appeal from whey 'e get spraddle-out to de referee who tell 'e dat 'e out!*—NaT (1999.04.28, p.9A, Lickmout' Lou) [< Br E dial; perh a blend of 'sprawl' + 'straddle'; see *EDD spraddle* (Dev., Amer) 'to stride; to straddle or stretch the legs apart; to sprawl' + cit (Amer, 1896). To a baby: *"Crawl along and spraddle out"*]

spray.man *n* (StVn) [*IF*} (Collective name for) person(s) employed to spray insecticides (hence the name) to protect banana crops. *Day grow so handsome an' lusty / Day look so healthy an' green / De sprayman dey come / an' spray all aroun' / To keep me lacatan clean.*—SVFS:9, Care Yo' Lacatan.

squad.die [skwadi] *n* (Jmca) [*AF*] A policeman. *It look like dem a go rob everybody when a squaddie who was sitting behind the one with the gun just pop off one inna the gunman back.*—DaG (short story) [IAE *squad* 'a police division' + familiarity suff -*ie* (cp *auntie*.)]

squin.gee [skwɪnʤi] *adj* (Trin) Squeezed up so as to occupy less space. *Squingee looking guy! He look like he can fight with somebody?*—Trinidad Dictionary. [Cp (*DCEU*) Jmca: **quinge up** (Jmca); **squinge** *vb* (US) **2.** Intr]

step *vb intr* **Phrase step out** *vb phr* (Bdos) [*IF*] To have or seek sexual relationships outside of marriage; to be unfaithful to your spouse. **a.** *"Stepping-out" is the problem much of the time in troubled marriages in Barbados ... "It is mainly infidelity that brings couples to psychiatrists" said the psychiatrist. ... "It is usually the man who has stepped out," the professional added. "Their justification usually is that is what men do', as fickle as that."*—SuS (1993.04.11, p.7A) **b.** *The feeling is that men are now more likely to forgive women who "step out" and women are less likely to tolerate "wayward" men.*—NaT (2000.04.21, p.17) [By extension of the sense (Bdos) 'to go out temporarily'. See *DCEU* **step** Phr 2.2]

still *adv* (Jmca) [*IF/AF*] Anyway; nevertheless; all the same. *You know wha' me da like know still, is why the Ministry come tear down some of the houses and leave some'.*—DaG [Perh a survival of EE usage. Cp Shak, *Henry IV.I,* III.3: "Hostess, I forgive thee ... Thou seest I am pacified still."—(Falstaff, l.66)]

stilt.walk.er *n* (ECar) A masquerade dancer on stilts. *Stiltwalkers—also called Tiltmen or Moko Jumbies, are widely scattered throughout the Caribbean islands, having their origin in West Africa. Towering above the crowds at popular festivals, these figures are regaining their popularity. Indeed, they may very well be the success story among efforts to revive some of our cultural heritage. No street festival nowadays seems complete without the Stiltwalkers in their long, colourful trousers; and even special costumes, ducking under the telephone wires.*—(Folk Character of the Caribbean Almanac, 2001) □ See (*DCEU*) **stiltman**.

stone *vb tr* (Jmca) [*AF—Joc*] **Phrase tek it stone dawg** To have enough (of sth) to throw away. *Im ave so much money im can tek it stone dawg.*—DPJP:40 [*stone dog,* 'to pelt (it) at stray dogs']

stool *n* (Gren) (*Obs*) A small private shrine set aside in a room, for ritual use. *And the making of the stool for Ogun, she tell me how to do that for the first three days feast. Her stool (shrine) was put up first for the first three days.*—SDP:86 [< (W Afr.) *stool,* 'a throne', by extension] □ Restricted usage, African religious survivals.

string *vb tr* (Jmca) [*AF*] To thread. *Me Granny still a gi me more needle fi string.*—DaG (2001.04.23) [Perh by extension of sense of stringing beads, i.e. 'passing a thread through the eye']

stump your toe *vb phr* (ECar) // **bounce your foot** (Gren) // **buck your foot/toe** (Baha, Jmca) To stub or hit your toe against sth. *Mind you stump your toe if you don' look where you going.*—(Trin)

stupe *n* (Bdos, Guyn) [*AF—Derog*] A stupid person; an idiot; a fool. **a.** *He's a real stupe, putting on earing like a girl.*—(Guyn) **b.** *They're quitting school like a bunch of stupes,/Breaking in places stealing fruits, ...*—AdV (1990.06.06, p.1B, Li'l Rick) [Abbr back-formation + functional adj >n shift < IAE *stupid* 'foolish', wh is common spoken usage] □ Inoffensive, mildly pejorative.

stupse *n* (Bdos) // ***suck-teeth*** (CarA) [AF] The salivary sound made by sucking air in through the closed teeth; also called a ***suck-teeth***. *If you just heard a stupse that was Al Gilkes; don't pay he no mind.* —AdV (1993.11.05, p.9, Eric Lewis) [Functional shift of ideoph **stupse** into usage as n, vb] □ See *DCEU* **steups**, of which this is a common alternative spelling.

sup.port.ance *n* (Jmca) // **child money** (Bdos, Guyn) // **child support** (ECar) [AF] Money (usu a regular sum, often as required by order of a court), due to an unmarried mother from her child's father. *This time now David and his wife, Pansy, had separated ... although he always used to carry his supportance to give Pansy.* —RLTJWS:102 [< IAE *support* (vb) + *ance* denoting 'resulting action', but sense prob influenced by 'importance'] □ See *DCEU* **child-support**.

SVG *abbr* (StVn) St Vincent and the Grenadines. *The people of SVG should consider whether they wish to retain the British Sovereign as Head of State of SVG or whether they want SVG to break away from the Crown and opt for republican status; thereby electing a Head of State to the office of President.* —Ned (CRC) Governor-General (2003.08.02, p.27)

sweet *vb tr* (Bdos) To sweeten (sth). *So I en mekkin' nuh sugar-cakes nor sweetin' my corn flakes wid nuh good-fuh-nutten Guatemala crap!* —AdV (2003.05.28, J. Layne-Clarke) [By functional/adj>vb/shift of 'sweet' adj, reinforced by / cc- / reduction < sweet(en)ing] □ Cp *DJE Jmca*, **sweet**, vb, 'To please (sb) greatly'. Also *OED sweet* vb1 **1.** To sweeten **2.** To delight.

T

take; tek *vb* (CarA) *Phrases* **1. take in short** *vb phr* (Guyn) [*IF*] // *answer a call of nature* (Guyn) To have a strong sudden urge to defecate. *(H)e [the carpenter] take in short on the roof an(d) in rushin(g) to get do(w)ng to de latrine (h)e fall an(d) hurt (h)imself and (h)e do (h)is business right dere!*—(Guyn) **2. tek it stone dog** *id phr* (Jmca) See **stone** *Phr* ... **3. tek set pon (sb)** *vb phr* (Jmca) [*AF*] To harass (sb); to bother (sb) persistently. *Dem two tek set (u)pon (h)im an(d) (h)im shoot at dem.*—(Jmca)

talk *vb Phrase* **talk yo(ur) talk** *vb phr* (CarA) [*AF/IF*] To speak your mind; to speak out (on a contentious matter). *Bishop Brume, uh cud shake yuh hand! Guh long an talk yuh talk! Uh glad to hear yuh. Wunna Bajans, pay attenshun to dis man!*—MMSC:31 □ Often used by sb in audience participation to emphasize endorsement of something being said from a public platform.

tap.an.ar.is (top.an.ar.is) *n* (Jmca) [*AF—Joc*] An upper-class person. *Mind you, plenty bhutto go see Pavarotti and nuff topanaris visit Rae Town.*—DaG (2001.08.16) [Abbr < top an(d) aris (to crat)]

tar brush *n phr Phrases* **1. touch of the tar brush** *n phr* (ECar) [*IF—Joc/Derog*] The physical appearance of a person of mixed race, with evidence of a black forebear. *The objection to the negro taint, the "touch of the tar brush" as it is locally called, is not so strong as in America and some of the West Indian islands.*—KTYBG:34 [A metaphorical ref to the irremovable blackness of tar, wh was usu brush-painted on to the staves of a barrel] **2. to have a touch of the tar brush** *vb phr* (ECar) [*IF—Joc/Derog*] To have, though unacknowledged, a black forebear far back in one's family line, although one's skin colour and hair texture may not indicate this fact. *Many 'local white' West Indians, like many white Americans in the Southern US, have a touch of the tar brush hidden in their history which, of course, they would fiercely deny at any suggestion.*—(Bdos) **3. (to be) tarred with the same brush** *vb phr* [*IF—Derog*] [By extension, of persons] To be of the same bad sort. *Of course, the one got off, but both of them shoulda been jailed — they are tarred with same brush.*—(Bdos) □ This id derives from characteristic colonialist association of badness with black people.

teach.ment *n* (Jmca) [*AF*] Schooling; regular education. *Mama did really waan lickle teachment for she did backward. Inna Mama time if yuh no white, yuh couldn't go a high school and so all dem tings mussy*

mek her believe di colour of yuh skin haffi do wid yuh ability.—SLHG: [A blend of *teach(ing)* + MENT] □ See special entry at -MENT.

tek *vb* (CarA) See **take**

tell *vb Phrase* **tell (sb) back** *vb phr* (Bdos) [*AF*] To answer (sb). *And she tell me she read them in English, and then the Eye-talian. And I 'shame. I can't tell-she-back not one damn word in Eye-talian.*—SuS (1994.10.30, p.21A) [*Back*, with the sense 'in return', by analogy with IAE phr vbs *hit back, pay back, etc.*]

tex.tur.ised (-ized) hair *n phr* (Bdos) A black person's hair that has been treated with a relaxant to soften its texture, then variously styled, usu with a regular pattern displaying the shape of the head. *Short texturised hair can be very flattering.*—AdV (1999.09.02, p.35) [< *texture* (see cit) + suff *-ize* as COD *-ize*.4 'affect or provide with'. Prob of AmE source]

thick-leaf thyme *n phr* (Guyn) // BROAD-LEAF/LEAVED THYME (Bdos) A straggling, rhizomous herb, with thick stems reaching about 2 ft in height; it is strongly aromatic, with thick, fleshy stems and leaves; it is used for seasoning and also as a herbal tea reputed to relieve menstrual pains; *Plectranthus amboinicus* or *coleus aromaticus*. □ See FINE-LEAF THYME.

thief; tief *vb Phrase* **get t(h)ief out** *Passive vb phr* (Bdos, Guyn) [*AF*] [Cricket, of a batsman] To be cheated (by the umpire). *Um is true de way 'e get out din too certain, but even ef 'e did feel 'e get t'ief out 'e en had nuh right gine in de Orstalian dressin'-room an' getting on like a idiot.*—AdV (1996.12.07, p.12) [IAE passive marker **get**, as in 'get killed, get soaked, etc., widely used in *AF/IF* CE + Cr *tief-out* (vb tr) 'to cheat (sb)']

Third Night *n phr* (Gren) A night of ceremonial singing and feasting invoking the safety of the soul of a dead person, three days after death. *I haven't tombed her yet, but I paid all the funeral expense. We had a Third Night for her, but no Nine Night, no Forty Night. And up to this I never make an offering for her, not yet.*—SDP:104 [A reference to the sacred resurrection of Jesus Christ]

threads *n pl* (Gren) [*AF—Joc*] (A man's) elegant wear, (usu) fashionable clothing. *Even at the office he would come out in his threads enough to make the ladies look twice.*—(Trin) [COD 10 *thread(s)* n. **5.** (chiefly N. Amer.) 'clothes']

throw away *vb phr* (Bdos) To dispose of; to throw (sth) out. *Christine, I am still coming to you and your kind readers for some more help. I need some pots and pans, a small fridge and a small stove. I believe there are lots of people who throw away still usable stoves and fridges.*—NaT (2005.06.14, p.21)

thyme *n* (Guyn) See FINE-LEAF THYME, THICK-LEAF THYME, GUYANA THYME. □ Note IAE pronunc [taɪm]

tief *n; vb* (CarA) [AF] See **thief**

tief.a.ble *adj* (Bdos) [AF—Joc] Likely, suitable to be stolen. *So you would know that anything and everything is tiefable, big or small. Look, no matter how much the farmers threaten the thieves with herbicides or pesticides 'pon duh crops, duh still getting tief.*—SaS (2007.06.30, Mavis Beckles, p.11) [< [AF—Cr] *tief*, by n > vb shift 'to steal' + IAD suff *-able* 'fit to' as in *eatable*, etc.]

tiefin(g) [ti.fin] /1′2/ *adj* (ECar) [AF—Derog] [Of persons] Being a thief; thieving; [of cats, dogs] that steal from one's premises; [of umpires, referees] cheating. *Look, the farmers does work long, hard, back-breaking hours in the hot broiling sun and sometimes the pouring rain to get their crops to grow, only for some tiefing body to come along, reap the people things and go pon the road and sell them off just so without a conscience.*—SaS (2006.04.22, p.9) [< 'thieving' with AF-Cr pronunc + functional stress shift] □ The cit represents a spelling regularization of the AF—Cr term in common use; IAE 'thieving' does not cover the connotative field shown in the Gloss. See DCEU **t(h)iefin(g)**²

tim.ber(s) *n pl* (Bdos) [Boat building] The rib(s) strapping the body of a wooden fishing boat, on to which the planking is nailed. *He uses local mahogany for the "floors" and the "timbers" (side strips) while the rest of the boat is constructed of silverballi, a Guyanese hardwood, and Honduras pine.*—NaT (1998.11.20, p.19) [OED 2 *timber* 6.b. pl. spec Naut. 'The pieces of wood composing the ribs, bends or frames of a ship's hull' + cits 1748–1885. The Bdos usage is restricted to boat-building]

time *introd adv* (Bdos, Guyn) By the time that. *Time dis letter reach you, I en know how de West Indies gine be doin' in de t'ird tes'.*—AdV (1996.12.28, p.12) **2. Phrases 2.1. en ha(ve) no time wid that** *neg id phr* (CarA) Not have any interest in or concern for sth. *One of the things that I found curious was that February 18 last year, the 200th anniversary of that capture of Trinidad by the English, passed apparently unrecognised, far less celebrated, in Trinidad. I mentioned this to a young Trinibagonian woman who replied—Man, people en ha no time wid that: that happen a long time ago; it has no relevance for Trinidad and Tobago today.*—AdV (1998.05.03, p.9) [A blend of 'no time (for) + (no concern) with'] □ Phrasal and prep **with** functions widely as a general connective in CE. See DCEU **with. 2. 2. from time** *adv phr* (Jmca) [IF] For a long time (in the past); for some time now. ... [E]

specially when you consider that the two of them had not spoken from time.—ObS (2002.04.23)

tin.nin-ba.do/-ba.doo *n* [AF—Joc] (Bdos) A small poor dwelling, often one room, under a corrugated galvanized roof. **a.** *Now look, the other day I decided that it would be good if I could get a few dollar bills, both to do some repairs to my li'l tinnin-ba-do, as well as add on another room to the place to rent out a nice two-bedroom apartment.*—SaS (2007.01.20, p.11) **b.** *But 'e culda tek a leaf outa Clydie book, doh, 'cause ef um is one thing I got to say in Clydie favour is that 'e don' ever fuhget to talk 'bout 'e roots an' 'bout the lil tinnin-badoo that 'e grew up in.*—NaT (2007.03.21, p.9A, Lickmout' Lou) [< *Tinnin(tinnen)* 'made of tin' hence 'cheap, lowly' + *badoo (ba-do)* perh of W Afr origin]

tis.ic; tiz.zic *n* (Bdos, Guyn) **1.** (Obs, Guyn) A persistent, throaty cough. **2.** [Perh by extension] A sickness affecting cats, causing continual sneezing. Only cats suffer from the "tisic" nowadays.—CGBD6:109 [< IAE *phthisic* adj. < *phthisis* 'pulmonary tuberculosis or a similar progressive wasting disease'.—(COD 10)] **2. Phrase 2.1. give sb tizzic** To harass sb. *He did start out gie-ing me tizzic. Me and he did come wrong, wrong.*—MMM:17

to(o).muchy *adj; adv; pron* (Guyn) [AF—Cr] Very (adj); too much (adv, pron) *"Disi disi something, tomuchy nice"*—Joc mimickery of early immigrant open-air marketplace vendors in Georgetown) [< IAE too much + paragogic / -i /. Cp **somuchy**] □ Now obsolete in dial speech.

tour.ism *n* (Bdos) [Hotel Ind] The business of attracting paying visitors from overseas to spend time at leisure and pleasure in a (Caribbean) territory; it is organized as a large-scale national and regional industry. *Ah hear you say de crime on tourist down / But that's because now less tourist come / If there's to be hope for tourism, / They must foster better relations.*—Cso, "Red"—RPB (2002) □ Note the CarA difference in this usage from the US (WCD 10) and Br (COD 10) senses which focus on outgoing travelling, in marked contrast to the CarA's industralized gaining of incoming travellers.

tra.vaux /1′2/ [travo] *n* (Gren) Government road work, esp. such that employs many hand-labourers. *They wish they could do something that I could go and work, even in the road, in the travaux.*—SDP:96 [< *travaux* 'public works']

trav.el (in spir.it) *vb intr (phr)* (CarA) [Religion] To make a spiritual journey under a supernatural influence. **a.** *And she tell me to put a bandage on my hand, that would help me to travel farther. But the Powers told me not to do that, she wanted to get me to the madhouse.*—SDP:90 **b.** *I come to know all this about the Baptists by travelling in spirit. I see.*—SDP:89 □ This sense is often extended outside the strict domain of spiritualist religion, to apply to a dying person's last hours. See DCEU.

tuck.o-tuck.o [tʌkʌ-tʌkʌ] *adj* (Jmca) [AF] [Of a person] Of short and squat build. *She was a short tucko-tucko gal with not too much commonsense.*— RLTJWS:58 [Perh from Ewe *túku-tukui* 'small, little'. See *DJE* **tuku-tuku**]

turn cat.gut *v phr* (Baha) See CATGUT Phr.

twists *n pl* (Bdos) [Hairstyling] Multiple short turnings of (a black woman's) hair, usu over the whole head, as a manner of expressing Africanness. *Some women go even further in the expression of their heritage and "grow out" the chemically processed hair choosing this road to unprocessed hair, including twists and in some cases, locks.*—AdV (1999.09.12, p.32)

U

u.ba cane *n phr* (Jmca) [*IF*] A variety of sugar cane. [The name apparently stems from an error. According to Thomas Lecky, a label marked 'DURBAN' was illegible except for the letters 'D', 'R and 'N', as the package which had been imported from Natal and Zululand arrived water-soaked in Jamaica during World War I—J.P. Lecky *Cattle and I,* Kingston, 1996, p.272]

up.hol.ste.ry *n* (CarA) [By extended sense] An upholsterer's workshop. □ See JOINERY.

V

voop [vʊp] *vb intr* (Trin) [Cricket, of a batsman] To hit out recklessly; to swipe. *He was caught out vooping wildly.*—(Trin) [An image word]

W

wag.ga-wag.ga *n; adj* (Jmca) // *wopsy* (Bdos) (One who is) fat and sloppy. [< (*DYL*) Yoruba, *wagawaga* 'clumsy; awkward in shape and motion']

walk *vb tr* **Phrase walk.ing the dog** *vb phr* (Bdos) [*AF*] See cit. *For those that are still in the dark as to what 'walking the dog' is, the explanation following should make it clear. From what is understood, the driver of the particular van would wait until he is approaching an incline, put the van in neutral, remove the keys and throw them in the back of the van and walk alongside the van while passengers look for the keys. When the passengers locate the keys, they throw them to the driver who gets back in the van and continues his destination.*—NaT (Mag) (1999.02.19, p.3)

wa.ra.wa.ra *n* (Jmca) Bits and pieces. *Like the lady say "Is lil scraps a dis, lil scraps a dat, lil scraps a warawara".*—BJLSCH:40 [Perh via (*DYL*) Yoruba *warawara* (adv) 'hastily, quickly'. See also *DJE wara-wara* 'miscellaneous small things'; + cp *DCEU* '*wara-wara*' (Guyn) (adj) 'cheap looking']

war.ri.some *adj* [*AF*] (StVn) Trouble-making and cantankerous; noisily quarrelsome. *The mother said her son was not a warrisome sort of person, he never troubled people, and she did not know why anyone would want to murder him.*—(StVn) [Perh—blend of *warri*(or) + (quarrel)*some*]

was *introductory vb* (Jmca) It was; there was/were. **a.** *I had a three day feast, and on the last night, was a Friday night, I heard how she went on with a Power they call Wereh.*—SDP:89 **b.** *We uses to live on a sugar-estate name La Romain.* [*W*]*as a set of Indians living on the estate, and all of we was labourers.*—SWOS:82 [Pa.t. (*DCEU is*[1] 2 (i). Introducing a n phr or clause]

wash *n* (CarA) [*AF—Joc*] [Cricket] The winning by one side of the entire series of Test and/or One-Day cricket matches in a Tour. *It is a situation Hooper, just nine weeks into the post, has come to appreciate. His uncomplicated message to his players was not to concern themselves with washes of any colour but to raise their game "by ten to 15 percent, for everyone to play to potential or close to it on a consistent basis".*—NaT (2001.11.29, p.46) [Back-formation, with analogy, from WHITEWASH, BLACKWASH, BROWNWASH, + functional vb > n shift of IAE *wash* as in vb phrs *wash(ed) away, wash(ed) out, wash(ed) up*, connoting 'complete wiping']

wa.ter *vb tr* **Phrase wa.ter her garden** *vb phr* (Jmca) [*AF—Joc*] To have sex with her. *Dem would chat about who bubby dem like and about who garden dem done water.*—(Jmca, 1999) [Metaph of the male and female genitals in intercourse]

wa.ter-grass *n phr* (Jmca) // *pond grass* (Bdos) *But we still had Granny Tucker's wiry black hands, strong enough to scrub away khaki suds, so why not to pull water-grass.*—BJLSCH:146 [From the wetness of its favoured habitat] □ With '*pull water grass*' in cit, cp PICK POND GRASS.

wa.ter yam *n phr* (Belz, Guyn, Jmca, StVn) /// *crop Lisbon* (Bdos)

way.lay-way.lay [welewele] /1122/ (Trin) (Not quite a BACHANNAL, but) a disorderly situation out of wh could come violence. *There was a lot of shouting and bottle-throwing, and a whole big welewele.*—(Trin) [Cp (*DYL*) Yoruba *wéléwélé* adv 'with ripples']

weave[1]**, weaves, weaved, weaving, weave on** *vb tr* (CarA) **1.** [Of hair] To add strands of artificial hair by interlacing them with the natural hair on a black woman's head so as to give her hairstyle an appearance of natural abundance. **a.** *Her hair hung shoulder length with such a sleek smooth finish, you couldn't tell she'd had it weaved.*—(Bdos) **b.** *Best hair to weave on.*—Ad (Bdos) [Extension of the sense of IAE *weave*, as distinct from 'plait'] □ The related past tense is *weaved* not *woven*. **2.** [Of wood] To interlace millimetre thin slats of processed wood to produce a tight surface. *This unique teak 7-piece dining room set with weaved and pineapple style chairs can be yours for only $152/month.*—Ad, SuS (1999.09.19, p.21A)

weave(s)[2]**; weave-on(s)** *n (pl)* (CarA) [Of hair] Long smooth strands of (usu black) synthetic hair plaited on to a black woman's normal hair to create an appearance of natural length. **a.** *The weave is currently reigning supreme and comes in a vast variety: basket weave, straight weave, wet n' wavy, corkscrew and curly.*—NaT (1996.05.10, p.24) **b.** *Very short texturised hair or long weaves are favoured by a lot of Barbadian women.*—AdV (1999.09.12, p.35) **c.** *Only the whites of Celestine's eyes were visible as she jerked her head from side to side, as if somehow she was trying to dislodge it. Miraculously, she broke out of the Spirit just as her weave-on began to weave off.*—SuS (2000.06.11, p.10) [By functional of vb > n shift of *weave*[1]*, weave on*]

weav.ing *n* (CarA) The adding of long strands of artificial (usu black) hair to the body of a black woman's own straightened hair to create an appearance of natural length. See WEAVE ON. *The trend today is also very long hair. With the great use of hair pieces and other forms of hair additions like weaving (which has a place since they can serve to alleviate baldness) they give the wearer the opportunity to have any length or any style they desire, she said.*—AdV (1999.09.12, p.34)

we.reh [wɛrɛ] *n* (Gren) [Religion] One of the manifestations of spirit possession. *I had a three day feast, and on the last night, I heard how she went on with a Power they call Wereh. That Wereh would be with her the whole day, she can see, she can tell you things.*—SDP:89 [Cp (*ADMY*), Yoruba *were* 'madness']

West In.di.an fruit fly *n phr* (Bdos) A small brown fly with distinctive yellowish brown patterning on the wings; the adult fly is about 8—10 mm long, with iridescent eyes, and its larvae are yellowish white; *Anastrepha obliqua diptera (Tephritidae)*. See cit. *The West Indian Fruit Fly was first discovered in Florida in 1930. It is a medium-sized, yellow-brown fly which feeds on the pulp of the fruit. Secondary organisms like bacteria and fungi can move in, causing the fruit to rot. The female lays the eggs in groups beneath the skin of the fruits and when fully grown, they penetrate the fruit skin, fall to the ground and pupate in the soil.*—AdV (2002.10.11, p.7)

what-not *n* (Bdos) A piece of wooden furniture consisting of 4 or 5 small open triangular ledges, of lessening size, with the smallest at the top, mounted spaced on three slender, carved stems; it stands in the corner of a drawing-room, used for displaying a variety of small ornaments or framed photographs. □ The item is a particularly popular piece of furniture, identified as described, in Bdos. Cp *COD* 10 **whatnot**.

which.in *conj* (Bdos) [AF] Of whom/which. *De lates' deaf (de Guyanese woman whichin duh fin' she body in a cart road in de Belle few days ago) remin' me o' dem canefiel' murders.*—NaT (1998.02.25, p.9A, Lickmout' Lou) □ See *DCEU*.

white Lis.bon *n phr* (Bdos) /// CROP LISBON (Bdos)

white.wash¹ *vb tr* (CarA) [AF—Joc] [Of touring white teams i.e. English or Australian cricketers] To win an entire series of matches against an opposing side of black players (i.e. from the West Indies). *Cock-a-hoop England whitewash Windies.*—SuS (H, 2004.08.22, p.15B) [Metaph usage: to be washed out by a team of white players.' Prob orig AmE. Cp *OED* 2 *whitewash* vb 3. 'In baseball and other games: To beat (the opponents) so that they fail to score.' + cits 1867–1981]

white.wash² *n* (CarA) [AF—Joc] **1.** The winning of an entire series of matches by a touring team of English or Australian cricketers. **2.** [By extension] The loss of an entire series of matches of a tour by an opposng side of white players (i.e. from England or Australia). *They have been beaten in both previous Tests and, as in four of their overseas engagements in the past four years, again face the prospect of a clean sweep, the dreaded whitewash they were so adept at dishing out in their heyday in the 1980s when it became known as the "blackwash".*—SuS (H, 2004.08.22, p.15B) [By functional vb > n shift of WHITEWASH¹] □ Cp BLACKWASH, BROWNWASH.

white yam *n phr* (Dmca) /// CROP LISBON (Bdos)

wind.ball crick.et *n phr* (ECar) Cricket played with a tennis ball or rubber ball of similar size. *We would then go up to Montrose Pond Bottom (Christ Church where he lived) and play windball cricket, which is now called soft ball.*—SaS (1993.07.03, p.18) □ Sometimes also called **softball cricket**. See cit.

wind.ward side *n* (Dmca) /// AUVENT (Dmca)

wis.dom weed (Jmca) [IF] Another name for GANJA. [From the general feeling of euphoria, and well-being and sometimes hallucination produced by smoking GANJA]

with.er tip *n phr* (CarA) See DIE BACK.

wiz.zy-wiz.zy.ing *n* (Bdos) [AF—Joc] Whisperings; quiet gossip. *You mussee remember de business wid M—— S——, all de rumours an' wizzy-wizzying' dat did circulatin' roun' Buhbayduss at de time an' still to some extent upwards to now ... .*—NaT (1998.05.13, p.9A, Lickmout' Lou)

wop.sy *adj* (Bdos) [AF—Derog] [Usu of a woman] Very fat and ungainly. *Now, when I say overweight I ain't mean slightly plump or chubby or fairly fat, I mean big with a capital "B" and fat with a capital "F". The girl was 13 years old and weighed 300 and nuff, I talking 'bout big and wopsy'.*—AdV (1998.01.02, p.11, Eric Lewis) [Cp *EDD wopser*. 'Anything large of its kind']

worm oil plant *n phr* (Belz) /// APASOTE (Belz)

worm.wood *n* (Jmca) /// APASOTE (Belz)

wun [wʌn] *possessive pron particle* (Bdos) [AF—Cr] **Phrase dem/them wun** *pron phr* Own (in CE pron. Phr. **their own**). *Ting, the thieves does jump over people fences and tief their limes, mangoes and whatever they could get duh two hands 'pon and go 'long 'bout the place selling them like duh is them wun.*—SaS (2007.06.30, Mavis Beckles, p.11) □ This is a rare survival of Creole usage, in the **paradigm me wun, you wun, he/she wun, dem wun**.

X–Y

ya¹ *pron 2nd pers, subj & obj* (CarA) [*AF—Cr*] [Unstressed form of SE] You. *But life just won't give some people a easy break, it like to break ya, it like to the stuff that you made of, it like see ya fall down hard and wonder if you got the guts, willpower or determination to stand up and face it like a man.*—SaS (2007.10.27, p.11) [< yo, dial pronunc of you, with opening of vowel [u] > a] *EDD* notes the forms **ya**, **yah** (under the entry **you**) as occurring in e, w, and n in Yks in 19C.

ya² *pron, 2nd pers, possess* (CarA) [Unstressed form of SE]Your. *If wunna miss and move on just as soon as you see the green light, yo might find ya'self all the way down the road, skating pon ya side.*—SaS (2007.10.27, p.11) [< CarA Cr usage, yo < yo(ur), in possess function] **1.** *EDD* notes the forms ya, yah, (under the entry **your**), as occurring in Suf. **2.** Note the loose occurrence of this form interchangeably with *Bdos* dial **wunna** and IAE **you** in the same utterance.

ya³ *adv* (CarA) Here. (See *DCEU* **ya.**) □ **ya³** usually carries stress, in contast with **ya¹, ²**.

yam *vb tr* (Bdos) [*AF—Joc*] To eat voraciously. **a.** *Good, common sense would tell you that at Old Year's night when the hotel full of people looking to yam and cram that no tourism industry want to be hit by a strike.*—AdV (Eric Lewis) **b.** *Bud wid proper housing so that when the rain fall, they don't get wet; that they get something to eat when the day come, that the houses they live in ain't falling down 'round them because the wood ants yamming them down.*—SaS (2006.12.30, p.11) [< nyam 'eat' an *AF—Cr/Joc* African survival. See *DCEU*] □ This form, **yam** (vb) occurs rarely other than in *Joc* Bdos usage.

yard *n* [*By extension*] **1.** (Jmca) [*AF/IF*] Jamaica, as your homeland. *Missus, de woman look and sound like a head teacha who lef' yard and come to foreign fe mek life.*—DaG (Outlook, 1995.03.05, p.13) **2.** (Trin) The enclosed backyard used as the base of a STEEL-BAND group. **b.** *The whole development of the ping pong depended both on the exchange of ideas among tuners and on competition. There are many stories of panmen visiting each other's yards especially during the war years before band rivalry became particularly violent.* [An extension of (*DCEU*) **yard¹** sense 1, with specific ref to (*DCEU*) **pan-yard**] **3. Phrases 3.1. a yard; back a yard** (Jmca) At home; back home. **a.** *Some a we don't even ha passport fe come back a yard.*—ObS (1995.05.07, p.4) **b.** *This is to let you know how proud we are of you back a yard.*—(E-mail to Asafa Powell at 2004 Olympic Games)

yella [yɛla~yala] *adj* (Guyn) [*AF—Joc*] Light-skinned; of mixed (Afro-European) race but not dark-skinned. *Yalla nigga na know (h)e race till (h)e t(h)ief(= Yellow nigger doesn't know his race until he is a thief)*— Prov(SPBG no.1028) [Cp (SBT:262) AAVE: yellow/ yelluh/ high yelluh. 'A very light-complexioned African-American, praised in some quarters, damned in others'] □ The Guyn Prov proves the term to belong to very early Creole usage, though it is now rare, replaced by **light-skinned**, etc. (see *DCEU*).

you *pron* (Car—) *Phrase* **not you?** *terminal approval tag phr* (Bdos) [*AF*] Don't you agree? /wouldn't you agree? **a.** *Hey, I nearly fuhget to tell yuh—de big $75-a-ticket show, "The Great Classics", get cancel, whichin I could predick woulda happen, not you?*—AdV (1993.10.15, p.9) **b.** *Dem is de t'ings I does consider blessin's, de t'ings I does gi' praise to de Almighty fuh, not you?*—Nat (2000.09.06, p.9A, Lickmout' Lou)

Z

Zeek *Phrase* **hungry and tired as Zeek** *id phr* (Bdos) [*AF—Joc*] As exhausted as you could be. *And then as I said before back home to Dalkeith and my father's uncaring grace before (before meals) while my brothers and I remained as hungry and tired as Zeek.*— AdV (2003.12.25, p.25) [A surviving catch phrase (like 'tired as hell) but of unknown origin]

zep.po *n* (Trin) [*AF—Joc*] Scandalous rumour; significant gossip. *Yo hear de zeppo? Dey say Panday and dem got a ten million dollar account in London.*— (Trin)

zig-zag *adj* (Trin) Untrustworthy; never straight; scheming. *He's such a zig-zag man that no self-respecting woman should ever encourage his sweet talk.*— (Trin, 1986)

Zion *n* (Jmca) A folk-level cultist belief system particular to black Jamaicans, whose rituals include prayer-meetings, ceremonial feasts, etc., and whose devotees are given to spirit-possession and speaking in tongues. **a.** *Zion spirits do not reside at the "mission ground", because the Zion pantheon gives far less recognition to human spirits, and more to the heavenly or biblical host.*—SRCJ:6 **b.** *Soul train is coming our way / Zion train is coming our way. Two thousand years of history / Black History / could not be wiped away so easily. / Oh children Zion train is coming our way. / Get on board now / Zion train is coming our way.*—'Zion Train', Bob Marley reggae lyric 1980. [From long-standing post-emancipation identification of diasporic African peoples with Israel, delivered as God's chosen people, and by preference equated to 'Zion', the hill on which Jerusalem stands and home of the ancient Isrealites of the Bible. In Rastafari cultism, **Zion** becomes the desired religious goal. See cit **b**]

ZR cult.ure [zɛd–ar kʌlčʌr] *n phr* (Bdos) // MINIBUS CULTURE (Bdos) **a.** *The ZR culture in Barbados, which continues to attract the attention of the police, came into the spotlight in Kid Site's new dub number, 'ZR Van Run The Country'. The veteran also highlighted the scourge of drug addiction ...*—SaS (2004.06.26, p.16) **b.** *He also stressed that it was more important to socialise children correctly so they would not be drawn to negative behaviours associated with the ZR subculture.*—SaS (2004.08.21, p.36) [< ZR, the number-plate code identifying the smaller type of private service vehicles (PSVs) in Bdos. See gloss at MINIBUS CULTURE]

CITATION CODES FOR BIBLIOGRAPHICAL REFERENCES USED IN THE NEW REGISTER OF CARIBBEAN ENGLISH USAGE

The following is a list of abbreviated codes identifying all sources from which illustrative citations have been taken, and all works of reference cited within glosses, etymological or usage notes. The sources of citation include literary works, newspapers, journals, reports, etc. taken from all the English-speaking West Indian territories covered by this *New Register of Caribbean English Usage*. The reader may note, for convenience, that the coding is patterned as follows:

Upper case for books:	ACJPS	ANDERSON, Izett, and F. CUNDALL, *Jamaica Proverbs and Sayings.*
Upper + lower case for journals:	Bes	*Belizean Studies*
Upper + lower + upper for newspapers:	CaW	*Caribbean Week*

Each listing is accompanied by full bibliographical reference as available, and the territory to which the lexicon relates is given in each case, in the last column. Also in the last column, reference works are identified as Ref.

ACJPS	ANDERSON, Izett, and F. CUNDALL, *Jamaica Proverbs and Sayings.* 2nd ed., 1927; repr. Irish Univ. Press, Shannon, 1972.	Jmca
ADMY	ABRAHAM, R.C., *Dictionary of Modern Yoruba.* London, Univ. of London Press, 1958.	Ref.
AdV	*Barbados Advocate*	Bdos
AVB	*Authorised* (King James) *Version of the Bible.*	Ref.
BACP	ALLSOPP, S.R.R., *Book of Afric Caribbean Proverbs.* Kingston, Arawak, 2004.	CarA
BCSJ	BRATHWAITE, E.K., *The Development of Creole Society in Jamaica, 1770–1820.* Oxford Univ. Press, 1971.	Jmca
Bes	*Belizean Studies.* Belize Institute of Social Research and Action	Belz
BJLSCH	BRODBER, Erna, *Jane and Louisa Will Soon Come Home.* London, New Beacon Books, 1980.	Jmca
Cab	*Bwee Caribbean Beat.* Port of Spain, Media and Editorial Projects.	Trin
Caribbean Festival Arts	(almanac)	CarA

Caq	*Caribbean Quarterly.* Univ. of the West Indies, Mona, Jamaica.	CarA
CaW	*Caribbean Week.* Bridgetown, Barbados.	CarA
CBCD	CRAVEN, H., and J. BARFIELD, *English–Congo and Congo–English Dictionary.* London, 1883.	Ref.
CCD	CAYETANO, E. Roy, *Chuluha Dan.* Stencilled ms, 1977.	Belz
CDB (Ms)	*Caribbean Development Bank,* Barbados.	CarA
CDID	COULLS, F.L., *Down in Demerara.* London, 1944.	Guyn
CEDM	*Collins English Dictionary Millennium Edition.* 4th ed. Glasgow, HarperCollins, 1998.	Ref.
CGBD	COLLYMORE, Frank A., *Notes for a Glossary of Barbadian Dialect.* 4th ed., 1970; 5th ed., 1976. Bridgetown, Barbados National Trust.	Bdos
COD	*Concise Oxford Dictionary.* 10th ed., Oxford, Oxford Univ. Press, 1999; 11th ed., Oxford Univ. Press, 2004.	Ref.
CPH	CLARKE, Austin, *The Polished Hoe.* New York, HarperCollins, 2003.	Bdos
CrU	*The Crusader.* Castries.	StLu
Cso	*Calypso.* (+ Author)	
CWPEC	CARRINGTON, S., *Wild Plants of the Eastern Caribbean.* London, Macmillan Edu., 1998.	CarA
DAFL	CHRISTALLER, Rev. J.G., *Dictionary of the Asante and Fante Language Called Tshi (Twi).* Basel, Basel Evangelical Missionary Society, 1933.	Ref.
DaG	*The Daily Gleaner; The Sunday Gleaner.* Kingston.	Jmca
DARE	CASSIDY, F.G., *Dictionary of American Regional English.* Cambridge, Belknap Press, Harvard, 1985–2002.	Ref.
DCEU	ALLSOPP, S.R.R., *Dictionary of Caribbean English Usage.* Oxford, Oxford Univ. Press, 1996.	CarA
DBE	HOLM, J., and A.W. Shilling, *Dictionary of Bahamian English.* New York, Lexik House, 1982.	Baha
DJE	CASSIDY, F.G., and R.B. LePAGE, *Dictionary of Jamaican English.* Cambridge, Cambridge Univ. Press, 1967, 2nd edn, 1980.	Jmca
DKAEC	FONTAINE, Marcel, and P.A. Roberts, *Diksyonné Kwèyòl–Anglé, English–Creole.* Roseau, Folk Research Centre, 1991.	Dmca
DMEI	WARMAN, Adolpho I.V., *Diccionario Trilingue: Miskito–Español/Inglés.* Nicaragua, 1962.	Ref.
DNE2	STORY, G.M., W.J. KIRWIN and J.D.A. WIDDOWSON (eds.), *Dictionary of Newfoundland English.* 2nd edn, Univ. of Toronto Press, 1998 & 1999.	Ref.
DPJP	HENRY, Mike, *Dictionary of Popular Jamaican Phrases.* Kingston, LMH Publishing, 2002.	Jmca

DSAS	DUNN, Richard S., *Sugar and Slaves*. New York, Norton, 1972.	Ref.
DSUE 2	PARTRIDGE, Eric, *A Dictionary of Slang and Unconventional English*, vol. 2, 6th ed., London, Routledge & Kegan Paul, 1967.	Ref.
DSUE 8	PARTRIDGE, Eric, *A Dictionary of Slang and Unconventional English*. 8th ed., London, Paul Beale Routledge, 1984.	Ref.
DYL	*Dictionary of the Yoruba Language*, Ibadan, Univ. Press, Nigeria, 2001.	Ref.
ECDS	ELDER, J.D., *From Congo Drum to Steel Band*. Trinidad, Univ. of the West Indies, St Augustine, 1969.	Trin
EDD	WRIGHT, Joseph, *The English Dialect Dictionary*. Oxford, Oxford Univ. Press, 1898.	Ref.
Ema	*Emancipation: The African-Guyanese Magazine*. Georgetown, Free Press.	Guyn
ExP	*Express*. Port of Spain.	Trin
FAZBH	FRASER, H., S. CARRINGTON, S. FORDE, A. GILMORE and J. GILMORE, *A–Z of Barbadian Heritage*. Kingston, Heinemann Caribbean, 1990.	Bdos
FGBTT	FFRENCH, Richard, *A Guide to the Birds of Trinidad and Tobago*. Pennsylvania, Asa Wright Nature Centre, 1976.	Trin
FKD	FRANK, David (ed.), *Kwéyòl Dictionary*. Castries, Ministry of Education, 2001.	StLu
FSCD	FERGUSON, Tyrone. *To Survive Sensibly or Court Heroic Death*. Georgetown, Public Affairs, Consulting Enterprise, 1999.	Guyn
GCROG	GIBSON, Kean, *The Cycle of Racial Oppression in Guyana*. Lanham, New York, Univ. Press of America, 2003	Guyn
GMPP	GASKIN, Molly R., *Medicinal Plants at the Pointe-a-Pierre Wild Flower Trust*. Pointe-a-Pierrre Wild Fowl Trust, 1991.	Trin
GMTB	GLINTON-MEICHOLAS, Patricia, *Talkin' Bahamian*. Nassau, Guanima Press, 1994.	Baha
GMMTB	GLINTON-MEICHOLAS, Patricia, *More Takin' Bahamian*. Nassau, Guanima Press, 1995.	Baha
GMPCG	LACHMAN-WHITE, D.A., C.D. ADAMS and U.O.D. TROTZ, *A Guide to the Medicinal Plants of Coastal Guyana*. London, Commonwealth Science Council, 1992.	Guyn
Gyr	*Guyana Review*. Georgetown.	Guyn
HCWP	HONYCHURCH, P.N., *Caribbean Wild Plants and Their Uses*. Bridgetown, Honychurch, 1980.	CarA
HHWFB	HANDLER, J.S., R. HUGHES and E.M. WILTSHIRE, *Freedman of Barbados*. Charlottesville, Virginia Foundation for the Humanities and Public Policy, 1980.	Bdos

HPV	HOROWITZ, Michael, *Morne-Paysan: Peasant Village in Martinique*. New York, Holt, Rinehart & Winston, 1969.	Mart
HSOH	HINDS, Marcia H., *Saga of Hairoun*. M.H. Resourcentre, 2002.	StVn
HSPBC	HIGMAN, Barry W., *Slave Populations of the British Caribbean 1807–1834*. Baltimore, Johns Hopkins Univ. Press.	CarA
HTTD	HAYNES, Martin, *Trinidad and Tobago Dialect (Plus)*. San Fernando, Trinidad, 1987.	Trin
HTUP	HANDLER, Jerome S., *The Unappropriated People*. Baltimore, Johns Hopkins Univ. Press, 1974.	Bdos
HWW	HILL, Errol, *Wey-Wey*. St Augustine, Trinidad, Extra-Mural Studies Unit, 1978.	Trin
JASL	JESSE, C. Rev., *The Amerindians in St Lucia*. St Lucia Archaeological and Historical Society, 1968.	Trin
JCMAT	Jamaica Cultural Development Commission, *Mento an' Ting*. Kingston, 1990.	Jmca
JGRR	JACOBS, Richard W., and Ian JACOBS, *Grenada: The Route to Revolution*. Havana Cuba, Casa de Las Americas, 1980.	Gren
JJCM	JACOBS, C.M., *Joy Comes in the Morning*. Port of Spain, Caribbean Historical Society, 1996.	ECar
JJRW	JAHNIYA, I.C., *Jamaican Rastafarian Word Sound*. Bound typescript, 1987.	Jmca
JMRF	JOHNSON, Linton K., *Mi Revalushanary Fren*. London, Penguin, 2002.	Jmca
JPBC	JORDAN, Portia Brown, *A Potpourri in Bahamian Culture*. Nassau, Nassau Printing Press, 1986.	Baha
JTGDD	JAMES, Osmund, *Tough Girls Don't Dance*. Kingston, Kingston Publishers, 1996	Jmca
KACR	KREMSER, Manfred, *African-Caribbean Religions,* part 1. Vienna, WUV–Universitatsverlog	Ref.
KED	FYLE, Clifford N., and Eldred A. JONES, *A Krio–English Dictionary*. Oxford, Oxford Univ. Press, 1980.	Ref.
KTYBG	KIRKE, Henry, *Twenty Five Years in British Guiana*. London, Sampson Lon & Co., 1898; repr. Negro Univ. Press, 1970.	Guyn
LOFR	LABASTIDE, Neville, *One for the Road*. St Augustine, Trinidad, Extra-Mural Studies Unit, Univ. of the West Indies, 1978	Trin
LS	LOVELACE, Earl, *Salt*. London, Faber & Faber, 1996.	Trin
LSDSY	LOWE, S., *Shub Down and Small-Up Yuself*. Kingston, Polar Bear Press, 1999.	Jmca
LTS	LOVELACE, Earl G., *The School Master*. London, Heinemann, 1979.	Trin
Luk	*Lucian Kaiso*. Castries, Folk Research Centre.	StLu

MCUD	MACAFEE, Ci (ed.), *A Concise Ulster Dictionary.* Oxford, Oxford Univ. Press, 1996.	Ref.
MDSLC	MONDESIR, Jones E.; ed. L.D. CARRINGTON, *Dictionary of St Lucian Creole.* Berlin, Mouton de Gruyter, 1992.	StLu
MHJT	MAIS, Roger, *The Hills Were Joyful Together.* (In the edition: *The Three Novels of R. Mais.*) London, Jonathan Cape, 1966.	Jmca
MMM	MEEK, Norma, *Minibus Muse.* Bridgetown, Norma Meek, 1993.	Bdos
MMSC	MEEK, Norma, *In My Small Corner.* Bridgetown, Norma Meek, 1993.	Bdos
MSHPG	MENEZES, Mary Noel, *Scenes from the History of the Portuguese in Guyana.* London, M.N. Menezes, 1986.	Guyn
MSMCDB	MURREL, S.N., W.D. SPENCER and A.A. McFARLANE, *Chanting Down Babylon: The Rastafarian Reader.* Philadelphia, Temple Univ. Press, 1998.	Jmca
Nag	*National Geographic.* Washington, National Geographic Society.	Ref.
NaT	*The Nation.* Nation Publishing Co., Bridgetown.	Bdos
NeD	*Trinidad and Tobago's Newsday.*	Trin
NSOE	NAIPAUL, V.S., *The Suffrage of Elvira.* London, André Deutsch, 1958.	Trin
NSWOM	NYEELAH, *Someone to Watch Over Me.* Barbados, Homegrown Press, 2002.	Bdos
NTSM	NEWTON, Velma, *The Silver Men.* Bridgetown, Institute of Social and Economic Research, Univ. of the West Indies, 1984.	Bdos
OBCSS	BROWN, S. (ed.), and J. WICKHAM, *The Oxford Book of Caribbean Short Stories,* Oxford, Oxford Univ. Press, 1999.	CarA
ObS	*The Observer.* Kingston.	Jmca
OED	*Oxford English Dictionary.* Oxford, Clarendon Press, 1933.	Ref.
OED 2	*Oxford English Dictionary.* 2nd ed., vols 1–20. Oxford, Clarendon Press, 1989.	Ref.
OEDS	Supplements to *OED,* vols. 1–4, 1982–86.	Ref.
Outlook	*Jamaica Gleaner Outlook* in Jamaica *Sunday Gleaner.*	Jmca
PDKF	PELEMAN, Louis; ed. Roger DESIR, *Diksyonnè Kwéyòl–Fransé.* Port-au-Prince, Bon Nouvel, 1976.	Hait
PDT	POLLARD, Velma, *Dread Talk: The Language of Rastafari.* Montreal, McGill–Queen's Univ. Press; Kingston, Canoe Press, 2000.	Ref.
PRJW	PATRICK, Peter, *Recent Jamaican Words in Sociolinguistic Context, American Speech,* 70.3 (Fall 1995), 232–59.	Jmca
Q & CGEL	QUIRK, Randolph (et al.), *A Comprehensive Grammar of the English Language.* London, Longman, 1985.	Ref.

RHDAS	LIGHTER, J.E. (ed.), *Random House Historical Dictionary of American Slang*. New York, Random House, 1994.	Ref.
RHJSS	ROBINSON, Kim, and Leeta HEARNE, *Twenty-two Jamaican Short Stories*. Kingston, Kingston Publishers, 1987.	Ref.
RJH	ROBERTSON, Diane, *Jamaican Herbs*. Kingston, Jamaican Herbs Ltd., 1982/86.	Jmca
RLTJWS	REYNOLD, Nia Z., *Native Daughter: The Life and Times of a Jamaican Woman of the Soil*. London & Oxford, Macmillan Educ., 2000.	Jmca
RPP	ROTH, Vincent, *Roth's Pepper Pot*. Georgetown, Daily Chronicle, 1958.	Guyn
RPP	RYAN, Selwyn, *Pathways to Power*.	Trin
RTFR	RAMCHAND, K. (ed.), Eric ROACH, *The Flowering Rock: Collected Poems: 1938–1974*. Leeds, Peepal Tree Press, 1992.	Tbgo
SaS	*The Sun on Saturday*. Bridgetown.	Bdos
SAZJ	SENIOR, Olive, *A–Z of Jamaican Heritage*. Longman Caribbean, 1989.	Jmca
SBT	SMITHERMAN, G., *Black Talk*. New York, Houghton Mifflin, 1994.	Ref.
SBWW	STONE, Maureen, *Black Woman Walking*. BeaGay Publications, 2002.	Bdos
SCL	Society for Caribbean Linguistics	CarA
SDP	SMITH, M.G., *Dark Puritan*. Kingston, Dept. of Extra-Mural Studies, Univ. of the West Indies, 1963.	Gren
SeA	*The Searchlight*.	StVn
SGDA	SANTAMARIA, F.J., *Diccionario General de Americanismos*. Mexico, 1942.	Ref.
SGIS	SINCLAIR, Norma, *Grenada, Isle of Spice*. London, Macmillan Caribbean, 1987.	Gren
SHWI	STURGE, J., and T. HARVEY, *The West Indies in 1837*. London, Frank Cass, 1968.	Ref.
Sky Writings	Air Jamaica in-flight magazine. Kingston.	Jmca
SLK	*St Lucia Kaiso*, 2nd ed.	StLu
SOED	*Shorter Oxford English Dictionary*, 2nd ed., Oxford, Oxford Univ. Press, 1993.	Ref.
SPBG	SPIERS, Rev. James, *The Proverbs of British Guiana*, Demerara, Argosy Co., 1902.	Guyn
Sport & General	Georgetown, in the 1930s	Guyn
SRCJ	SEAGA, Edward, *Revival Cults in Jamaica*. Kingston, Institute of Jamaica [reprint of *Jamaica Journal* 3.2 (June 1969)] 1982.	Jmca
SRIC	SLONE, THOMAS, *Rasta Is Cuss: A Dictionary of Rastafarian Cursing*. Oakland, CA, Masalai Press, 2003.	Jmca

SRRA	ALLSOPP, Stanley Richard R.,	
SSE	SPEARS, Richard A., *Slang and Euphemism: A Dictionary of Oaths, Curses, etc., etc.* New York, Jonathan David, 1981.	Ref.
SSHL	SMITH, K.B., and F.C. SMITH, *To Shoot Hard Labour.* Scarborough, Ont., Edan, 1986.	Antg
SSLG	SISTREN; ed. H. FORD-SMITH, *Lionheart Gal.* London, Women's Press, 1986.	Jmca
StN	*Stabroek News.* Georgetown.	Guyn
SuG	*Sunday Guardian.* Port of Spain.	Trin
Suj	*BWIA Sunjet/Inflight Magazine.* Port of Spain.	Trin
SuS	*Sunday Sun.* Nation Publishing Co., Bridgetown.	Bdos
SVFS	SUTHERLAND, Junior, *A Collection of Vincentian Folk Songs,* vol. 1. Department of Culture: Ministry of Tourism and Culture, Kingstown, March, 2003.	StVn
SWOS	SELVON, Samuel, *Ways of Sunlight.* Longman Caribbean, 1973.	Trin
TrG	*Trinidad Guardian & Sunday Guardian.* Port of Spain.	Trin
ViN	*The Vincentian.* Kingstown.	StVn
WCD	Webster's Collegiate Dictionary.	Ref.
Xnews	Newspaper, Kingston.	Jmca
YFOC	YOUNG, Colville, *From One Caribbean Corner.* Belize, C.N. Young, 1983/1993.	Belz
YPF	YOUNG, Colville, *Pataki Full.*, Belize, 1993.	Belz
YRRC	YANSEN, C.A., *Random Remarks on Creolese.* Rev. ed., vols. 1 & 2. Chameleon Press, [1975] 1993.	Guyn

ABOUT THE EDITOR

Professor Richard Allsopp joined the fledgling College of Arts and Science in Barbados of the University of the West Indies as its first lecturer in English, in 1963, and serving soon after as a significant member of its development and management team in his capacities as vice dean and chairman of the Division of Survey Courses and Social Sciences. He would go on to serve the university in a variety of capacities: as the campus's first public orator, as a member of the university's council and senate, to name a few.

He designed and developed a first-year course in the use of English as a compulsory university-wide course, and with it developed a reputation for rigorous teaching and examining, and insistence on exacting standards. His pioneering role as a Caribbean linguist/creolist had earlier resulted in his membership of a group of thirteen scholars who gathered for the inaugural International Conference on Creole Languages held at the Mona, Jamaica, campus of the University of the West Indies in 1959. His dissertations at the master's and doctoral levels were the first known theses in any Caribbean creole. His seminal work in creole studies, and in particular on phonology, on structure and on the African origins of Caribbean creoles, would later bring prestige to him and to the University of the West Indies.

Not surprisingly, then, Professor Allsopp together with colleagues across the university was instrumental in the early 1970s in the introduction of linguistics studies at the University of the West Indies and in the design and teaching of a range of linguistics courses. His purpose, in his own words, was "to use the discipline of linguistics, never as an end in itself . . ., but as an instrument for the study and appreciation of the usage and structure of the English language as it has developed in the Caribbean; firstly as being basic to education in general and secondly as crucial to the proper acquisition of a foreign language by any Caribbean student".

In 1971, Professor Allsopp launched the Caribbean Lexicography Project and became its first director and coordinator. The product of this project, his landmark *Dictionary of Caribbean English Usage* (1996), was the culmination of over twenty years of dedicated and singular effort with limited resources. With this "stupendous work" (as described by the Economist) he sealed his reputation not only as a lexicographical scholar, but as a major contributor to Caribbean education and cultural understanding. His dictionary was followed in 2005 by his well-received *Book of Afric Caribbean Proverbs*.

Further, at the international level, Professor Allsopp was the first West Indian invited to serve on the editorial board of the *Oxford English Dictionary* and the *American Heritage Dictionary*. He also served as the English-language consultant to the Church of the Province of the West Indies for the *Book of Common Prayer*.

In 1958 he was awarded the Crane gold medal for the most outstanding contribution to education in British Guiana. In 2003 the University of the West Indies honoured his work and his signal contribution to Caribbean culture and scholarship by conferring on him the honorary degree of Doctor of Letters, an uncommon distinction for a member of its community. In his citation, the university's public orator aptly described Professor Allsopp as a "gentle giant of a scholar and gentleman, [an] eloquent epitome of Caribbean cultural expression..., [a] human computer of the language, passions and culture of Caribbean people". In 2004, the Government of Barbados awarded him the country's second highest national honour, Companion of Honour, for his distinguished contribution to education.

– University of the West Indies, Cave Hill, news release, 5 June 2009

www.ingramcontent.com/pod-product-compliance
Lightning Source LLC
Chambersburg PA
CBHW071057280326
41928CB00050B/2539